DATE DUE

THE LIFE

OF

GEORGE WASHINGTON

VOL. II.

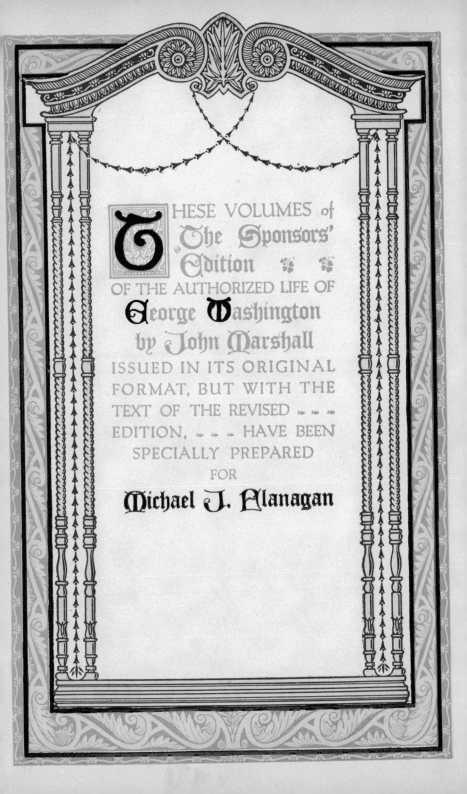

These Volumes of "The Sponsors' Edition" of the authorized life of George Washington by John Marshall issued in its original format, but with the text of the revised edition, have been specially prepared for

Michael J. Flanagan

THE

LIFE

OF

GEORGE WASHINGTON,

COMMANDER IN CHIEF

OF THE

AMERICAN FORCES,

DURING THE WAR WHICH ESTABLISHED THE INDEPENDENCE
OF HIS COUNTRY,

AND

FIRST PRESIDENT

OF THE

UNITED STATES.

COMPILED

UNDER THE INSPECTION OF

THE HONOURABLE BUSHROD WASHINGTON,

FROM

ORIGINAL PAPERS

BEQUEATHED TO HIM BY HIS DECEASED RELATIVE, AND NOW IN POSSESSION
OF THE AUTHOR.

TO WHICH IS PREFIXED,

AN INTRODUCTION,

CONTAINING

A COMPENDIOUS VIEW OF THE COLONIES PLANTED BY THE ENGLISH

ON THE

CONTINENT OF NORTH AMERICA,

FROM THEIR SETTLEMENT
TO THE COMMENCEMENT OF THAT WAR WHICH TERMINATED IN THEIR

INDEPENDENCE.

BY JOHN MARSHALL.

VOL. II.

THE CITIZENS' GUILD
OF WASHINGTON'S BOYHOOD HOME
FREDERICKSBURG, VA.

1926

CONTENTS

CHAPTER I.

CHAPTER II.

CHAPTER III.

CHAPTER IV.

CHAPTER V.

CHAPTER VI.

CHAPTER VII.

CHAPTER VIII.

CHAPTER IX.

CHAPTER X.

CHAPTER XI.

THE LIFE

OF

GEORGE WASHINGTON

THE LIFE

OF

GEORGE WASHINGTON

CHAPTER I.

Birth of Mr. Washington....His mission to the French
on the Ohio....Appointed Lieutenant Colonel of a
regiment of regular troops....Surprises Monsieur
Jumonville....Capitulation of fort Necessity...Is appointed aid-de-camp to General Braddock....Defeat
and death of that general....Is appointed to the command of a regiment....Extreme distress of the frontiers, and exertions of Colonel Washington to
augment the regular forces of the colony....Expedition
against fort Du Quesne....Defeat of Major Grant....
Fort Du Quesne evacuated by the French, and taken
possession of by the English....Resignation of Colonel
Washington....His marriage.

GEORGE WASHINGTON, the third son of   <u>1732</u>
Augustine Washington, was born on the 22d
of February, 1732, near the banks of the Po-   Birth of Mr.
Washington.
towmac, in the county of Westmoreland, in
Virginia. His father first married Miss Butler,
who died in 1728; leaving two sons, Lawrence
and Augustine. In 1730, he intermarried with
Miss Mary Ball, by whom he had four sons,
George, John, Samuel and Charles; and one

daughter, Betty, who intermarried with Colonel Fielding Lewis, of Fredericksburg.

His great grand-father, John Washington, a gentleman of a respectable family, had emigrated from the north of England about the year 1657, and settled on the place where Mr. Washington was born.

At the age of ten years he lost his father. Deprived of one parent, he became an object of more assiduous attention to the other; who continued to impress those principles of religion and virtue on his tender mind, which constituted the solid basis of a character that was maintained through all the trying vicissitudes of an eventful life. But his education was limited to those subjects, in which alone the sons of gentlemen, of moderate fortune, were, at that time, generally instructed. It was confined to acquisitions strictly useful, not even extending to foreign languages.

In 1743, his eldest brother intermarried with the daughter of the Honourable George William Fairfax, then a member of the council; and this connexion introduced Mr. Washington to Lord Fairfax, the proprietor of the Northern Neck of Virginia, who offered him, when in his eighteenth year, an appointment as surveyor, in the western part of that territory. His patrimonial estate being inconsiderable, this appointment was readily accepted; and in the performance of its duties, he acquired that information respect-

ing vacant lands, and formed those opinions
concerning their future value, which afterwards
contributed greatly to the increase of his private
fortune.

Those powerful attractions which the profes-
sion of arms presents to young and ardent minds,
possessed their full influence over Mr. Washington. Stimulated by the enthusiasm of military genius, to take part in the war in which
Great Britain was then engaged, he had pressed
so earnestly to enter into the navy, that, at the
age of fifteen, a midshipman's warrant was obtained for him. The interference of a timid and
affectionate mother deferred the commencement,
and changed the direction of his military career.
Four years afterwards, at a time when the militia were to be trained for actual service, he was
appointed one of the Adjutants General of Virginia, with the rank of Major. The duties annexed to this office soon yielded to others of a
more interesting character.

France was beginning to develop the vast plan
of connecting her extensive dominions in America, by uniting Canada with Louisiana. The
troops of that nation had taken possession of a
tract of country claimed by Virginia, and had
commenced a line of posts, to be extended from
the Lakes to the Ohio. The attention of Mr.
Dinwiddie, Lieutenant Governor of that Province, was attracted to these supposed encroachments; and he deemed it his duty to demand,

in the name of the King his master, that they should be suspended.

This mission was toilsome and hazardous. The Envoy would be under the necessity of passing through an extensive and almost unexplored wilderness, intersected with rugged mountains and considerable rivers, and inhabited by fierce savages, who were either hostile to the English, or of doubtful attachment. While the dangers and fatigues of this service deterred others from undertaking it, they seem to have possessed attractions for Mr. Washington, and he engaged in it with alacrity.

October 31.

His mission to the French on the Ohio.

On receiving his commission, he left Williamsburg and arrived, on the 14th of November, at Wills' creek, then the extreme frontier settlement of the English, where guides were engaged to conduct him over the Alleghany mountains. After surmounting the impediments occasioned by the snow and high waters, he reached the mouth of Turtle creek, where he was informed that the French General was dead, and that the greater part of the army had retired into winter quarters. Pursuing his route, he examined the country through which he passed with a military eye, and selected the confluence of the Monongahela and Alleghany rivers, the place where fort Du Quesne was afterwards erected by the French, as an advantageous position, which it would be adviseable to seize and to fortify immediately.

After employing a few days among the Indians in that neighbourhood, and procuring some of their chiefs to accompany him, whose fidelity he took the most judicious means to secure, he ascended the Alleghany river. Passing one fort at the mouth of French creek, he proceeded up the stream to a second, where he was received by Monsieur Le Gardeur de St. Pierre, the commanding officer on the Ohio, to whom he delivered the letter of Mr. Dinwiddie, and from whom he received an answer with which he returned to Williamsburg. The exertions made by Mr. Washington on this occasion, the perseverance with which he surmounted the difficulties of the journey, and the judgment displayed in his conduct towards the Indians, raised him in the public opinion, as well as in that of the Lieutenant Governor. His journal,* drawn up for the inspection of Mr. Dinwiddie, was published, and impressed his countrymen with very favourable sentiments of his understanding and fortitude.

As the answer from the commandant of the French forces on the Ohio indicated no disposition to withdraw from that country, it was deemed necessary to make some preparations to maintain the right asserted over it by the British crown; and the assembly of Virginia authorized the executive to raise a regiment for that purpose, to consist of three hundred men. The

* See note No. I, at the end of the volume.

CHAP. I

1754

Appointed
lieutenant
colonel of
a regiment
of regular
troops.

command of this regiment was given to Mr. Fry, † and Major Washington was appointed Lieutenant Colonel. Anxious to be engaged in active service, he obtained permission, about the beginning of April, to advance with two companies to the Great Meadows in the Alleghany mountains. By this movement he hoped to cover that frontier, to make himself more perfectly acquainted with the country, to gain some information respecting the situation and designs of the French, and to preserve the friendship of

---

† With an unaffected modesty which the accumulated honours of his after life could never impair, Major Washington, though the most distinguished military man then in Virginia, declined being a candidate for the command of this regiment. The following letter written on the occasion to Colonel Richard Corbin, a member of the council, with whom his family was connected by the ties of friendship and of affinity, was placed in the hands of the author by Mr. Francis Corbin, a son of that gentleman.

"DEAR SIR,—In a conversation at Green Spring you gave me some room to hope for a commission above that of a Major, and to be ranked among the chief officers of this expedition. The command of the whole forces is what I neither look for, expect, or desire; for I must be impartial enough to confess, it is a charge too great for my youth and inexperience to be intrusted with. Knowing this, I have too sincere a love for my country, to undertake that which may tend to the prejudice of it. But if I could entertain hopes that you thought me worthy of the post of Lieutenant-colonel, and would favour me so far as to mention it at the appointment of officers, I could not but entertain a true sense of the kindness.

I flatter myself that under a skilful commander, or man of sense, (which I most sincerely wish to serve under,) with my own application and diligent study of my duty, I shall be able to conduct my steps without censure, and in time, render myself worthy of the promotion that I shall be favoured with now."

The commission he solicited was transmitted to him by Mr. Corbin, in the following laconic letter:

"DEAR GEORGE,—I inclose you your commission. God prosper you with it.

Your friend, RICHARD CORBIN."

the savages. Soon after his arrival at that place, he was visited by some friendly Indians, who informed him that the French, having dispersed a party of workmen employed by the Ohio company to erect a fort on the south-eastern branch of the Ohio, were themselves engaged in completing a fortification at the confluence of the Alleghany and Monongahela rivers: a detachment from which place was then on its march towards his camp. Open hostilities had not yet commenced; but the country was considered as invaded: and several circumstances were related, confirming the opinion that this party was approaching with hostile views. Among others, it had withdrawn itself some distance from the path, and had encamped for the night in a bottom, as if to ensure concealment. Entertaining no doubt of the unfriendly designs with which these troops were advancing, Lieutenant Colonel Washington resolved to anticipate them. Availing himself of the offer made by the Indians to serve him as guides, he proceeded through a dark and rainy night to the French encampment, which he completely surrounded. At daybreak, his troops fired and rushed upon the party, which immediately surrendered. One man only escaped capture, and M. Jumonville alone, the commanding officer, was killed.

Surprises
Monsieur
Jumonville.

While the regiment was on its march to join the detachment advanced in front, the command devolved on Lieutenant Colonel Washington by the death of Colonel Fry. Soon after its arrival, it was reinforced by two independent companies of regulars. After erecting a small stockade at the Great Meadows, Colonel Washington commenced his march towards fort Du Quesne, with the intention of dislodging the French from that place. He had proceeded about thirteen miles, when he was met by some friendly Indians, who informed him that the French and their savage allies, "as numerous as the pigeons in the woods," were advancing rapidly to meet him. Among those who brought this information was a trusty chief, only two days from the fort on the Ohio, who had observed the arrival of a considerable reinforcement at that place, and had heard their intention of marching immediately to attack the English, with a corps composed of eight hundred French and four hundred Indians. This intelligence was corroborated by information previously received from deserters, who had reported that a reinforcement was expected.

The troops commanded by Colonel Washington were almost destitute of provisions; and the ground he occupied was not adapted to military purposes. A road at some distance, leading through other defiles in the mountains, would enable the French to pass into his rear, intercept his supplies, and starve him into a surrender, or fight him with a superiority of three to one.

In this hazardous situation, a council of war unanimously advised a retreat to the fort at the Great Meadows, now termed fort Necessity; where the two roads united, and where the face of the country was such as not to permit an enemy to pass unperceived. At that place, it was intended to remain, until reinforcements of men, and supplies of provisions, should arrive.

In pursuance of this advice, Colonel Washington returned to fort Necessity, and began a ditch around the stockade. Before it was completed, the French, amounting to about fifteen hundred men, commanded by Monsieur de Villier, appeared before the fort, and immediately commenced a furious attack upon it. They were received with great intrepidity by the Americans, who fought partly within the stockade, and partly in the surrounding ditch, which was nearly filled with mud and water. Colonel Washington continued the whole day on the outside of the fort, encouraging the soldiers by his countenance and example. The assailants fought under cover of the trees and high grass, with which the country abounds. The engagement was continued with great resolution from ten in the morning until dark; when Monsieur de Villier demanded a parley, and offered terms of capitulation. The proposals first made were rejected; but, in the course of the night, articles were signed, by which the fort was surrendered, on condition that its garrison should be allowed

CHAP. I

1754

June 23.

July 2.

Third.

Capitulation of fort Necessity.

Fourth.

the honours of war—should be permitted to retain their arms and baggage, and be suffered to
march without molestation into the inhabited
parts of Virginia. The capitulation being in
French—a language not understood by any person in the garrison, and being drawn up hastily
in the night, contains an expression which was
inaccurately translated at the time, and of which
advantage has been since taken, by the enemies
of Mr. Washington, to imply an admission on
his part, that Monsieur Jumonville was assas-
sinated. An account of the transaction was published by Monsieur de Villier, which drew from
Colonel Washington a letter to a friend, completely disproving the calumny. Though entirely discredited at the time, it was revived at
a subsequent period, when circumstances, well
understood at the date of the transaction, were
supposed to be forgotten.*

The loss of the Americans in this affair is not
ascertained. From a return made on the 9th
of July, at Wills' Creek, it appears that the
killed and wounded, of the Virginia regiment,
amounted to fifty-eight; but the loss sustained
by the two independent companies is not stated.
That of the assailants was supposed to be more
considerable.

Great credit was given to Colonel Washington
by his countrymen, for the courage displayed on
this occasion. The legislature evinced its satis-

* See note No. II, at the end of the volume.

faction with the conduct of the whole party, by passing a vote of thanks † to him, and the officers under his command; and by giving three hundred pistoles, to be distributed among the soldiers engaged in the action.

The regiment returned to Winchester, to be recruited; soon after which it was joined by a few companies from North Carolina and Maryland. On the arrival of this reinforcement, the Lieutenant Governor, with the advice of council, regardless of the condition or number of the forces, ordered them immediately to march over the Alleghany mountains, and to expel the French from fort Du Quesne, or to build one in its vicinity.

The little army in Virginia, which was placed under the command of Colonel Innes, from North Carolina, did not, as now reinforced, exceed half the number of the enemy, and was neither provided with the means of moving, nor with supplies for a winter campaign. With as little consideration, directions had been given

---

† To the vote of thanks, the officers made the following reply:

"We, the officers of the Virginia regiment, are highly sensible of the particular mark of distinction with which you have honoured us, in returning your thanks for our behaviour in the late action; and can not help testifying our grateful acknowledgments, for your 'high sense' of what we shall always esteem a duty to our country and the best of kings.

"Favoured with your regard, we shall zealously endeavour to deserve your applause, and, by our future actions, strive to convince the worshipful house of burgesses, how much we esteem their approbation, and, as it ought to be, regard it as the voice of our country.

Signed for the whole corps,
GEO: WASHINGTON."

for the immediate completion of the regiment, without furnishing a single shilling for the recruiting service. Although a long peace may account for many errors at the commencement of war, some surprise will be felt at such ill-considered and ill-judged measures. Colonel

Washington remonstrated strongly against these orders, but prepared to execute them. The assembly, however, having risen without making any provision for the farther prosecution of the war, this wild expedition was laid aside, and the Virginia regiment was reduced to independent companies.

In the course of the winter, orders were received "for settling the rank of the officers of his majesty's forces when serving with the provincials in North America." These orders directed "that all officers commissioned by the King, or by his General in North America, should take rank of all officers commissioned by the Governors of the respective provinces; and farther, that the general and field officers of the provincial troops should have no rank when serving with the general and field officers commissioned by the crown; but that all captains, and other inferior officers of the royal troops, should take rank over provincial officers of the same grade, having senior commissions."

Strong as was his attachment to a military life, Colonel Washington possessed in too eminent a degree the proud and punctilious feelings of a soldier, to submit to a degradation so humiliating as was produced by his loss of rank. Professing his unabated inclination to continue in the service, if permitted to do so without a sacrifice too great to be made, he retired indignantly from the station assigned him, and answered the various letters which he received, pressing him still to hold his commission, with assurances that he would serve with pleasure, when he should be enabled to do so without dishonour.

His eldest brother had lately died, and left him a considerable estate on the Potowmac. This gentleman had served in the expedition against Carthagena; and, in compliment to the admiral who commanded the fleet engaged in that enterprise, had named his seat *Mount Vernon!* To this delightful spot Colonel Washington withdrew, resolving to devote his future attention to the avocations of private life. This resolution was not long maintained.

General Braddock, being informed of his merit, his knowledge of the country which was to be the theatre of action, and his motives for retiring from the service, gratified his desire to make one campaign under a person supposed to possess some knowledge of war, by inviting him to enter his family as a volunteer aid-de-camp.

Having determined to accept this invitation, he joined the commander-in-chief, immediately

Is appointed aid-de-camp to General Braddock.

after his departure from Alexandria, and proceeded with him to Wills' Creek. The army,
consisting of two European regiments and a few
corps of provincials, was detained at that place
until the 12th of June, by the difficulty of procuring wagons, horses, and provisions. Colonel
Washington, impatient under these delays, suggested the propriety of using pack-horses instead of wagons, for conveying the baggage.

The commander-in-chief, although solicitous to
hasten the expedition, was so attached to the
usages of regular war, that this salutary advice
was at first rejected; but, soon after the commencement of the march, its propriety became
too obvious to be longer neglected.

On the third day after the army had moved
from its ground, Colonel Washington was seized
with a violent fever, which disabled him from
riding on horseback, and was conveyed in a
covered wagon. General Braddock, who found
the difficulties of the march greater than had
been expected, continuing to consult him privately, he strenuously urged that officer to leave
his heavy artillery and baggage with the rear
division of the army; and with a chosen body
of troops and some pieces of light artillery, to
press forward with the utmost expedition to
fort Du Quesne. In support of this advice, he
stated that the French were then weak on the
Ohio, but hourly expected reinforcements. During the excessive drought which prevailed at

that time, these could not arrive; because the river Le Bœuf, on which their supplies must be brought to Venango, did not then afford a sufficient quantity of water for the purpose. A rapid movement therefore might enable him to carry the fort, before the arrival of the expected aid; but if this measure should not be adopted, such were the delays attendant on the march of the whole army, that rains sufficient to raise the waters might reasonably be expected, and the whole force of the French would probably be collected for their reception; a circumstance which would render the success of the expedition doubtful.

This advice according well with the temper of the commander-in-chief, it was determined in a council of war, held at the Little Meadows, that twelve hundred select men, to be commanded by General Braddock in person, should advance with the utmost expedition against fort Du Quesne. Colonel Dunbar was to remain with the residue of the two regiments, and all the heavy baggage.

Although this select corps commenced its march with only thirty carriages, including ammunition wagons, the hopes which had been entertained of the celerity of its movements were not fulfilled. "I found," said Colonel Washington, in a letter to his brother, written during the march, "that instead of pushing on with

June 19.

vigour, without regarding a little rough road, they were halting to level every mole-hill, and to erect bridges over every brook." By these means they employed four days in reaching the great crossings of the Yohiogany, only nineteen miles from the Little Meadows.

Colonel Washington was obliged to stop at that place;—the physician having declared that his life would be endangered by continuing with the army. He obeyed, with reluctance, the positive orders of the general to remain at this camp, under the protection of a small guard, until the arrival of Colonel Dunbar; having first received a promise that means should be used to bring him up with the army before it reached fort Du Quesne.

The day before the action of the Monongahela he rejoined the general in a covered wagon; and, though weak, entered on the duties of his station.

In a short time after the action had commenced, Colonel Washington was the only aid remaining alive, and unwounded. The whole duty of carrying the orders of the commander-in-chief, in an engagement with marksmen who selected officers, and especially those on horseback, for their objects, devolved on him alone. Under these difficult circumstances, he manifested that coolness, that self-possession, that fearlessness of danger which ever distinguished him, and which are so necessary to the character of a consummate soldier. Two horses were killed under him, and four balls passed through his coat; but, to the astonishment of all, he escaped unhurt,—while every other officer on horseback was either killed or wounded. "I expected every moment," says an eye-witness,* "to see him fall. His duty and situation exposed him to every danger. Nothing but the superintending care of Providence could have saved him from the fate of all around him."

At length, after an action of nearly three hours, General Braddock, under whom three horses had been killed, received a mortal wound; and his troops fled in great disorder. Every effort to rally them was ineffectual until they had crossed the Monongahela, when, being no longer pursued, they were again formed. The general was brought off in a small tumbril by Colonel Washington, Captain Stewart of the guards, and his servant. The defeated detachment retreated with the utmost precipitation to the rear division of the army; soon after which, Braddock expired. In the first moments of alarm, all the stores were destroyed, except those necessary for immediate use; and not long afterwards, Colonel Dunbar marched the remaining European troops to Philadelphia, in order to place them in, what he termed, winter quarters.

Defeat and death of that general.

August.

* Dr. Craik.

Colonel Washington was greatly disappointed and disgusted by the conduct of the regular troops in this action. In his letter to Lieutenant Governor Dinwiddie, giving an account of it, he said, "They were struck with such an inconceivable panic, that nothing but confusion and disobedience of orders prevailed among them. The officers in general behaved with incomparable bravery, for which they greatly suffered; there being upwards of sixty killed and wounded—a large proportion out of what we had.

"The Virginia companies behaved like men, and died like soldiers; for, I believe, out of three companies on the ground that day, scarce thirty men were left alive. Captain Peronny, and all his officers down to a corporal, were killed. Captain Poulson had almost as hard a fate, for only one of his escaped. In short, the dastardly behaviour of the regular troops (so called,) exposed those who were inclined to do their duty, to almost certain death; and, at length, in spite of every effort to the contrary, they broke, and ran as sheep before hounds; leaving the artillery, ammunition, provisions, baggage, and in short every thing, a prey to the enemy: and when we endeavoured to rally them, in hopes of regaining the ground, and what we had left upon it, it was with as little success as if we had attempted to have stopped the wild bears of the mountains, or the rivulets with our feet: for they

Wakefield - the Birthplace of George Washington

This is from an etching made in idealization of the original house, situated on the banks of the Potomac, 38 miles from Fredericksburg, in Westmoreland County, Virginia, where our First President was born, February 22, 1732. The original house, which was built by Washington's father, Augustine, was destroyed by fire more than 150 years ago, before the Declaration of Independence was signed.

Wakefield—the Birthplace of George Washington

This is from an etching made in idealization of the original house, situated on the banks of the Potomac, 38 miles from Fredericksburg, in Westmoreland County, Virginia, where our First President was born, February 22, 1732. The original house, which was built by Washington's father, Augustine, was destroyed by fire more than 150 years ago, before the Declaration of Independence was signed.

would break by, in spite of every effort to prevent it."*

Colonel Washington had long been the favourite soldier of Virginia; and his reputation grew with every occasion for exertion. His conduct in this battle had been universally extolled; † and the common opinion of his countrymen was, that, had his advice been pursued, the disaster had been avoided. The assembly was in session, when intelligence was received of this defeat, and of the abandonment of the colony by Colonel Dunbar. The legislature, perceiving the necessity of levying troops for the defence of the province, determined to raise a regiment, to consist of sixteen companies, the command of which was offered to Colonel Washington; who was also designated, in his commission, as the Commander-in-chief of all the forces raised and to be raised in the colony of Virginia. The uncommon privilege of naming

August.

Is appointed to the command of a regiment.

* In another letter, he says, "We have been beaten, shamefully beaten—shamefully beaten by a handful of men, who only intended to molest and disturb our march! Victory was their smallest expectation! But see the wondrous works of Providence, the uncertainty of human things! We, but a few moments before, believed our numbers almost equal to the force of Canada; they only expected to annoy us. Yet, contrary to all expectation and human probability, and even to the common course of things, we were totally defeated, and have sustained the loss of every thing."

† In a sermon preached not long after the defeat of General Braddock, the Rev. Mr. Davies, speaking of that disaster, and of the preservation of Colonel Washington, said: "I can not but hope that Providence has preserved that youth to be the saviour of this country." These words were afterwards considered as prophetic; and were applied by his countrymen to an event very opposite to that which was contemplated by the person who uttered them.

his Field Officers was added to this honourable manifestation of the public confidence.

Retaining still his prepossessions in favour of a military life, he cheerfully embraced this opportunity of re-entering the army. After making the necessary arrangements for the recruiting service, and visiting the posts on the frontiers, which he placed in the best state of defence of which they were susceptible; he set out for the seat of government, where objects of the first importance required his attention; but was overtaken below Fredericksburg by an express, carrying the intelligence, that a large number of French and Indians, divided into several parties, had broken up the frontier settlements; were murdering and capturing men, women, and children; burning their houses, and destroying their crops. The troops stationed among them for their protection, were unequal to that duty; and, instead of being able to afford aid to the inhabitants, were themselves blocked up in their forts.

Extreme distress of the frontiers and exertions of Colonel Washington to augment the regular forces of the colony.

Colonel Washington hastened back to Winchester, where the utmost confusion and alarm prevailed. His efforts to raise the militia were unavailing. Attentive only to individual security, and regardless of the common danger, they could not be drawn from their families. Instead of assembling in arms, and obtaining safety by meeting their invaders, the inhabitants fled into the lower country, and increased the general terror. In this state of things, he en-

deavoured to collect and arm the men who had
abandoned their houses, and to remove their
wives and children to a distance from this scene
of desolation and carnage. Pressing orders were
at the same time despatched to the newly appointed officers, to forward their recruits; and
to the county lieutenants, east of the Blue
Ridge, to hasten their militia to Winchester: but
before these orders could be executed, the party
which had done so much mischief, and excited
such alarm, had re-crossed the Alleghany mountains.

Early in the following spring, the enemy
made another irruption into the inhabited country, and did great mischief. The number of
troops on the regular establishment was totally
insufficient for the protection of the frontier,
and effective service from the militia was
found to be unattainable. The Indians, who
were divided into small parties, concealed themselves with so much dexterity, as seldom to be
perceived until the blow was struck. Their
murders were frequently committed in the very
neighbourhood of the forts; and the detachments
from the garrisons, employed in scouring the
country, were generally eluded, or attacked to
advantage. In one of these skirmishes, the
Americans were routed, and Captain Mercer was
killed. The people either abandoned the country, or attempted to secure themselves in small
stockade forts, where they were in great distress

for provisions, arms, and ammunition; were often surrounded, and sometimes cut off. Colonel Washington was deeply affected by this state of things. "I see their situation," said he, in a letter to the Lieutenant Governor, "I know their danger, and participate their sufferings, without having it in my power to give them farther relief than uncertain promises. In short, I see inevitable destruction in so clear a light, that unless vigorous measures are taken by the assembly, and speedy assistance sent from below, the poor inhabitants now in forts must unavoidably fall, while the remainder are flying before the barbarous foe. In fine, the melancholy situation of the people; the little prospect of assistance; the gross and scandalous abuses cast upon the officers in general, which is reflecting upon me in particular for suffering misconduct of such extraordinary kind; and the distant prospect, if any, of gaining reputation in the service, cause me to lament the hour that gave me a commission, and would induce me, at any other time than this of imminent danger, to resign, without one hesitating moment, a command from which I never expect to reap either honour or benefit; but, on the contrary, have almost an absolute certainty of incurring displeasure below, while the murder of helpless families may be laid to my account here."

Colonel Washington had been prevented from taking post at fort Cumberland by an unfortunate and extraordinary difficulty, growing out of an obscurity in the royal orders, respecting the relative rank of officers commissioned by the king, and those commissioned by the governor. A Captain Dagworthy, who was at that place, and of the former description, insisted on taking the command, although it had been committed to Lieutenant Colonel Stevens; and, on the same principle, he contested the rank of Colonel Washington also. This circumstance had retained that officer at Winchester, where public stores to a considerable amount were deposited, with only about fifty men to guard them. In the deep distress of the moment, a council of war was called, to determine whether he should march this small body to some of the nearest forts, and, uniting with their petty garrisons, risk an action; or wait until the militia could be raised. The council unanimously advised a continuance at Winchester. Lord Fairfax, who commanded the militia of that and the adjacent counties, had ordered them to his assistance; but they were slow in assembling. The unremitting exertion of three days, in the county of Frederick, could produce only twenty men.

The incompetency of the military force to the defence of the country having become obvious, the assembly determined to augment the regiment to fifteen hundred men. In a letter addressed to the house of burgesses, Colonel Washington urged the necessity of increasing it still farther, to two thousand men; a less number than which could not possibly, in his opinion, be sufficient to cover the extensive frontier of Virginia, should the defensive system be continued. In support of this demand, he stated, in detail, the forts which must be garrisoned; and observed, that, with the exception of a few inhabitants in forts on the south branch of the Potowmac, the north mountain near Winchester had become the frontier; and that, without effectual aid, the inhabitants would even pass the Blue Ridge. He farther observed that the woods seemed "alive with French and Indians;" and again described so feelingly the situation of the inhabitants, that the assembly requested the governor to order half the militia of the adjoining counties to their relief; and the attorney general, Mr. Peyton Randolph, formed a company of one hundred gentlemen, who engaged to make the campaign, as volunteers. Ten well trained woodsmen, or Indians, would have rendered more service.

The distress of the country increased. As had been foreseen, Winchester became almost the only settlement west of the Blue Ridge, on the northern frontier; and fears were entertained that the enemy would soon pass even that barrier, and ravage the country below. Express after express was sent to hasten the militia, but sent in vain. At length, about the last of April, the French and their savage allies, laden with

plunder, prisoners, and scalps, returned to fort
Du Quesne.

Some short time after their retreat, the militia appeared. This temporary increase of strength was employed in searching the country for small parties of Indians, who lingered behind the main body, and in making dispositions to repel another invasion. A fort was commenced at Winchester, which, in honour of the general who had been appointed to the command of the British troops in America, was called fort Loudoun; and the perpetual remonstrances of Colonel Washington at length effected some improvement in the laws for the government of the troops.

Instead of adopting, in the first instance, that military code which experience had matured, the assembly passed occasional acts to remedy particular evils as they occurred; in consequence of which, a state of insubordination was protracted, and the difficulties of the commanding officer increased. Slight penalties were at first annexed to serious military offences; and when an act was obtained to punish mutiny and desertion with death, such crimes as cowardice in action, and sleeping on a post, were pretermitted. It was left impossible to hold a general court martial, without an order from the governor; and the commanding officer was not at liberty to make those arrangements in other respects which his own observation suggested, but shackled by the control of others, who could neither judge so correctly, nor be so well informed, as himself.

These errors of a government unused to war, though continually remarked by the officer commanding the troops, were slowly perceived by those in power, and were never entirely corrected.

Successive incursions continued to be made into the country by small predatory parties of French and Indians, who kept up a perpetual alarm, and murdered the defenceless, wherever found. In Pennsylvania, the inhabitants were driven as far as Carlisle; and in Maryland, Fredericktown, on the eastern side of the Blue Ridge, became a frontier. With the Virginia regiment, which did not yet amount to one thousand men, aided occasionally by militia, Colonel Washington was to defend a frontier of near four hundred miles in extent, and to complete a chain of forts. He repeatedly urged the necessity and propriety of abandoning fort Cumberland, which was too far in advance of the settlements, and too far north, to be useful, while it required for its defence a larger portion of his force than could be spared with a proper regard to the safety of other and more advantageous positions. The governor, however, thought the abandonment of it improper, since it was a *"king's fort,"* and Lord Loudoun, on being consulted, gave the same opinion.

Among the subjects of extreme chagrin to the commander of the Virginia troops, was the practice of desertion. The prevalence of this crime was ascribed, in a considerable degree, to the ill-judged parsimony of the assembly. The daily pay of a soldier was only eight pence, out of which two pence were stopped for his clothes. This pay was inferior to what was received in every other part of the continent; and, as ought to have been foreseen, great discontents were excited by a distinction so invidious. The remonstrances of the commanding officer, in some degree, corrected this mischief; and a full suit of regimentals was allowed to each soldier, without deducting its price from his pay.

This campaign furnishes no event which can interest the reader; yet the duties of the officer, though minute, were arduous; and the sufferings of the people, beyond measure afflicting. It adds one to the many proofs which have been afforded, of the miseries to be expected by those who defer preparing the means of defence, until the moment when they ought to be used; and then, rely almost entirely, on a force neither adequate to the danger, nor of equal continuance.

It is an interesting fact to those who know the present situation of Virginia, that, so late as the year 1756, the Blue Ridge was the north-western frontier; and that she found immense difficulty in completing a single regiment to protect the inhabitants from the horrors of the scalping knife, and the still greater horrors of being led into captivity by savages who added terrors to death by the manner of inflicting it.

As soon as the main body of the enemy had withdrawn from the settlements, a tour was made by Colonel Washington to the south-western frontier. There, as well as to the north, continued incursions had been made; and there too, the principal defence of the country was entrusted to an ill-regulated militia. The fatal consequences of this system are thus stated by him, in a letter to the lieutenant governor: "The inhabitants are so sensible of their danger, if left to the protection of these people, that not a man will stay at his place. This I have from their own mouths, and the principal inhabitants of Augusta county. The militia are under such bad order and discipline, that they will come and go, when and where they please, without regarding time, their officers, or the safety of the inhabitants, but consulting solely their own inclinations. There should be, according to your honour's orders, one-third of the militia of these parts on duty at a time; instead of that, scarce one-thirtieth is out. They are to be relieved every month, and they are a great part of that time marching to and from their stations; and they will not wait one day longer than the limited time, whether relieved or not, however urgent the necessity for their continuance may

be." Some instances of this, and of gross mis-
behaviour, were then enumerated; after which,
he pressed the necessity of increasing the number of regulars to two thousand men.

After returning from this tour, to Winchester,
he gave the Lieutenant Governor, in curious detail, a statement of the situation in which he
found the country, urging, but urging in vain,
arguments which will always be suggested by
experience, against relying chiefly on militia for
defence.

Sensible of the impracticability of defending
such an extensive frontier, Colonel Washington
continued to press the policy of enabling him
to act on the offensive. The people of Virginia,
he thought, could be protected only by entering
the country of the enemy; giving him employment at home, and removing the source of all
their calamities by taking possession of fort Du
Quesne.

"As defensive measures," he observed in a
letter to the Lieutenant Governor, "are evidently
insufficient for the security and safety of the
country, I hope no arguments are necessary to
evince the necessity of altering them to a vigorous offensive war, in order to remove the cause."
But in the event, that the assembly should still
indulge their favourite scheme of protecting the
inhabitants by forts along the frontiers, he presented a plan, which, in its execution, would
require two thousand men—these were to be

distributed in twenty-two forts, extending from the river Mayo to the Potowmac, in a line of three hundred and sixty miles. In a letter written about the same time to the speaker of the assembly, he said, "The certainty of advantage, by an offensive scheme of action, renders it, beyond any doubt, preferable to our defensive measures. Our scattered force, so separated and dispersed in weak parties, avails little to stop the secret incursions of the savages. We can only perhaps put them to flight, or frighten them to some other part of the country, which answers not the end proposed. Whereas, had we strength enough to invade their lands, we should restrain them from coming abroad, and leaving their families exposed. We should then remove the principal cause, and have stronger probability of success; we should be free from the many alarms, mischiefs, and murders, that now attend us; we should inspirit the hearts of our few Indian friends, and gain more esteem with them. In short, could Pennsylvania and Maryland be induced to join us in an expedition of this nature, and to petition his Excellency Lord Loudoun for a small train of artillery, with some engineers, we should then be able, in all human probability, to subdue the terror of fort Du Quesne; retrieve our character with the Indians; and restore peace to our unhappy frontiers."

His total inability to act offensively, or even to afford protection to the frontiers of Virginia,

was not the only distressing and vexatious circumstance to which he was exposed. The Lieutenant Governor, to whose commands he was
subjected in every minute particular, and who
seems to have been unequal to the difficulties
of his station, frequently deranged his system by
orders which could not be executed without considerable hazard and inconvenience. Colonel
Washington could not always restrain his chagrin on such occasions; and, on one of them,
observed in a letter to an intimate friend, who
possessed great influence in the country, "whence
it arises, or why, I am truly ignorant, but my
strongest representations of matters relative to
the peace of the frontiers are disregarded, as idle
and frivolous; my propositions and measures,
as partial and selfish; and all my sincerest endeavours for the service of my country, perverted
to the worst purposes. My orders are dark,
doubtful, and uncertain: to-day approved, to-
morrow condemned; left to act and proceed at
hazard; accountable for the consequences, and
blamed without the benefit of defence. If you
can think my situation capable of exciting the
smallest degree of envy, or of affording the least
satisfaction, the truth is yet hid from you, and
you entertain notions very different from the
reality of the case. However, I am determined
to bear up under all these embarrassments some
time longer, in the hope of better regulations

under Lord Loudoun, to whom I look for the future fate of Virginia."

Not long after this letter was written, Lord Loudoun, in whose person the offices of Governor and Commander-in-chief were united, arrived in Virginia. A comprehensive statement of the situation of the colony, in a military point of view, and of the regiment in particular, was drawn up and submitted to him by Colonel Washington. In this he enumerated the errors which had prevented the completion of his regiment, showed the insufficiency of the militia for any military purpose, and demonstrated the superiority of an offensive system over that which had been pursued.

This statement was probably presented by Colonel Washington in person, who was permitted, during the winter, to visit Lord Loudoun in Philadelphia, where that nobleman met the Governors of Pennsylvania, Maryland, and North Carolina, and the Lieutenant Governor of Virginia, in order to consult with them on the measures to be taken, in their respective Provinces, for the ensuing campaign. He was, however, disappointed in his favourite hope of being able to act offensively against the French on the Ohio. Lord Loudoun had determined to direct all his efforts against Canada, and to leave only twelve hundred men in the middle and southern colonies. Instead of receiving assistance, Virginia was required to send four hundred men to South Carolina. Not discouraged by these disappointments, Colonel Washington continued indefatigable in his endeavours to impress on Mr. Dinwiddie, and on the assembly, the importance of reviving, and properly modifying their military code, which had now expired, of making a more effective militia law, and of increasing their number of regular troops.

So far from succeeding on the last subject, he had the mortification to witness a measure which crushed his hopes of an adequate regular force. Being unable to complete the regiment by voluntary enlistment, the assembly changed its organization, and reduced it to ten companies; each to consist of one hundred men. Yet his anxious wishes continued to be directed towards fort Du Quesne. In a letter written about this time to Colonel Stanwix, who commanded in the middle colonies, he said, "You will excuse me, sir, for saying, that I think there never was, and perhaps never again will be, so favourable an opportunity as the present for reducing fort Du Quesne. Several prisoners have made their escape from the Ohio this spring, and agree in their accounts, that there are but three hundred men left in the garrison; and I do not conceive that the French are so strong in Canada, as to reinforce this place, and defend themselves at home this campaign: surely then this is too precious an opportunity to be lost."

But Mr. Pitt did not yet direct the councils of Britain; and a spirit of enterprise and heroism did not yet animate her generals. The campaign to the north was inglorious; and to the west, nothing was even attempted, which might relieve the middle colonies.

Large bodies of savages, in the service of France, once more spread desolation and murder over the whole country, west of the Blue Ridge. The regular troops were inadequate to the protection of the inhabitants; and the incompetency of the defensive system to their security became every day more apparent. "I exert every means," said Colonel Washington, in a letter to Lieutenant Governor Dinwiddie, "to protect a much distressed country; but it is a task too arduous. To think of defending a frontier of more than three hundred and fifty miles extent, as ours is, with only seven hundred men, is vain and idle; especially when that frontier lies more contiguous to the enemy than any other.

October 8.

"I am, and for a long time have been, fully convinced, that if we continue to pursue a defensive plan, the country must be inevitably lost."

October 24.

In another letter he said, "The raising a company of rangers, or augmenting our strength in some other manner, is so far necessary, that, without it, the remaining inhabitants of this once fertile and populous valley will scarcely be detained at their dwellings until the spring. And if there is no expedition to the westward then, nor a force more considerable than Virginia can support, posted on our frontiers; if we still adhere, for the next campaign, to our destructive defensive schemes, there will not, I dare affirm, be one soul living on this side the Blue Ridge the ensuing autumn, if we except the troops in garrison, and a few inhabitants of this town, who may shelter themselves under the protection of this fort. This I know to be the immoveable determination of all the settlers of this country."

To the Speaker of the assembly he gave the same opinion; and added, "I do not know on whom these miserable undone people are to rely for protection. If the assembly are to give it to them, it is time that measures were at least concerting, and not when they ought to be going into execution, as has always been the case. If they are to seek it from the Commander-in-chief, it is time their condition was made known to him. For I can not forbear repeating again, that, while we pursue defensive measures, we pursue inevitable ruin."

It was impossible for Colonel Washington, zealous in the service of his country, and ambitious of military fame, to observe the errors committed in the conduct of the war, without censuring them. These errors were not confined to the military affairs of the colony. The Cherokee and Catawba Indians had hitherto remained faithful to the English, and it was very desirable to engage the warriors of those tribes heartily in their service; but so miserably was the intercourse with them conducted, that, though a considerable expense was incurred, not much assistance was obtained, and great disgust was excited among them. The freedom with which the Commander-in-chief of the Virginia forces censured public measures, gave offence to the Lieutenant Governor, who considered these censures as manifesting a want of respect for himself. Sometimes he coarsely termed them *impertinent;* and at other times, charged him with looseness in his information, and inattention to his duty. On one of these occasions, Colonel Washington

thus concluded a letter of detail, "Nothing remarkable has happened, and therefore I have nothing to add. I must beg leave, however, before I conclude, to observe, in justification of my own conduct, that it is with pleasure I receive reproof when reproof is due, because no person can be readier to accuse me, than I am to acknowledge an error, when I have committed it; nor more desirous of atoning for a crime, when I am sensible of being guilty of one. But, on the other hand, it is with concern I remark, that my best endeavours lose their reward; and that my conduct, although I have uniformly studied to make it as unexceptionable as I could, does not appear to you in a favourable point of light. Otherwise, your honour would not have accused me of *loose* behaviour, and *remissness* of duty, in matters where, I think, I have rather exceeded than fallen short of it. This, I think, is evidently the case in speaking of Indian affairs at all, after being instructed in very express terms, 'Not to have any concern with, or management of Indian affairs.' This has induced me to forbear mentioning the Indians in my letters to your honour of late, and to leave the misunderstanding, which you speak of, between Mr. Aikin and them, to be related by him."

Not long after this, he received a letter informing him of some coarse calumny, reflecting on his veracity and honour, which had been reported to the Lieutenant Governor. He enclosed a copy of this letter to Mr. Dinwiddie, and thus addressed him,—"I should take it infinitely kind if your honour would please to inform me whether a report of this nature was ever made to you; and, in that case, who was the author of it.

"It is evident from a variety of circumstances, and especially from the change in your honour's conduct towards me, that some person, as well inclined to detract, but better skilled in the art of detraction than the author of the above stupid scandal, has made free with my character. For I can not suppose, that malice so absurd, so barefaced, so diametrically opposite to truth, to common policy, and, in short, to everything but villany, as the above is, could impress you with so ill an opinion of my honour and honesty.

"If it be possible that ****, for my belief is staggered, not being conscious of having given the least cause to any one, much less to that gentleman, to reflect so grossly; I say, if it be possible that **** could descend so low as to be the propagator of this story, he must either be vastly ignorant of the state of affairs in this country *at that time*, or else, he must suppose that the whole body of the inhabitants had combined with me in executing the deceitful fraud. Or why did they, almost to a man, forsake their dwellings in the greatest terror and confusion; and while one half of them sought shelter in paltry forts, (of their own building,) the other should flee to the adjacent counties for refuge; numbers of them even to Carolina, from whence they have never returned?

"These are facts well known; but not better known than that these wretched people, while they lay pent up in forts, destitute of the common supports of life, (having in their precipitate flight forgotten, or rather, been unable to secure any kind of necessaries,) did despatch messengers of their own, (thinking I had not represented their miseries in the piteous manner they deserved,) with addresses to your honour and the assembly, praying relief. And did I ever send any alarming account, without sending also the original papers (or the copies) which gave rise to it?

"That I have foibles, and perhaps many of them, I shall not deny. I should esteem myself, as the world also would, vain and empty, were I to arrogate perfection.

"Knowledge in military matters is to be acquired only by practice and experience; and if I have erred, great allowance should be made for want of them; unless my errors should appear to be wilful; and then, I conceive, it would be more generous to charge me with my faults, and to let me stand or fall according to evidence, than to stigmatize me behind my back.

"It is uncertain in what light my services may have appeared to your Honour: but this I know, and it is the highest consolation I am capable of feeling, that no man that ever was employed in a public capacity, has endeavoured to discharge the trust reposed in him with greater honesty, and more zeal for the country's interest than I have done; and if there is any person living, who can say with justice that I have offered any intentional wrong to the public, I will cheerfully submit to the most ignominious punishment that an injured people ought to inflict. On the other hand, it is hard to have my character arraigned, and my actions condemned, without a hearing.

"I must therefore again beg in *more plain*, and in very *earnest* terms, to know if * * * * has taken the liberty of representing my conduct to your Honour with such ungentlemanly freedom as the letter implies. Your condescension herein will be acknowledged a singular favour."

In a letter, some short time after this, to the Lieutenant Governor, he said, "I do not know that I ever gave your Honour cause to suspect me of ingratitude; a crime I detest, and would most carefully avoid. If an open, disinterested behaviour carries offence, I may have offended; for I have all along laid it down as a maxim, to represent facts freely and impartially, but not more so to others than to you, sir. If instances of my ungrateful behaviour had been particularized, I would have answered them. But I have been long convinced that my actions and their motives have been maliciously aggravated." A request that he might be permitted to come to Williamsburg for the settlement of some accounts, which he was desirous of adjusting under the inspection of the Lieutenant Governor, who proposed to leave the province in the following November, was refused in abrupt and disobliging terms. In answer to the letter containing the refusal, Colonel Washington, after stating the immoveable disposition of the inhabitants to leave the country unless more sufficiently protected, added, "To give a more succinct account of their affairs than I could in writing, was the principal, among many other reasons, that induced me to ask leave to come down. It was not to enjoy a party of pleasure that I asked leave of absence. I have indulged with few of those, winter or summer."

Mr. Dinwiddie soon afterwards took leave of Virginia, and the government devolved on Mr. Blair, the President of the Council. Between him and the commander of the colonial troops the utmost cordiality existed.

After the close of this campaign, Lord Loudoun returned to England, and General Abercrombie succeeded to the command of the army. The department of the middle and southern provinces was committed to General Forbes, who, to the inexpressible gratification of Colonel Washington, determined to undertake an expedition against fort Du Quesne.

He urged an early campaign, but he urged it ineffectually; and, before the troops were assembled, a large body of French and Indians broke into the country, and renewed the horrors of the tomahawk and scalping-knife. The county of Augusta was ravaged and about sixty persons were murdered. The attempts made to intercept these savages were unsuccessful; and they recrossed the Alleghany, with their plunder, prisoners, and scalps.

At length, orders were given to assemble the regiment at Winchester, and be in readiness to march in fifteen days. On receiving them, Colonel Washington called in his recruiting parties; but so inattentive had the government been to his representations that, previous to marching

his regiment, he was under the necessity of repairing to Williamsburg, personally to enforce
his solicitations for arms, ammunition, money,
and clothing. That these preparations for an
expedition vitally interesting to Virginia, should
remain to be made after the season for action
had commenced, does not furnish stronger evidence of the difficulties encountered by the chief
of the military department, than is given by another circumstance of about the same date. He
was under the necessity of pointing out and
urging the propriety of allowing to his regiment, which had performed much severe service,
the same pay which had been granted to a second regiment, voted the preceding session of Assembly, to serve for a single year.

Among other motives for an early campaign,
Colonel Washington had urged the impracticability of detaining the Indians. His fears were
well founded. Before a junction of the troops
had been made, these savages became impatient
to return to their homes; and, finding that the
expedition would yet be delayed a considerable
time, they left the army, with promises to rejoin it at the proper season.

In pursuance of the orders which had been received, the Virginia troops moved in detachments
from Winchester to fort Cumberland, where
they assembled early in July: after which, they
were employed in opening a road to Raystown,
where Colonel Bouquet was stationed. As the

English were continually harassed by small parties of French and Indians, the general had contemplated advancing a strong detachment over
the Alleghany mountains, for the purpose of
giving them employment at home. By the advice of Colonel Washington this plan was relinquished. In support of his opinion, he stated
the probability that a large force was collected
at fort Du Quesne, and the impracticability of
moving a strong detachment, without such a
quantity of provisions, as would expose it to the
danger of being discovered and cut to pieces. He
advised to harass them with small parties, principally of Indians; and this advice was pursued.

Colonel Washington had expected that the
army would march by Braddock's road: but, late
in July, he had the mortification to receive a letter from Colonel Bouquet, asking an interview
with him, in order to consult on opening a new
road from Raystown, and requesting his opinion on that route. "I shall," says he, in answer
to this letter, "most cheerfully work on any road,
pursue any route, or enter upon any service, that
the general or yourself may think me usefully
employed in, or qualified for; and shall never
have a will of my own, when a duty is required
of me. But since you desire me to speak my
sentiments freely, permit me to observe, that,
after having conversed with all the guides, and
having been informed by others acquainted with
the country, I am convinced that a road, to be

compared with General Braddock's, or indeed that will be fit for transportation even by pack-horses, can not be made. I own I have no pre-dilection for the route you have in contempla-tion for me."

A few days after writing this letter, he had an interview with Colonel Bouquet, whom he found decided in favour of opening the new road. After their separation, Colonel Washing-ton, with his permission, addressed to him a let-ter to be laid before General Forbes, then indis-posed at Carlisle, in which he stated his reasons against this measure. He concluded his argu-ments against the new road: arguments which appear to be unanswerable, by declaring his fears that, should the attempt be made, they would be able to do nothing more than fortify some post on the other side of the Alleghany, and pre-pare for another campaign. This he prayed Heaven to avert.

He was equally opposed to a scheme which had been suggested of marching by the two dif-ferent routes, and recommended an order of march by Braddock's road, which would bring the whole army before fort Du Quesne in thirty-four days, with a supply of provisions for eighty-six days.

In a letter of the same date addressed to Ma-jor Halket, aid of General Forbes, Colonel Washington thus expressed his forebodings of the mischiefs to be apprehended from the adoption of the proposed route. "I am just returned from a conference held with Colonel Bouquet. I find him fixed—I think I may say unalterably fixed—to lead you a new way to the Ohio, through a road, every inch of which is to be cut at this advanced season, when we have scarcely time left to tread the beaten track, universally confessed to be the best passage through the mountains.

"If Colonel Bouquet succeeds in this point with the general, all is lost! all is lost indeed! our enterprise is ruined! and we shall be stopped at the Laurel hill this winter; but not to gather laurels, except of the kind which cover the mountains. The southern Indians will turn against us, and these colonies will be desolated by such an accession to the enemy's strength. These must be the consequences of a miscarriage; and a miscarriage, the almost necessary consequence of an attempt to march the army by this route."

Colonel Washington's remonstrances and arguments were unavailing; and the new route was adopted. His extreme chagrin at this measure, and at the delays resulting from it, was expressed in anxious letters to Mr. Fauquier, then governor of Virginia, and to the speaker of the house of burgesses.

In a letter to the speaker, written while at fort Cumberland, he said: "We are still encamped here; very sickly, and dispirited at the prospect before us. That appearance of glory which we

September 2.

once had in view—that hope—that laudable ambition of serving our country, and meriting its
applause, are now no more: all is dwindled into
ease, sloth, and fatal inactivity. In a word, all
is lost, if the ways of men in power, like certain
ways of Providence, are not inscrutable. But
we who view the actions of great men at a distance can only form conjectures agreeably to a
limited perception; and, being ignorant of the
comprehensive schemes which may be in contemplation, might mistake egregiously in judging
of things from appearances, or by the lump. Yet
every f**l will have his notions—will prattle
and talk away; and why may not I? We seem
then, in my opinion, to act under the guidance
of an evil genius. The conduct of our leaders,
if not actuated by superior orders, is tempered
with something—I do not care to give a name
to. Nothing now but a miracle can bring this
campaign to a happy issue." He then recapitu-
lated the arguments he had urged against attempting a new road, and added, "But I spoke
unavailingly. The road was immediately begun; and since then, from one to two thousand
men have constantly wrought on it. By the last
accounts I have received, they had cut it to the
foot of the Laurel hill, about thirty-five miles;
and I suppose, by this time, fifteen hundred men
have taken post about ten miles further, at a
placed called Loyal Hanna, where our next fort
is to be constructed.

"We have certain intelligence that the French strength at fort Du Quesne did not exceed eight hundred men, the thirteenth ultimo; including about three or four hundred Indians. See how our time has been misspent—behold how the golden opportunity is lost—perhaps, never to be regained! How is it to be accounted for? Can General Forbes have orders for this?—Impossible. Will then our injured country pass by such abuses? I hope not. Rather let a full representation of the matter go to his majesty; let him know how grossly his glory and interests, and the public money have been prostituted."

Colonel Washington was soon afterwards ordered to Raystown. Major Grant had been previously detached from the advanced post at Loyal Hanna, with a select corps of eight hundred men, to reconnoitre the country about fort Du Quesne. In the night he reached a hill near the fort, and sent forward a party for the purpose of discovery. They burnt a log house, and returned. Next morning, Major Grant detached Major Lewis, of Colonel Washington's regiment, with a baggage guard, two miles into his rear; and sent an engineer, with a covering party, within full view of the fort, to take a plan of the works. In the mean time he ordered the *reveillée* to be beaten in different places. An action soon commenced, on which Major Lewis, leaving Captain Bullett, with about fifty Virginians to guard the baggage, advanced with the utmost celerity to support Major Grant. The English were defeated with considerable loss; and both Major Grant and Major Lewis were taken prisoners. In this action, the Virginians evidenced the spirit with which they had been trained. Out of eight officers, five were killed, a sixth wounded, and a seventh taken prisoner. Captain Bullett, who defended the baggage with great resolution, and contributed to save the remnant of the detachment, was the only officer who escaped unhurt. Of one hundred and sixty-two men, sixty-two were killed on the spot, and two wounded. This conduct reflected high honour on the commanding officer of the regiment as well as on the troops; and he received, on the occasion, the compliments of the general. The total loss was two hundred and seventy-three killed, and forty-two wounded.

October 8.

It was at length determined that the main body of the army should move from Raystown; and the general called on the colonels of regiments, to submit severally to his consideration, a plan for his march. That proposed by Colonel Washington has been preserved, and appears to have been judiciously formed.

They reached the camp at Loyal Hanna, through a road indescribably bad, about the fifth of November; where, as had been predicted, a council of war determined that it was unadviseable to proceed farther this campaign. It would have been almost impossible to winter an army in that position. They must have retreated from the cold inhospitable wilderness into which they had penetrated, or have suffered immensely; perhaps have perished. Fortunately, some prisoners were taken, who informed them of the extreme distress of the fort. Deriving no support from Canada, the garrison was weak; in great want of provisions; and had been deserted by the Indians. These encouraging circumstances changed the resolution which had been taken, and determined the general to prosecute the expedition.

Colonel Washington was advanced in front; and, with immense labour, opened a way for the main body of the army. The troops moved forward with slow and painful steps until they reached fort Du Quesne, of which they took peaceable possession; the garrison having on the preceding night, after evacuating and setting it on fire, proceeded down the Ohio in boats.

To other causes than the vigour of the officer who conducted this enterprise, the capture of this important place is to be ascribed. The naval armaments of Britain had intercepted the reinforcements designed by France for her colonies; and the pressure on Canada was such as to disable the governor of that province from detaching troops to fort Du Quesne. Without the aid of these causes, the extraordinary and

CHAP. I

1758

Fort Du Quesne evacuated by the French, and taken possession of by the English.

November 25.

unaccountable delays of the campaign must have defeated its object.

The works were repaired, and the new fort received the name of the great minister, who, with unparalleled vigour and talents, then governed the nation.

After furnishing two hundred men from his regiment as a garrison for fort Pitt, Colonel Washington marched back to Winchester; whence he soon afterwards proceeded to Williamsburg, to take his seat in the General Assembly, of which he had been elected a member by the county of Frederick, while at fort Cumberland.

A cessation of Indian hostility being the consequence of expelling the French from the Ohio, Virginia was relieved from the dangers with which she had been threatened; and the object for which alone he had continued in the service, after perceiving that he should not be placed on the permanent establishment, was accomplished. His health was much impaired, and his domestic affairs required his attention.

Resignation and marriage of Colonel Washington.

Impelled by these and other motives of a private nature, he determined to withdraw from a service, which he might now quit without dishonour; and, about the close of the year, resigned his commission, as colonel of the first Virginia regiment, and commander-in-chief of all the troops raised in the colony.

The Washington Family Burial Ground

Wakefield, Westmoreland County, Virginia

Here rest the mortal remains of George Washington's great-grand-father, Colonel John Washington, who came to Virginia in 1658 and was buried here in 1677; of his grandfather, Lawrence Washing-ton, buried in 1697; of his grandmother, Jane (Butler), in 1729; of his father, Augustine Washington, in 1743; and other members of the Washington family.

The officers whom he had commanded were greatly attached to him. They manifested their esteem and their regret at parting, by a very affectionate address,* expressive of the high opinion they entertained both of his military and private character.

This opinion was not confined to the officers of his regiment. It was common to Virginia; and had been adopted by the British officers with whom he served. The duties he performed, though not splendid, were arduous; and were executed with zeal, and with judgment. The exact discipline he established in his regiment, when the temper of Virginia was extremely hostile to discipline, does credit to his military character, and the gallantry the troops displayed, whenever called into action, manifests the spirit infused into them by their commander.

The difficulties of his situation, while unable to cover the frontier from the French and Indians, who were spreading death and desolation in every quarter, were incalculably great; and no better evidence of his exertions, under these distressing circumstances, can be given, than the undiminished confidence still placed in him, by those whom he was unable to protect.

The efforts to which he incessantly stimulated his country for the purpose of obtaining possession of the Ohio; the system for the conduct of the war which he continually recommended; the

* See note No. III. at the end of the volume.

vigorous and active measures always urged upon those by whom he was commanded; manifest an ardent and enterprising mind, tempered by judgment, and quickly improved by experience.

Not long after his resignation, he was married to Mrs. Custis; a young lady to whom he had been for some time attached; and who, to a large fortune and fine person, added those amiable accomplishments which ensure domestic happiness, and fill, with silent but unceasing felicity, the quiet scenes of private life.

CHAPTER II.

Colonel Washington appointed commander-in-chief of
the American forces....Arrives at Cambridge....Strength
and disposition of the two armies....Deficiency of the
Americans in arms and ammunition....Distress of
the British from the want of fresh provisions....
Falmouth burnt....Success of the American cruisers....
Measures to form a continental army....Difficulty of
re-enlisting the troops....Plan for attacking Boston....
General Lee detached to New York....Possession
taken of the heights of Dorchester....Boston evacuated....Correspondence respecting prisoners.

THE attention of Colonel Washington, for   1775
several years after his marriage, was principally
directed to the management of his estate. He
continued a most respectable member of the
legislature of his country, in which he took an
early and a decided part against the claims of
supremacy asserted by the British Parliament.
As hostilities approached, he was chosen by the
independent companies, formed through the
northern parts of Virginia, to command them;
and was elected a member of the first congress
which met at Philadelphia. The illustrious
patriots who composed it, soon distinguished him
as the soldier of America, and placed him on all
those committees whose duty it was to make arrangements for defence. When it became necessary to appoint a commander-in-chief, his military character, the solidity of his judgment, the

steady firmness of his temper, the dignity of his person and deportment, the confidence inspired by his patriotism and integrity, and the independence of his fortune, combined to designate him, in the opinion of all, for that important station. Local jealousy was suppressed, not only by the enthusiasm of the moment, but by that policy which induced the sagacious delegation from New England, to prefer a commander-in-chief from the south.

Colonel
Washington
appointed
Commander-
in-chief
of the
American
forces.

June 15.

On the 14th of June, he was unanimously chosen "General, and Commander-in-chief of the armies of the United Colonies, and all the forces now raised, or to be raised by them."*

On the succeeding day, when the President communicated this appointment to him, he expressed his high sense of the honour conferred upon him, and his firm determination to exert every power he possessed in the service of his country and of her "glorious cause." At the same time he acknowledged the distress he felt from a consciousness that his abilities and military experience might not be equal to the extensive and important trust.

He declined all compensation for his services; and avowed an intention to keep an exact account of his expenses, which he should rely on Congress to discharge.

A special commission was directed, and a resolution unanimously passed, declaring that "Con-

---

* See note No. IV. at the end of the volume.

gress would maintain, assist, and adhere to him, as the General and Commander-in-chief of the forces raised, or to be raised, for the maintenance and preservation of American liberty, with their lives and fortunes."

He prepared, without delay, to enter upon the arduous duties of his office; and, remaining only a few days in New York, where several important arrangements were to be made, proceeded to the head quarters of the American army.

As all orders of men concurred in approving his appointment, all concurred in expressing their satisfaction at that event, and their determination to afford him entire support. A committee of the Congress of Massachusetts waited to receive him at Springfield, on the confines of the colony, and to escort him to the army. On his arrival, an address was presented to him by the House of Representatives, breathing the most cordial affection, and testifying the most exalted respect. His answer* was well calculated to keep up impressions essential to

Arrives at
Cambridge.

---

* It is in the following terms:
"Gentlemen,—Your kind congratulations on my appointment and arrival, demand my warmest acknowledgments, and will be ever retained in grateful remembrance. In exchanging the enjoyments of domestic life for the duties of my present honourable but arduous situation, I only emulate the virtue and public spirit of the whole Province of Massachusetts, which, with a firmness and patriotism without example, has sacrificed all the comforts of social and political life, in support of the rights of mankind, and the welfare of our common country. My highest ambition is to be the happy instrument of vindicating these rights, and to see this devoted Province again restored to peace, liberty, and safety.
"GEO: WASHINGTON."

CHAP. II

1775

July 3.

Strength and
disposition
of the
two armies.

the success of that arduous contest into which
the United Colonies had entered.

The first moments after his arrival in camp
were employed in reconnoitring the enemy, and
examining the strength and situation of the
American troops.

The main body of the British army, under
the immediate command of General Howe, was
entrenching itself strongly on Bunker's hill.
Three floating batteries lay in Mystic river, near
the camp, and a twenty gun ship below the
ferry, between Boston and Charlestown.   A
strong battery on the Boston side of the water,
on Cop's or Cope's hill, served to cover and
strengthen the post on Bunker's hill.   Another
division was deeply entrenched on Roxbury
neck.   The light horse, and an inconsiderable
body of infantry, were stationed in Boston.

The American army lay on both sides of
Charles river.   The right occupied the high
grounds about Roxbury; whence it extended towards Dorchester; and the left was covered by
Mystic or Medford river, a space of at least
twelve miles.   These extensive lines could not
be contracted without opening to the British
general a communication with the country.

For the purpose of a more distinct arrangement, the army was thrown into three grand
divisions.   That part of it which lay about Roxbury constituted the right wing, and was commanded by Major General Ward; the troops

near Mystic or Medford river formed the left, which was placed under Major General Lee. The centre, including the reserve, was under the immediate command of General Washington, whose head quarters were at Cambridge.

The army consisted of fourteen thousand five hundred men; but several circumstances combined to render this force less effective than its numbers would indicate.

So long had the hope of avoiding open hostilities been indulged, that the time for making preparations to meet them had passed away unemployed, and the neglect could not be remedied. On General Washington's arrival in camp, he had ordered a return of the ammunition to be made; and the report stated three hundred and three barrels of powder to be in store. A few days after this return, the alarming discovery was made, that the actual quantity was not more than sufficient to furnish each man with nine cartridges. This mistake had been produced by a misapprehension of the committee of supplies, (for the magazines were not yet in possession of military officers,) who, instead of returning the existing quantity, reported the whole which had been originally furnished by the Province. Though the utmost exertions were made, this critical state of things continued about a fortnight, when a small supply of powder was received from Elizabethtown, in New

Deficiency of the Americans in arms and ammunition.

Jersey.* The utmost address was used to conceal from the enemy this alarming deficiency;
but when it is recollected, in how many various
directions, and to what various bodies, application for assistance was unavoidably made, it
will appear scarcely possible that those efforts
at concealment could have been completely successful. It is more probable that the communications which must have been made to the British general were discredited; and that he could
not permit himself to believe, that an army without bayonets would be hardy enough to maintain the position occupied by the Provincials,
if destitute of ammunition.

The troops were also in such need of tents,
as to be placed in barracks, instead of being
encamped in the open field; and were almost
destitute of clothing. They had, too, been raised
by the colonial governments; each of which or-
ganized its quota on different principles. From
this cause resulted not only a want of uniform-
ity, but other defects which were much more
important. In Massachusetts, the soldiers had
chosen their platoon officers, and generally lived
with them as equals. This unmilitary practice

---

* A circumstance attending this transaction, will furnish
some idea of the difficulties encountered by those who then
conducted the affairs of America. All-important to the general safety as was the speedy replenishment of the magazines
of that army which lay encamped in front of the enemy, the
committee of Elizabethtown was under the necessity of transmitting this powder secretly, lest the people of the neighbourhood should seize and detain it for their own security.

was the certain index of that general insubordination which pervaded every department. The difficulty of establishing principles of order and obedience, always considerable among raw troops, was increased by the short terms for which enlistments had been made. The quotas of some of the colonies would be entitled to a discharge in November; and none were engaged to continue in service longer than the last of December. The early orders evidence a state of things still more loose and unmilitary than was to be inferred from the circumstances under which the war had been commenced.

An additional inconvenience, derived from this mixed agency of local governments with that of the Union, was thus stated by General Washington in a letter addressed to congress:—"I should be extremely deficient in gratitude as well as justice, if I did not take the first opportunity to acknowledge the readiness and attention which the congress and different committees have shown to make every thing as convenient and agreeable as possible; but there is a vital and inherent principle of delay, incompatible with military service, in transacting business through such various and different channels.* I esteem it my duty, therefore, to represent the inconvenience that must unavoidably ensue from a

---

* The General was under the necessity of carrying on a direct correspondence, not only with the several colonial governments, but with the committees of all the important towns and some inferior places.

dependence on a number of persons for supplies; and submit it to the consideration of congress, whether the public service will not be best
promoted by appointing a Commissary General
for the purpose." †

Every military operation was also seriously
affected by the total want of engineers, and
the deficiency of working tools.

To increase difficulties already so considerable,
the appointment of general officers, made by
congress, gave extensive dissatisfaction, and determined several of those who thought themselves injured, to retire from the service.

These disadvantages deducted essentially
from the capacity of the American force: but
under them all, the General observed with pleasure "the materials for a good army." These
were "a great number of men, able bodied, active, zealous in the cause, and of unquestionable
courage." Possessed of these materials, he employed himself indefatigably in their organization. The army was arranged into divisions and
brigades; and congress was urged to the appointment of a Paymaster, Quarter-master General,
and such other general staff as are indispensable
in the structure of a regular military establishment.

The two armies continued to work on their
respective fortifications, without seriously mo-

---

† It is strange that an army should have been formed without such an officer.

lesting each other. Slight skirmishes occasionally took place, in which little execution was done; and, although the Americans made some advances, no attempt was made to dislodge them.

The Commander-in-chief submitted with reluctance to this state of apparent inactivity. He felt the importance of destroying the army in Boston, before it should be strengthened by reinforcements in the ensuing spring; and with a view to this object, frequently reconnoitred its situation, and was assiduous in collecting every information respecting its strength. The result of his observations and inquiries seems to have been, a strong inclination to the opinion, that to carry the works by storm, though hazardous, was not impracticable. A council of general officers being unanimously of opinion, that for the present at least, the attempt ought not to be made, it was laid aside.

September.

A rigorous blockade being maintained, the British army began to suffer considerably for fresh meat and vegetables. The small parties which sailed from Boston, in quest of these articles, were frequently disappointed by the vigilance of the minute men. But the continuance of active exertion, which this service required on the part of the inhabitants of the sea coast, soon became burdensome; and the governors of the several colonies pressed for detachments from the main army. Although it was impossible

Distress of the British from the want of fresh provisions.

to spare the troops required, without hazarding the cause of the colonies, great irritation was excited by the refusal to comply with these demands of particular protection. They at length became so importunate, and the unavoidable refusal to comply with them was so ill received, that congress was induced to pass a resolution, declaring that the army before Boston was designed only to oppose the enemy at that place, and ought not to be weakened by detachments for the security of other parts of the country. At Newport, in Rhode Island, the committee sought to secure the place, by entering into a compromise with Captain Wallace, who commanded the ships of war on that station, stipulating that he should be furnished with provisions on condition of his sparing the town, and committing no depredations on the country. This compromise contravened so essentially the general plan of distressing the British forces, that General Washington deemed it necessary to interpose, and represent to the Governor of that province, the mischief to be apprehended from so dangerous a practice.

While the blockade of Boston was thus perseveringly maintained, other events of considerable importance took place elsewhere.

In July, Georgia joined her sister colonies, and chose delegates to represent her in congress: after which, the style of "The thirteen United Colonies" was assumed; and by that title, the

English Provinces, confederated and in arms, were thenceforward designated.

After a recess of one month, congress again assembled at Philadelphia. The state of the colonies, and the letters of the Commander-in-chief being immediately taken into consideration, the scarcity of arms and ammunition engaged their most serious attention. Great exertions * had been made, by importation and by domestic manufacture, to extricate the country from this perilous situation; but the supplies were unequal to the necessities of the army; and the danger resulting from the want of articles, so vitally essential in war, still continued to be great.

The importance of a maritime force to the military operations of a country possessing an immense extent of sea coast must always be sensibly felt; and, in an early stage of the contest, the particular attention of the United Colonies was directed more immediately to this interesting object, by an event not very unusual in war, but which, at this time, excited no ordinary degree of resentment.

Orders had been issued to the commanders of the British ships of war to proceed, as in the case of actual rebellion, against those seaport towns

---

* The agents of congress had the address to purchase all the powder on the coast of Africa, and that within the British forts, without attracting notice; and to seize the magazine in the island of Bermuda. Great exertions were also made in the interior to obtain saltpetre and sulphur, for the manufacture of that important article.

which were accessible, and in which any troops should be raised, or military works erected.

Falmouth, a flourishing village on the sea coast of Massachusetts, having given some particular offence, a small naval force, commanded by Captain Mowat, was, under colour of these

orders, detached for its destruction. After making an ineffectual effort to induce the inhabitants to deliver up their arms and ammunition, and four of the principal citizens as hostages, he

commenced a furious cannonade and bombardment, by which the town was reduced to ashes. An attempt was then made to penetrate into the country; but the militia and minute men, rather irritated than intimidated by this wanton act of unavailing devastation, drove the party, which had landed, back to their ships.

This measure was loudly reprobated throughout America, and contributed, not a little, to turn the attention of the United Colonies to their marine. It was one immediate motive with the convention of Massachusetts, for granting letters of marque and reprisal; and was assigned by congress, in addition to the capture of American merchantmen on the high seas, as an inducement for fitting out some ships of war; to man which they directed two battalions of marines to be recruited.

Though congress deferred granting general letters of reprisal, they adopted a measure of equal efficacy, but less hostile in appearance.

Their ships of war were authorized to capture all vessels employed in giving assistance to the enemy; the terms used in their resolution were such as comprehended every possible capture. A few small cruisers had already been fitted out by the directions of General Washington; and the coasts soon swarmed with the privateers of New England. These naval exertions were attended Success of the American cruisers. with valuable consequences. Many captures were made; and important supplies of ammunition were thus obtained.

Although the British army had manifested no intention to evacuate Boston, fears were continually entertained for New York. Mr. Tryon, who was popular in that province, had been lately recalled from North Carolina, and appointed its governor. His utmost influence was employed in detaching that colony from the union; and his exertions were seconded by the Asia man of war, whose guns commanded the town. The consequence of these intrigues and of this terror was, that even in the convention, disaffection to the American cause began openly to show itself; and a determination to join the king's standard is said to have been expressed with impunity. These threatening appearances were rendered the more serious by some confidential communications from England, stating the intention of administration to send a fleet into the Hudson, and to occupy both New York and Albany. Under the alarm thus excited, an effort was made in congress to obtain a resolution for seizing the governor. He had, however, been artful enough to make impressions in his favour; and he was defended by a part of the delegation from New York with so much earnestness that, for a time, the advocates of the proposition forbore to press it. Afterwards, when the increasing defection in that province induced Congress to resume the subject, the resolution was expressed in general terms; and assumed the form of a recommendation, to those who exercised the legislative and executive functions in the several provinces, "to arrest and secure every person in the respective colonies, whose going at large might, in their opinion, endanger the safety of the colony, or the liberties of America." Intelligence of this resolution is supposed to have been received by the governor, who, after some correspondence with the mayor of the city respecting his personal safety, retired for security on board the Halifax packet, and continued to carry on his intrigues with nearly as much advantage as while on shore.

But the subject which, next to the supply of arms and ammunition, most interested the American government, was the re-enlistment of the army.

Measures
to form a
continental
army.

On the 29th of September, at the earnest solicitation of General Washington, a committee had been appointed by congress, with directions to repair to the camp at Cambridge; there to con-

The Historic Washington Elm at Cambridge, Massachusetts.

The Historic Washington Elm at Cambridge, Massachusetts

"Under this tree," as the granite tablet states, *"Washington first took command of the American army, July 3d, 1775."* This picture is from a photograph taken about the year 1900. In spite of the most determined efforts to preserve this historic relic, the tree fell in November, 1923.

© U&U

In the commencement of the contest, while the minds of many were undetermined, it was of vast importance to secure the public confidence, and it was necessary to pay some attention even to the public caprice. The real difficulties under which he laboured were not generally known. His numbers were exaggerated, and his means of carrying on offensive operations were magnified. The expulsion of the British army from Boston had been long since anticipated by many; and those were not wanting, who endeavoured to spread discontent by insinuating that the Commander-in-chief was desirous of prolonging the war, in order to continue his own importance. To these symptoms of impatience, and to the consequences they might produce, he could not be insensible; but it was not in his power to silence such complaints, by disclosing to the world his real situation. His views still continued to be directed towards Boston; and, congress having manifested a disposition favourable to an attack on that place, the general officers had been again assembled, and had again advised unanimously against the measure. Supposing that fears for the safety of the town might embarrass the proceedings of the army, congress resolved, "that if General Washington and his December. council of war should be of opinion that a successful attack might be made on the troops in Boston, he should make it in any manner he might think expedient, notwithstanding the town and property in it might be thereby destroyed."

Whilst waiting for a favourable opportunity to execute this bold plan, the American general availed himself of the occasional aids received from the militia, to make advances on the besieged, and to seize positions which would favour ulterior operations. Ploughed Hill, Cobble Hill, and Lechmere's Point, were successively occupied and fortified. His approaches were carried within half a mile of the works on Bunker's Hill; and his guns drove their floating batteries from their stations, and protected others constructed under his orders.

Plans for attacking Boston.

Hitherto, the object of the war had been a redress of grievances. The language, that it was a war against a corrupt administration, had been carefully observed; and allegiance to the British crown was universally avowed. The progress, however, of the public mind towards independence, though slow, was certain; and measures were necessarily taken, which apparently tended to that object. Among these, was the act of establishing temporary governments in place of that revolutionary system which followed the suspension of the ancient institutions.

The first application on this subject was made by Massachusetts; * and her example was soon

---

* On this application congress recommended that an assembly and council should be chosen in the usual way, who should exercise the powers of government until a Governor of his Majesty's appointment should consent to govern the colony according to its charter.

followed by other colonies. These applications could not fail to draw forth the sentiments of members on the very interesting question of separation from the mother country. They who wished to lead public opinion to independence, were desirous of establishing a regular government in each province, entirely competent to the administration of its affairs; while they who were hostile to that event, opposed every measure which might either incline the colonies towards it, or strengthen the opinion in Great Britain, that it was the real object of all who had resisted the legislative supremacy of parliament. A resolution was with difficulty obtained in the case of New Hampshire, which formed a precedent for others of the same nature, recommending to the provincial convention to call a full and free representation of the people, who should establish such form of government as would best promote the general happiness, and most effectually secure peace and good order in the colony, during the continuance of the present dispute with Great Britain. Without this last clause, which still maintained the appearance of preserving the ancient connexion with the parent state, the recommendation would not have been made. About the same time, congress also resolved that it would be extremely dangerous to the liberties and welfare of America, for any colony separately to petition the king or either house of parliament.

Having taken into consideration a proclamation, declaring certain persons in the colonies to have forgotten their allegiance, and to be in a state of open rebellion, and threatening with punishment those who should be found carrying on correspondence with them;—congress declared, "in the name of the people of these United Colonies, and by the authority according to the purest maxims of representation derived from them, that whatever punishment shall be inflicted upon any persons in the power of their enemies, for favouring, aiding, or abetting the cause of American liberty, shall be retaliated in the same kind, and in the same degree, upon those in their power, who have favoured, aided, or abetted, or shall favour, aid, or abet the system of ministerial oppression."

The British army, the command of which, on the recall of General Gage, had devolved upon General Howe, still remained inactive in Boston; and was still closely blocked up on the land side. The history of this winter campaign, is a history of successive struggles on the part of the American general, with the difficulties imposed by the want of arms, ammunition, and permanent troops, on a person extremely solicitous, by some grand and useful achievement, to prove himself worthy of the high station to which the voice of his country had called him.

Considering the resolution relative to the attack on Boston as indicating the desire of congress on that subject, he assured the president that an attempt would be made to put it in execution the first moment he should perceive a probability of success. If this should not occur, as soon as might be expected or wished, he prayed that his situation might be recollected, and that congress would do him the justice to believe, that circumstances, not inclination on his part, occasioned the delay. "It is not," said he, "in the pages of history to furnish a case like ours. To maintain a post within musket shot of the enemy for six months together, without *ammunition;* and at the same time, to disband one army and recruit another, within that distance of twenty-odd British regiments, is more than, probably, ever was attempted. But if we succeed as well in the latter, as we have hitherto done in the former, I shall think it the most fortunate event of my whole life."

In the month of January a council of war, at which Mr. John Adams, a member of congress, and Mr. Warren, president of the provincial congress of Massachusetts, assisted: Resolved, "that a vigorous attempt ought to be made on the ministerial troops in Boston, before they can be reinforced in the spring, if the means can be provided, and a favourable opportunity should offer." It was farther advised, "that thirteen regiments of militia should be asked for from Massachusetts and the neighbouring colonies, in order to put the army in a condition to make the attempt. The militia to assemble on the first of February, and to continue in service, if necessary, until the first of March." The colonies readily complied with these requisitions; but so mild had the season hitherto been, that the waters about Boston continued open. "Congress would discover in my last," said the general, on the nineteenth of January, "my motives for strengthening these lines with militia. But whether, as the weather turns out exceedingly mild, (insomuch as to promise nothing favourable from ice,) and there is no appearance of powder, I shall be able to attempt any thing decisive, time only can determine. No man upon earth wishes to destroy the nest in Boston more than I do; no person would be willing to go greater lengths than I shall to accomplish it, if it shall be thought adviseable; but if we have no powder to bombard with, nor ice to pass on, we shall be in no better situation than we have been all the year: we shall be in a worse, as their works are stronger."

Early in January, the Commander-in-chief received unquestionable intelligence that an armament was equipping in Boston, to sail under General Clinton on a secret expedition. Many considerations induced him to believe that New York was its destination. He thought the possession of the Hudson of great importance to the British: and that the numerous adherents to the royal cause in New York, furnished an additional reason for transferring the seat of war to that colony. Whilst deliberating on this subject, he received a letter from General Lee, requesting to be detached to Connecticut, for the purpose of assembling a body of volunteers, who should march into New York, and be employed both for the security of that place, and the expulsion or suppression of a band of tories collecting on Long Island. Though inclined to the adoption of this measure, delicacy towards those who exercised the powers of civil government in the colony, suspended his decision on it. Mr. John Adams, who possessed great and well merited influence, was then at Watertown, attending the provincial convention; and with him, the general held some communications respecting his powers. That gentleman being decidedly of opinion that they extended to the case, General Lee was detached, with instructions to raise a body of volunteers in Connecticut, to reinforce the battalions of New Jersey and New York, which were placed under his command. His orders were to proceed to New York; to examine the fortifications of the city, and up the river; to put them in the best possible state of defence; to disarm all persons whose conduct rendered them justly suspected of designs unfriendly to the government, especially those on Long Island; and to collect the arms and ammunition in their possession, for the use of the army.

General Lee
detached to
New York.

No difficulty was found in raising the volunteers required from Connecticut. The people of that province were zealous and enterprising, and Governor Trumbull having sanctioned the measure, troops were immediately embodied, and Lee commenced his march for New York at the head of twelve hundred men.

The inhabitants of that place were much alarmed at his approach. Captain Parker of the Asia man of war had threatened that he would destroy the town in the event of its being entered by any considerable body of provincials; and it was believed that these threats would be executed.

A committee of safety, which had been appointed to exercise the powers of government during the recess of the provincial congress, addressed a letter to General Lee, expressing astonishment at the report that he was about to enter the town without previously intimating his design, and pressing him earnestly not to pass the confines of Connecticut, until they could have further explanations with him.

Holding in utter contempt the threats of Captain Parker, Lee continued his march; and, in a letter * to congress, represented in such strong terms the impolicy of leaving the military arrangements for New York under the control of the local government, that congress appointed three of their own body, to consult with him

---

* See note No. V. at the end of the volume.

and the council of safety, respecting the defence of the place; and instructed him to obey the directions of that committee.

Lee soon acquired that ascendancy which is the prerogative of a superior mind, over those who were sent for his government, and they directed him to execute whatever he suggested. A plan recommended by him, for fortifying the city and preserving its connexion with Long Island, was adopted, and prosecuted with vigour.

General Clinton arrived almost at the same instant with General Lee, but without troops. He said openly, that none were coming; that no hostilities were contemplated against New York; and that he was, himself, merely on a visit to his friend Tryon. "If it be really so," added General Lee, in his letter containing this communication, "it is the most whimsical piece of civility I ever heard of." General Clinton did not affect to conceal that his real object was to proceed to North Carolina, where he expected that five regiments from Europe would join the small force he should carry with him.

About the middle of February, the cold was intense, and the ice became sufficiently firm to bear the troops. General Washington was now disposed to execute the bold plan he had formed, of attacking General Howe in Boston; but a council of war being almost unanimous against the measure, it was abandoned. The want of

ammunition for the artillery was a principal inducement to this opinion.

The attempt, probably, would not have succeeded, and must certainly have been attended
with considerable loss. But the advice of the
council seems to have been adopted with regret.
In communicating their opinion to congress, the
general observed, "Perhaps the irksomeness of
my situation may have given different ideas to
me, from those which influence the gentlemen I
consulted; and might have inclined me to put
more to the hazard than was consistent with
prudence. If it had this effect, I am not sensible
of it, as I endeavoured to give the subject all
the consideration a matter of such importance
required. True it is, and I can not help acknowledging, that I have many disagreeable sensations on account of my situation; for, to have
the eyes of the whole continent fixed on me,
with anxious expectation of hearing some great
event, and to be restrained in every military operation for want of the necessary means to carry
it on, is not very pleasing; especially as the
means used to conceal my weakness from the
enemy, conceal it also from our friends, and add
to their wonder."

Late in February, various appearances among
the British troops indicated an intention to evacuate Boston; but as these appearances might
be deceptive, and he had now received a small
supply of powder, General Washington deter-

mined to prosecute vigorously a plan he had formed, to force General Howe either to come to an action, or to abandon the town.

Since the allowance of a bounty, recruiting had been more successful; and the regular force had been augmented to rather more than fourteen thousand men. In addition to these troops, the Commander-in-chief had called to his aid about six thousand of the militia of Massachusetts. Thus reinforced, he determined to take possession of the heights of Dorchester, and to fortify them. As the possession of this post would enable him to annoy the ships in the harbour and the soldiers in the town, he was persuaded that a general action would ensue. But if this hope should be disappointed, his purpose was to make the works on the heights of Dorchester only preparatory to seizing and fortifying Nook's Hill, and the points opposite the south end of Boston, which commanded the harbour, a great part of the town, and the beach from which an embarkation must take place in the event of a retreat.

To facilitate the execution of this plan, a heavy bombardment and cannonade were commenced on the town and on the British lines, which were repeated the two succeeding nights. On the last of them, immediately after the firing had begun, a strong detachment, under the command of General Thomas, took possession of the heights without opposition. Such was their ac-

March.

Possession taken of the heights of Dorchester.

tivity and industry through the night that, although the ground was almost impenetrable, the works were sufficiently advanced by the morning, nearly to cover them. When daylight disclosed their operations to the British, a considerable degree of embarrassment appeared, and an ineffectual fire was commenced on the party in possession of the heights, who in turn opened a battery on the besieged; and continued with unremitting labour to strengthen their position.

It was necessary to dislodge the Americans from the heights, or to evacuate the town; and General Howe, as had been foreseen, determined to embrace the former part of the alternative. Three thousand chosen men, to be commanded by Lord Percy, were ordered on this service. These troops were embarked, and fell down to the castle, in order to proceed up the river to the intended scene of action; but were scattered by a furious storm, which disabled them from immediately prosecuting the enterprise. Before they could again be in readiness for the attack, the works were made so strong, that the attempt to storm them was thought unadviseable, and the evacuation of the town became inevitable.

In the expectation that the flower of the British troops would be employed against the heights of Dorchester, General Washington had concerted a plan for availing himself of that occasion, to attack Boston itself. The storm which defeated the proposed attack on the heights defeated this enterprise also.

The determination to evacuate Boston was soon communicated. A paper signed by some of the select men of the town, and brought out with a flag, stated the fact. This paper was accompanied by propositions said to be made on the part of General Howe, but not signed by him, relative to the security of the town, and the peaceable embarkation of his army. As these propositions were not addressed to the Commander-in-chief, and were not authenticated by the signature of General Howe, nor by any act obligatory on him, General Washington thought it improper directly to notice them; and ordered the officer to whom they were delivered to return an answer stating the reasons why they were not treated with more attention. The determination, however, to continue his advances and to secure Nook's Hill, was changed; and considerable detachments were moved towards New York, before the actual evacuation of Boston. This event took place on the 17th of March; and, in a few days, the whole fleet sailed out of Nantasket road, directing its course eastward.

Boston evacuated.

March 17.

The recovery of this important town gave great joy to the United Colonies. Congress passed a vote of thanks to the General and his army, "for their wise and spirited conduct in the siege and acquisition of Boston;" and directed a medal of gold to be struck in commemoration of the event.

As soon as the British fleet had put to sea, the American army proceeded by divisions to New York, where it arrived on the 14th of April.

During the siege of Boston, an altercation concerning prisoners took place between the commanders of the respective armies, which was viewed with great interest throughout America. The character of the war—a war between a sovereign and those who professed to be his subjects, led to a course of conduct on the part of the British General, which the actual state of things did not justify.

General Gage, as Governor of Massachusetts, had received all the irritations of which his mind was susceptible—irritations which seemed to have had no inconsiderable influence over his conduct as Commander-in-chief. He regarded the Americans nearly as rebels; and treated them as if the great national resistance they were making on principle, was to be viewed as the act of a few daring and turbulent individuals, rising against laws of unquestionable obligation, who would soon be quelled, and punished for their disobedience of legitimate authority. In this spirit, he threw some distinguished gentlemen of Boston, and the American officers and soldiers who fell into his hands, into the common jail of felons; and treated them, without respect to military rank or condition, not as prisoners of war, but as state criminals.

General Washington remonstrated very seriously against this unjustifiable measure. Considering political opinion entirely out of the question, and "conceiving the obligations of humanity, and the claims of rank, to be universally binding, except in the case of retaliation;" he expressed the hope he had entertained, "that they would have induced, on the part of the British General, a conduct more conformable to the rights they gave." While he claimed the benefits of these rights, he declared his determination "to be regulated entirely, in his conduct towards the prisoners who should fall into his hands, by the treatment which those in the power of the British General should receive."

To this letter, a haughty and intemperate answer was returned, retorting the complaints concerning the treatment of prisoners, and affecting to consider it as an instance of clemency, that the cord was not applied to those whose imprisonment was complained of. To this answer, General Washington gave a manly and dignified reply, which was, he said, "to close their correspondence perhaps forever;" and which concluded with saying, "If your officers, our prisoners, receive from me a treatment different from what I wished to show them, they and you will remember the occasion of it."

The result of this correspondence was communicated to the council of Massachusetts,* who were requested to order the British officers then on parole to be confined in close jail, and the soldiers to be sent to such place of security as the general court should direct.

On the recall of General Gage, the command devolved on General Howe, whose conduct was less exceptionable; and this rigorous treatment of prisoners was relaxed.

Not long after this correspondence with General Gage, while Montgomery was employed in the siege of St. John's, Colonel Ethan Allen was captured in a bold and rash attempt on Montreal. Under the pretext of his having acted without authority, he was put in irons, and sent to England as a traitor.

While he was yet in Canada, congress requested the Commander-in-chief to inquire into the fact. He addressed a letter to Sir William Howe, requiring explanations on it, and assuring him that General Prescot, who had been taken in Canada, and was understood to have contributed to the severities inflicted on Colonel Allen, should receive exactly the fate of that officer.

---

* In the early part of the war, congress had appointed no commissary of prisoners; nor had the government taken upon itself the custody of them. They were entrusted for safe keeping to the respective legislatures and committees, to whom it was necessary to apply for the execution of every order respecting them.

General Howe, not holding any authority in Canada, or not choosing to enter fully into this subject, General Schuyler was directed to make particular inquiries into the conduct of Prescot; and congress, on being informed of the inefficacy of the application to General Howe, ordered that officer into close jail.

CHAPTER III.

Invasion of Canada meditated....Siege of St. John's....
Capture of fort Chamblée....Carleton defeated at
Longueisle....St. John's capitulated....Montreal sur-
renders....Arnold's expedition....He arrives before
Quebec....Retires to Point Aux Trembles....Mont-
gomery lays siege to Quebec....Unsuccessful attack on
that place....Death of Montgomery....Blockade of
Quebec....General Thomas takes command of the
army....The blockade raised....General Sullivan takes
the command....Battle of the Three Rivers....Canada
evacuated....General Carleton constructs a fleet....En-
ters lake Champlain....Defeats the American flotilla....
Takes possession of Crown Point....Retires into winter quarters.

1775   DURING these transactions, events of great
interest were passing still further north.

Serious dissatisfaction prevailed in Canada.
The measures of administration had disquieted
the British settlers, without conciliating the
ancient inhabitants. At the same time, the regular troops had been chiefly ordered to Boston,
and the province left almost entirely undefended. These facts were known in the United
Colonies. It was also known that military stores
to an immense amount had been deposited in
Quebec, and that preparations were making to
invade the colonies from that quarter. The possession of that country was believed to be all important; and its present temper countenanced
the opinion, that its weight would be thrown into
the scale of that party, which should first show a

force in it sufficient for the protection of its inhabitants. The facility with which Crown Point and Ticonderoga had been taken, and the command of the lakes George and Champlain acquired, added to the motives already stated, inspiring congress with the daring design of anticipating the plans meditated in Canada, by taking possession of that province.

In June, 1775, a resolution passed that body, directing General Schuyler to repair to Ticonderoga, and take the proper measures for securing that post and Crown Point, and for retaining the command of the lakes. He was, at the same time authorized, if he should find the measure not disagreeable to the Canadians, to take possession of St. John's and Montreal, and to pursue any other steps which might have a tendency to promote the peace and security of the United Colonies.

Near three thousand men from New England and New York were designed for this service. A number of batteaux were directed to be built at Ticonderoga and Crown Point, to convey them along lake Champlain, and fifty thousand dollars in specie were voted for the expenses of the army in Canada.

General Schuyler, who was at New York when this important command was confided to him, hastened to Ticonderoga, in order to make the necessary arrangements for the enterprise.

The troops of that department, belonging to different colonies, stationed at different places, and acknowledging no one commanding officer, were found in a state of entire disorganization. The stores were misapplied, or wasted; no subordination nor camp discipline was observed; and had the enemy been in a condition to attempt a *coup de main*, Ticonderoga and Crown Point would have been lost, with as much facility as they had been acquired.

Schuyler immediately commenced the task of preparing vessels for the transportation of the troops; a task the more laborious and tedious, as the timber for the batteaux was then to be procured from the woods. Before the preparations were complete, or the soldiers destined for the expedition were assembled, the impatience expressed by the discontented in Canada rendered an immediate movement adviseable.

Orders were therefore given to General Montgomery to embark with the troops then in readiness; and General Schuyler having directed the expected reinforcements to rendezvous at the Isle Aux Noix, followed and joined him before he reached that place.

Circular letters to the Canadians, exhorting them to rouse and assert their liberties, and declaring, that the Americans entered their country, not as enemies, but as friends and protectors, were immediately dispersed among them; and to improve the favourable impression which had

been made, it was determined to advance directly
to St. John's. On the sixth of September, the
American army, amounting to about one thousand men, entirely destitute of artillery, embarked on the Sorel, and proceeding down that
river, landed within a mile and a half of the fort.
The intelligence received during the evening,
determined them to return to the Isle Aux Noix,
and wait for their remaining troops and artillery.

The Isle Aux Noix lies at the junction of the
Sorel with lake Champlain; and to prevent the
armed vessels at St. John's from entering the
latter, a boom was drawn across the narrow
channel, at the point of union between those
waters.

While at that place, General Schuyler became so ill as to be confined to his bed; and
the command devolved on Montgomery.

Late in September the artillery was brought
up; and reinforcements arrived, which aug- September 25
mented the army to nearly two thousand men;—
upon which Montgomery again proceeded to the Siege of St. Johns.
investment of St. John's. This place was gar-
risoned by five or six hundred regulars, with
about two hundred Canadian militia, and was
well provided with artillery and military stores
The army of Canada, as well as the other armies
of the United Colonies, was almost entirely
without powder; and, of consequence, the siege
advanced slowly. Its necessities in this respect
were fortunately relieved by the capture of fort

CHAP. III

1775

October.

Capture of
Fort
Chamblée.

Chamblée, which being supposed to be covered by St. John's, was not in a defensible condition. In this place, about one hundred and twenty barrels of gunpowder were taken, after which the siege of St. John's was prosecuted with vigour; but the garrison made a resolute defence, and for some time indulged the hope of being relieved.*

Colonel· M'Clean, a veteran officer, with his regiment of royal highland emigrants, and a few hundred Canadians, was posted near the junction of the Sorel with the St. Lawrence. General Carleton was at Montreal, where he had collected about a thousand men, chiefly Canadians. At the head of these troops, he hoped to effect a junction with M'Clean, after which he designed to march with his whole force against Montgomery, and endeavour to raise the siege; but, on attempting to cross over from
Montreal, he was encountered and entirely defeated at Longueisle by a detachment of the American troops under Colonel Warner. Another party advanced on M'Clean. Being entirely abandoned by his Canadians so soon as they were informed of the defeat of the governor, and having also received information that Arnold was approaching Point Levi, M'Clean retreated to Quebec. The Americans occupied the post he had abandoned, and erected batteries on a point of land at the junction of the Sorel with the

* Annual Register.

St. Lawrence; where they also constructed several armed rafts and floating batteries, in order to prevent Carleton with the vessels at Montreal from escaping down the river.

Montgomery was pressing the siege of St. John's with great vigour, and had advanced his works near the fort, when the account of the success at Longueisle reached him. On receiving this intelligence, he sent a flag by one of the prisoners, with a letter to Major Preston, the commanding officer, demanding a surrender of the place. All hopes of relief having now vanished, the garrison capitulated, on being allowed the honours of war.

Scarcely was this first success obtained, when the consequences of short enlistments began to be felt. The time of service for which the troops had engaged being about to expire, great difficulty was experienced in prevailing on them to proceed farther; and before the General could induce them to march against Montreal, he was under the necessity of stipulating explicitly, that all who wished it should be discharged at that place. Having effected this compromise, he proceeded against Montreal; while his floating batteries, under Colonel Easton, advanced up the St. Lawrence, and not only prevented the armed vessels of the enemy from escaping to Quebec, but drove them still higher up the river.

Montreal was not in a condition to be defended. After engaging to allow the Canadians their own laws, the free exercise of their religion, and the privilege of governing themselves, Montgomery took peaceable possession of the town; and Governor Carleton retired to his flotilla.

While preparations were making to attack these vessels, the Governor was conveyed in a boat with muffled oars down the river, in a dark night, and made his escape to Quebec. The fleet soon afterwards surrendered, and the General prepared, with the utmost expedition, to proceed with the few troops who were willing to follow him, to the capital of Canada.

Diminished as his army was by the discharge of those who claimed the performance of his engagements made at St. John's, it was necessary to leave a part of it at Montreal, St. John's, and Chamblée to garrison those places—keep open the communication between Quebec and the United Colonies—preserve the dependence of the Canadians—overawe the Indians, and hold in check the garrisons above him at Detroit and Niagara. These essential objects, though provided for with the utmost possible economy of men, formed such deductions from his force, as to leave little more than three hundred soldiers to follow their General in the enterprise against Quebec.

Foreseeing that the whole force of Canada would be concentrated about Montreal, General

Washington had planned an expedition against Quebec, to be carried on by a detachment from his camp before Boston, which was to march by the way of Kennebec river; and, passing through the dreary wilderness lying between the settled parts of Maine and the St. Lawrence, to enter Canada about ninety miles below Montreal.

The object of this hardy enterprise was to compel Carleton, either to draw his troops from the upper country and leave the passage open to the army invading the province by the way of the river Sorel, or, if he should maintain that position, to take possession of Quebec. All his accounts assured him that this place was unable to hold out against the force which would appear before it; and, if attacked by an American army before the return of Carleton, would surrender without firing a shot.

This arduous enterprise was committed to Colonel Arnold. About a thousand men, consisting of New England infantry, some volunteers,* a company of artillery under Captain Lamb, and three companies of riflemen, were selected for the service.

Such delays in expediting this detachment were occasioned by the derangements of the army, that Arnold could not commence his march until the middle of September.

Arnold's expedition by the way of the Kennebec.

The success of the expedition depending in a great measure on the friendly temper of the

---

* Colonel Burr, since Vice President of the United States, was of this number.

province against which it was directed, the instructions given to Arnold earnestly inculcated the cultivation of a good understanding with the Canadians; and even enjoined an abandonment of the enterprise, should this sudden invasion of their country threaten to irritate them, and induce them to take up arms against the United Colonies. He was furnished with about one thousand pounds in specie to defray contingent expenses, and with a cargo of manifestoes to be dispersed through Canada.

The opinion which had been formed of the favourable disposition of the Canadians was not disproved by the event. They gave essential aid to the Americans, and cheerfully facilitated their march through that province. But the previous difficulties to be surmounted were much greater than had been apprehended. The intermediate country, which had never been well explored, opposed obstacles to the march, which only perseverance like that of Arnold and of his brave and hardy followers, could have conquered. Colonel Enos, who commanded the rear division, consisting of one third of the detachment, returned from the Dead River, a branch of the Kennebec. At first, his appearance excited the utmost indignation in the army; yet, on being arrested, he was acquitted by a court martial, on the principle that it was absolutely impracticable to obtain provisions on the route to preserve the troops from perishing with famine.

Arnold, who at the head of the first two divisions, still prosecuted his march, was thirty-two days traversing a hideous wilderness, without seeing a house, or any thing human. Notwithstanding the zealous and wonderfully persevering exertions of his men, the obstacles he encountered so protracted his march, that he did not reach the first settlements on the Chaudière, which empties itself into the St. Lawrence, near Quebec, until the 3d of November.

On the high grounds which separate the waters of the Kennebec from those of the St. Lawrence, the scanty remnant of provisions was divided among the companies; each of which was directed, without attempting to preserve any connexion with the other, to march with the utmost possible celerity into the inhabited country. Whilst those who gained the front were yet thirty miles from the first poor and scattered habitations which composed that frontier of Canada, their last morsel of food was consumed. But, preceded by Arnold, who went forward for the purpose of procuring for them something which might satisfy the demands of nature, the troops persevered in their labours with a vigour unimpaired by the hardships they had encountered, until they once more found themselves in regions frequented by human beings.

After a march of such unexampled fatigue, no more time was allowed for repose than was barely sufficient to collect the rear, and to refresh

the men. During this short respite from toil,
the address signed by General Washington was
published, and every assurance given to the people, that they came to protect, and not to plunder
them. The line of march was resumed; and, on
the 9th of November, this gallant corps reached
Point Levi, opposite Quebec.

He arrives
before
Quebec.

The town was almost entirely without a garrison, and nothing could exceed the astonishment
of its inhabitants. Could Arnold have immediately crossed the St. Lawrence, and have
availed himself of the first consternation, it is
believed that he might have entered the place
without opposition; but a high wind, and the
want of boats, rendered the passage of the river
impossible.

One of his Indian messengers, despatched with
letters to General Schuyler, had either betrayed
him or been intercepted; and thus intelligence
of his approach was communicated to Colonel
M'Clean who was then at the mouth of the Sorel.
Trembling for the capital of the province, that
gallant veteran determined to throw himself
into it, and endeavour to defend it. In the
mean time, the winds continued so high for several nights as to render the passage of the river
in the canoes which had been collected, too hazardous to be attempted; and it was only in
the night that the Americans could hope to cross,
because four ships of war were distributed at
different stations in the river, and armed boats

were employed to ply around them. Whilst the Americans were thus unavoidably detained on the south side of the St. Lawrence, Colonel M'Clean, with his corps of emigrants, entered the city.

At length the wind moderated; and Arnold determined to attempt the river. Eluding the armed vessels, and conquering a rapid current, he, with great difficulty and danger, crossed over in the night, and landed his little army about a mile and a half above the place which is rendered memorable by the disembarkation of Wolfe. The passage of the rugged cliffs which continue on the northern bank of the St. Lawrence for some distance above Quebec, being impracticable at this place, he marched down on the shore to Wolfe's Cove, and ascending with his band of hardy followers the same precipice which had opposed such obstacles to the British hero; he, too, formed his small corps on the heights near the plains of Abraham.

The dangerous and difficult operations of crossing the river in canoes, whilst the passage was vigilantly guarded by ships of war, and of gaining the almost perpendicular heights of the opposite shore, were completed, soon after midnight, by the advance party, consisting of the rifle companies. While waiting for the residue of the detachment, a council of all the officers was held for the purpose of determining on their future measures. Although destitute of every

implement required for an assault, Arnold proposed to march immediately against Quebec. He
counted on surprising the place, and finding the
gates open; but this opinion, which was not
earnestly pressed, was overruled.

Though disappointed in the expectation of
surprising Quebec, Arnold did not immediately
relinquish the hope of obtaining possession of
that important place. Not superior to the garrison in point of numbers, and without a single
piece of artillery, he was obviously incapable
of acting offensively; but he flattered himself
that a defection in the town might yet put it
in his hands. With this view, he paraded on
the adjacent heights for some days, and sent two
flags to demand a surrender. But the presence
of Colonel M'Clean restrained those measures
which the fears of the inhabitants dictated.
Deeming any communication with the assailants
dangerous, he refused to receive the flag, and
fired on the officer who bore it. Intelligence was
soon obtained, that the first alarm was visibly
wearing off, and giving place to other sentiments
unfavourable to the hope of gaining Quebec.
Fears for the vast property contained in the town
had united the disaffected; who were, at their
own request, embodied and armed. The sailors
too were landed, and placed at the batteries;
and, by these means, the garrison had become
more numerous than the American army.

After collecting those who had been left on the south side of the St. Lawrence, Arnold could not parade more than seven hundred men, and they were in no condition to risk an action. In their laborious march through the wilderness, nearly one third of their muskets had been rendered useless; and their ammunition had sustained such damage that the riflemen had not more than ten, nor the other troops more than six rounds for each man. Under these circumstances, it was thought most adviseable to retire to Point Aux Trembles, twenty miles above Quebec, and there await the arrival of Montgomery. On their march, they saw the vessel which conveyed General Carleton; and afterwards found he had been on shore at Point Aux Trembles, a few hours before they reached that place.*

In war, the success of the most judicious plans often depends on accidents not to be foreseen nor controlled. Seldom has the truth of this proposition been more clearly demonstrated, than in the issue of the expedition conducted by Colonel Arnold. The situation of Canada conformed exactly to the expectations of the American general. Not suspecting that so bold and difficult an enterprise could be meditated, its Governor had left Quebec entirely defenceless, and had drawn the strength of the province towards the

And retires to Point Aux Trembles.

November 19.

---

* In the account of this expedition much use has been made of a journal kept by Colonel Heth who served in it as a Lieutenant in Morgan's company of riflemen.

lakes. Could Arnold have reached that place a few days sooner—could he even have crossed the river on his first arrival at Point Levi—or had Colonel Enos been able to follow the main body with his division of the detachment—every probability favours the opinion, that this hardy and well conceived expedition would have been crowned with the most brilliant success. Nay, more—had Arnold been careful to relieve the inhabitants of the town from all fears respecting their property, there is reason to believe, they would have refused to defend it. But although this bold enterprise was planned with judgment, and executed with vigour; although the means employed were adequate to the object; yet the concurrence of several minute and unfavourable incidents entirely defeated it, and deprived it of that éclat to which it was justly entitled.

Having clothed his almost naked troops at Montreal, General Montgomery, at the head of about three hundred men, proceeded with his usual expedition to join Colonel Arnold at Point Aux Trembles, where he supplied the troops of that officer with clothes provided at Montreal; and afterwards marched with their united forces

December 5.   directly to Quebec. But, before his arrival, Governor Carleton, who had entered the town, was making every preparation for a vigorous defence. The garrison now consisted of about fifteen hundred men, of whom eight hundred were militia, and between four and five hundred were seamen. Montgomery's effective force was stated, by himself, at only eight hundred. His situation would have filled with despair a mind less vigorous, less sanguine, and less brave. His numbers were not sufficient to render success probable, according to any common principle of calculation; and the prospect of their being diminished might be rationally entertained. But, relying on their courage, on himself and his fortune, and on the fears of the garrison; stimulated, too, by the high expectations formed throughout America of his success, and by the dread of disappointing those expectations, he determined to lay immediate siege to the town.

In a few days he opened a six gun battery within seven hundred yards of the walls; but his artillery was too light to make a breach, and he did not calculate on any effect from it. His object was to amuse the garrison, and conceal his real design.

Montgomery lays siege to Quebec.

Although the troops supported the excessive hardships to which they were exposed, with constancy and firmness, Montgomery feared that such continued sufferings would overcome them; and, as he would soon have no legal authority to retain a part of them, he apprehended that he should be abandoned by that part. Impressed with the real necessity of taking decisive steps, and impelled by his native courage, this gallant officer determined to risk an assault.

Of such materials was his little army composed, that the most desperate hardihood could not hope to succeed in the purposed attempt, unless it should receive the approbation of all his troops. It was therefore necessary, not only to consult the officers individually on this delicate subject, but to obtain also the cheerful assent of the soldiers to the meditated enterprise. The proposition was at first received coldly by a part of Arnold's corps, who were, by some means, disgusted with their commanding officer; but the influence of Morgan, who was particularly zealous for an assault, and who held up as a powerful inducement, the rights conferred by the usages of war on those who storm a fortified town, at length prevailed; and the measure was almost unanimously approved.

Whilst the general was preparing for the assault, the garrison received intelligence of his design from a deserter. This circumstance induced him to change the plan, which had originally been to attack both the upper and lower towns at the same time. That finally adopted, was to divide the army into four parts; and while two of them, consisting of Canadians under Major Livingston, and a small party under Major Brown, were to distract the garrison by making two feints against the upper town at St. John's and Cape Diamond; the other two, led, the one by Montgomery in person, and the other by Arnold, were to make real attacks on

opposite sides of the lower town. After gaining
that, it would yet be extremely difficult to conquer the obstacles to be surmounted in forcing
their way to the upper town; but, as all the
wealth of the city would then be in their power,
it was confidently expected that the inhabitants,
to secure their property, would compel the governor to capitulate.

Between four and five in the morning, the December 31.
signal was given; and the several divisions moved Unsuccessful attack on that place.
to the assault under a violent storm of snow.
The plan was so well concerted, that from the
side of the river St. Lawrence, along the fortified
front round to the basin, every part seemed
equally threatened.* Montgomery advanced
at the head of the New York troops, along the
St. Lawrence, by the way of Aunce de Mere,
under Cape Diamond. The first barrier on this
side, at the Pot Ash, was defended by a battery,
in which a few pieces of artillery were mounted;
about two hundred paces in front of which was
a block-house and picket. The guard placed at
the block-house being chiefly Canadians, after
giving a random and harmless fire, threw away
their arms, and fled in confusion to the barrier.
Their terrors were communicated to those who
defended this important pass; and from the intelligence afterwards received by the American
prisoners in Quebec, it appears that the battery
was for a time deserted.

* Letter of Governor Carleton.

Unfortunately, the difficulties of the route rendered it impossible for Montgomery to avail himself instantly of this first impression. Cape Diamond, around which he was to make his way, presents a precipice, the foot of which is washed by the river, where such enormous and rugged masses of ice had been piled on each other, as to render the way almost impassable.† Along the scanty path leading under the projecting rocks of the precipice, the Americans pressed forward in a narrow file, until they reached the block-house and picket. Montgomery, who was himself in front, assisted with his own hand to cut down or pull up the pickets, and open a passage for his troops: but the roughness and difficulty of the way had so lengthened his line of march, that he found it absolutely necessary to halt a few minutes. Having re-assembled about two hundred men, he advanced boldly and rapidly at their head, to force the barrier. One or two persons had now ventured to return to the battery, and seizing a slow-match, discharged a gun, when the American front was within forty paces of it. This single and accidental fire proved fatal to the enterprise. The general, with Captains M'Pherson and Cheeseman, the first of whom was his aid, together with his orderly sergeant and a private, were killed upon the spot. The loss of their general, in whom their confidence had been so justly

**Death of
Montgomery.**

† Annual Register.

placed, discouraged the troops; and Colonel Campbell, on whom the command devolved, made no attempt to reanimate them. This whole division retired precipitately from the action, and left the garrison at leisure to direct its undivided force against Arnold.

At the common signal for the attack, the division commanded by this officer moved in files along the street of St. Roques towards the Saut de Matelots, where the first barrier had been constructed, and a battery of two twelve pounders erected. In imitation of Montgomery, he too led the forlorn hope in person, and was followed by Captain Lamb with his company of artillery, and a field piece mounted on a sled. Close in the rear of the artillery was the main body, in front of which was Morgan's company of riflemen, commanded by himself. The path along which the troops were to march was so narrow, that the two pieces of artillery in the battery were capable of raking with grape shot every inch of the ground; whilst the whole right flank was exposed to an incessant fire of musketry from the walls, and from the pickets of the garrison.

In this order Arnold advanced along the St. Charles with the utmost intrepidity. The alarm was immediately given, and the fire on his flank commenced. As he approached the barrier, he received a musket ball in the leg which shattered the bone, and was carried off the field. Morgan rushed forward to the battery at the head of his company, and received from one of the pieces, almost at its mouth, a discharge of grape shot, which killed only one man. The barricade was instantly mounted, on which the battery was deserted without a discharge from another gun. The captain of the guard, with the greater number of his men, were made prisoners.

Morgan formed his troops in the streets within the barrier, and took into custody several English and Canadian burghers; but his situation soon became extremely critical. He was not followed by the main body of the division—he had no guide—and was, himself, totally ignorant of the situation of the town. It was yet dark— and he had not the slightest knowledge of the course to be pursued, or of the defences to be encountered. Under these circumstances, it was thought unadviseable to advance farther. They were soon joined by Lieutenant Colonel Green, and Majors Bigelow and Meigs, with several fragments of companies, so as to constitute altogether about two hundred men.

As the light of day began to appear, this gallant party was again formed, with Morgan's company in front; and, with one voice, loudly called on him to lead them against the second barrier, which was now known to be less than forty paces from them, though concealed by an angle of the street from their immediate view. Seizing the few ladders brought with them, they

again rushed forward; and under an incessant
fire from the battery, and from the windows
overlooking it, applied their ladders to the barricade; and maintained for some time a fierce,
and, on their part, a bloody contest. Exposed
thus, in a narrow street, to a galling fire, and
finding themselves unable to force the barrier,
or to discharge more than one in ten of their
fire arms—the violence of the storm having un-
fitted them for service; many of the assailants
threw themselves into the stone houses on each
side, which afforded them a shelter both from
the storm and from the enemy. After continuing some time in this situation, Morgan proposed
to cut their way back to the American camp.
They were prevented from adopting this daring
resolution, only by the suggestion that the attack
led by Montgomery, of whose fate they were
ignorant, might possibly be successful; and that,
in the event of his having entered the opposite
part of the town, their co-operation might be
useful to him. On this account, they determined
still to maintain their situation. But the force
of the enemy increasing considerably, they soon
perceived that they were no longer masters of
their own destinies, and surrendered themselves
prisoners of war.*

In this bold attack on Quebec, the loss on the
part of the garrison was inconsiderable. That

---

* In this account of the attempt to storm Quebec, free use
is made of Colonel Heth's journal.

of the Americans was about four hundred men, three hundred and forty of whom were prisoners. It fell chiefly on Arnold's division. Captain Hendricks of the Pennsylvania riflemen, Lieutenant Humphries of Morgan's company, and Lieutenant Cooper of Connecticut, were among the slain. Captains Lamb and Hubbard, and Lieutenants Steele and Tisdale, were among the wounded. Every officer at the second barrier received several balls through his clothes, and some of them were severely scorched by the powder from the muzzles of the muskets discharged at them. But the loss most deplored, and most fatal to the hopes of the American army, was that of their general.

Richard Montgomery was a native of Ireland, and had served with reputation in the late war. After its conclusion he settled in New York, where he married an American lady, and took a decided part with the colonies in their contest with Great Britain. His military reputation was high throughout America. In the history of his achievements, while commanding in Canada, we perceive the bold, skilful, and active partisan; and, so far as a judgment can be formed of a capacity for conducting the movements of a large army from judicious management of a small one, we can not hesitate to allow him the talents of an able general. At the head of a small body of undisciplined troops, drawn from different colonies, unwilling to be commanded by a stranger, jealous of him in the extreme, often disposed to disobedience, and anxious for their homes, he conquered difficulties which not many would have ventured to meet; and, until his last fatal moment, was uniformly successful. In little more than two months, he made himself master of Canada, from the lakes to Quebec: and, as if determined to triumph over the climate itself, laid siege, in the depth of winter, to that important fortress. His measures seem to have been taken with judgment, and were certainly executed with great courage and unremitting exertion. When he appears to have risked much, and to have exposed his troops to excessive hardships, this line of conduct was not inconsiderately chosen. The state of his affairs left him only the alternative between attempting to storm Quebec, or abandoning the great object of the expedition. Nor was his attempt so hopeless a measure as the strength of the place, and the event might, at first view, induce us to suppose. The design was worthy of the lofty spirit which formed it; though hazardous, it was not desperate; and if great courage was required to crown it with success, great courage was employed in its execution. He counted, and with reason, on the fears of the garrison, and on the immense extent of ground to be guarded. Had he not fallen himself, or been deserted by his troops, it is even yet believed the enterprise would have succeeded. The progress made by Arnold's division gives great countenance to this opinion.

To manifest the high sense entertained of his services, congress directed a monument, expressing the circumstances of his death and the gratitude of his country, to be erected to his memory.

The Americans, being no longer in a condition to continue the siege, retired about three miles from the city; where, though inferior in numbers to the garrison, they maintained the blockade. By preserving this bold countenance, they retained the confidence of the Canadians; which saved their affairs, for a time, from total ruin.

Governor Carleton was content to preserve Quebec, until the reinforcements he expected in the spring should enable him to act on the offensive. He therefore determined not to hazard an attack, with a garrison on which it was unsafe to rely; and Arnold, on whom the command had devolved, remained undisturbed. Although badly wounded, he retained his courage and activity; and, though deserted by those whose terms of service had expired, so as to be reduced at one time to about five hundred effective men, he discovered no disposition to sink under the weight of adverse fortune.

While the affairs of the colonies wore this gloomy aspect in Canada, congress was indulging sanguine hopes of annexing that province to the union. Nine regiments, including one to be raised in that colony, were voted for its defence during the ensuing campaign; and General Schuyler was directed to construct a number of batteaux at Ticonderoga, for the purpose of transporting the troops to the scene of action.

Whilst adopting these measures, congress received the melancholy intelligence of the disaster of the 31st December. Far from being dispirited by this reverse of fortune, that body redoubled its exertions to hasten reinforcements to the army in Canada, and urged the several conventions to collect for its use all the specie they could obtain. These measures were, in some degree, accelerated by having been anticipated by the Commander-in-chief.*

The service in Canada being deemed of too much importance to be entrusted to Colonel, now Brigadier General Arnold, or to General Wooster; and the health of General Schuyler not admitting of his proceeding to Quebec; General Thomas, an officer who had acquired reputation at Roxbury, was ordered to take command of the army in that province.

---

* On the first intelligence received in the camp at Boston of the fate of Montgomery, General Washington, though extremely delicate respecting the assumption of power, without waiting for the orders of congress, had immediately requested the New England governments to raise several regiments to reinforce that army. This proceeding was approved by congress.

In the hope of exciting throughout Canada the sentiments which prevailed in the United Colonies, and of forming with it a perfect union, three commissioners, Mr. Franklin, Mr. Chase, and Mr. Carroll,† were deputed with full powers on this subject, and with instructions to establish a free press. These commissioners were directed to assure the people that they would be permitted to adopt such form of government as should be agreeable to themselves; to exercise freely all the rights of conscience; and to be considered as a sister colony, governed by the same general system of mild and equal laws which prevailed in the other colonies, with only such local differences as each might deem conducive to its own happiness. They were also instructed to inquire into the conduct of the American army, and to correct any irregularities which might be offensive to the people.

Congress seems to have entertained the opinion expressed by General Washington in a letter to General Schuyler, "that the Province could be secured only by laying hold of the affections of the people, and engaging them heartily in the common cause." In pursuance of this opinion, they adopted the magnanimous policy of compensating those individuals who had suffered for their adherence to the Americans.

Blockade
of Quebec
continued.

In the mean time Arnold maintained the blockade of Quebec. But reinforcements were slow

† They were accompanied by Mr. Carroll, a bishop of the Roman Catholic church.

in arriving, notwithstanding every exertion to hasten them, and from the first of January to the first of March, the effective force before that place had never exceeded seven hundred men, and had often been as low as five hundred. In March, reinforcements arrived in greater numbers, and the army was increased to seventeen hundred; but this number was soon reduced by the small-pox, which had made its way into camp, where, in contempt of orders, it was propagated by inoculation.

To render the blockade in any degree effectual, this small army, which occupied the island of Orleans and both sides of the St. Lawrence, was spread over a circuit of twenty-six miles, and divided by three ferries. The establishment of discipline had been impracticable, if attempted; and the Canadians were often injured and irritated. There is reason to believe that even General Arnold was disposed to think himself in the country of an enemy; and that, in repressing disorders, he did not exert that energy which he had always displayed conspicuously in the field.

Many causes combined to diminish the attachment originally manifested by the Canadians to the United Colonies. The necessities of his situation compelled General Arnold to issue a proclamation making paper money current, under the promise of redeeming it in four months, and denouncing those as enemies, who should

March 4.

refuse to receive it. The Canadians were unwilling to exchange their property or labour, for an article of such uncertain value; and the discontents excited by the attempt to force it on them were very considerable.

Another circumstance, which had great influence with reflecting men, was the obvious incompetence of the American force to its object. The Canadians had expected a powerful army—sufficient for the protection of the country; and their disappointment in this respect, produced a great change in their opinions and conduct.

The dissatisfaction arising from these causes was augmented by the priests. They, as a body, were never cordial in the American interest; and having been, since the death of Montgomery, very injudiciously neglected, had become almost universally hostile to the views of the United Colonies.

General Carleton was no stranger to the revolution which was taking place in the minds of the Canadians, and entertained the hope of raising the siege by their assistance. A detachment of about sixty men, from the garrison of Quebec, landed twelve leagues below the town on the south side of the river, and were joined by about two hundred and fifty Canadians, who were rapidly increasing in numbers, when they were suddenly attacked by a detachment sent by Arnold, which surprised their advance guard, killed a few, took some prisoners, and dispersed the residue.

As the season of the year approached when reinforcements from England might be expected, Arnold deemed it necessary to recommence active operations, and to resume the siege. His batteries were again erected, and were opened on the 2d of April, but without much effect. He had not weight of metal to make a breach in the wall, nor an engineer capable of directing a siege, nor artillerists who understood the management of the pieces.

On the 1st of April, Wooster had arrived, and, on the succeeding day, Arnold's horse fell with him, and so bruised one of his legs as to confine him to his bed for some time. Believing himself to be neglected, he obtained leave of absence as soon as he was able to move, and took the command at Montreal.

A considerable part of the army having become entitled to a discharge, no inducement could prevail on them to continue longer in so severe a service. This deduction from Wooster's force was the more sensibly felt, because the present situation of the roads, the lakes, and the St. Lawrence, suspended the arrival of the reinforcements destined for his aid.

Among the first who reached camp after this state of things took place, was General Thomas. He arrived on the 1st of May, and found an army consisting of nineteen hundred men; of

General Thomas takes command of the army.

whom, less than one thousand, including officers, were effective. Among these were three hundred entitled to discharge, who refused to do duty, and insisted importunately on being immediately dismissed. This small force was still more enfeebled by being so divided that it was impracticable to unite more than three hundred men at any one point. All the magazines contained but one hundred and fifty barrels of powder, and six days provisions; nor could adequate supplies from the country people be obtained, as the Canadians no longer manifested any disposition to serve them.

The river began to open below, and it was certain, that the British would seize the first moment of its being practicable, to relieve this important place. Amidst these unpromising circumstances, the hopes of taking Quebec appeared to General Thomas to be chimerical, and a longer continuance before the town both useless and dangerous. It was apparent that the first reinforcements which should arrive would deprive him entirely of the use of the river, and consequently would embarrass the removal of his sick, and military stores. No object remained to justify this hazard.

Under these impressions, he called a council of war, which unanimously determined, that the army was not in a condition to risk an assault —that the sick should be removed to the Three Rivers, and the artillery and other stores em-

The blockade
of Quebec
is raised.

barked in their boats, in order to move to a more
defensible position. On the evening of the
same day, intelligence was received that a British fleet was below; and, the next morning, five
ships, which had, with much labour and danger, made their way up the river through the
ice, appeared in sight. They soon entered the
harbour, and landed some men whilst the Americans were assiduously employed in the embarkation of their sick and stores—an operation carried on the more slowly, because the first appearance of the ships deprived them of the aid
expected from the teams and carriages of the
Canadians.

About noon, Carleton made a sortie at the
head of one thousand men, formed in two divisions, and supported by six field pieces. The
Americans had thrown up no intrenchments, and
could not bring into action more than three
hundred men. Under these circumstances, victory was scarcely possible, and could have produced no important effect. General Thomas,
therefore, with the advice of the field officers
about him, determined not to risk an action, and
ordered his troops to retreat up the river. This
was done with much precipitation, and many of
the sick, with all the military stores, fell into
the hands of the enemy. The army continued
its retreat to the Sorel, where General Thomas
was seized with the smallpox, of which he died.*

---

* Whilst the troops of the United Colonies were flying
from the vicinity of Quebec, an unexpected calamity befel

The Americans were much dissatisfied with the conduct of this gentleman. To him they, in some degree, attributed the disasters which ruined their affairs in Canada. But this censure was unjust. He took command of the army when it was too weak to maintain its ground, and when the time for saving the sick and the military stores had passed away.

The siege of Quebec, instead of being continued longer, ought to have been abandoned at an earlier period. This was the real fault of those who commanded in Canada. It is to be ascribed to the reluctance always felt by inexperienced officers to disappoint the public expectation, by relinquishing an enterprise concerning which sanguine hopes have been entertained; and to encounter the obloquy of giving

them in a different quarter of that province.

Colonel Bedel, with three hundred and ninety continental troops and two field pieces, had been stationed at the Cedars, a point of land about forty miles above Montreal, which projected far into the St. Lawrence, and could be approached only on one side. Early in the spring, General Carleton had planned an expedition against this post, the execution of which was committed to Captain Forster, who commanded at an English station on Oswegachie. At the head of a company of regulars and a body of Indians, amounting in the whole to six hundred men, he appeared before the American works early in May. Two days previous to his appearance, Colonel Bedel had received intelligence of his approach; and, leaving the fort to be commanded by Major Butterfield, had proceeded himself to Montreal, to solicit assistance. Arnold, who then commanded at that place, immediately detached Major Sherburne to the Cedars with one hundred men; and prepared to follow, in person, at the head of a much larger force.

Although the place could have been easily defended, the besiegers having no artillery—Major Butterfield, intimidated by the threat, that should any Indians be killed during the siege, it would be out of the power of Captain Forster

up a post, although it can no longer with prudence be defended. In the perseverance with
which the siege of Quebec was maintained, these
motives operated with all their force, and they
received an addition, from the unwillingness felt
by the Americans, to abandon those of their
friends who had taken so decisive a part in their
favour, as to be incapable of remaining in safety
behind them.

After the death of General Thomas, reinforcements assembled at the mouth of the Sorel, which
increased the army to four or five thousand men,
who were commanded by General Sullivan. The
friendly Canadians who had supposed themselves abandoned, manifested great joy at the
arrival of a force which appeared to them very
considerable; and offered every assistance in their

---

to restrain the savages from massacreing every individual of
the garrison, consented to a capitulation, by which the whole
party became prisoners of war. The next day, Major Sherburne approached without having received any information
that Butterfield had surrendered. Within about four miles
of the Cedars, he was attacked by a considerable body of
Indians; and, after a sharp conflict, surrendered at discretion.

On being informed of these untoward events, Arnold, at
the head of seven hundred men, marched against the enemy
then at Vaudreuil, in the hope of recovering the American
prisoners. When preparing for an engagement, he received
a flag, accompanied by Major Sherburne, giving him the
most positive assurances that if he persisted in his design,
it would be entirely out of the power of Captain Forster to
prevent his savages from pursuing their horrid customs, and
disencumbering themselves of their prisoners by putting every
man to death. This massacre was already threatened; and
Major Sherburne confirmed the information. Under the
influence of this threat, Arnold desisted from his purpose,
and consented to a cartel, by which the prisoners were delivered up to him; he agreeing, among other things, not only
to deliver as many British soldiers in exchange for them, but
also, that they should immediately return to their homes.

power. Sullivan calculated on their joining him in great numbers, and entertained sanguine hopes of recovering and maintaining the post of De Chambeau. As a previous measure, it was necessary to dislodge the enemy at the Three Rivers.

Carleton was not immediately in a situation to follow up the blow given the Americans at Quebec, and to drive them entirely out of the province; but the respite allowed them was not of long duration.

Towards the end of May large reinforcements arrived, which augmented the British army in Canada to about thirteen thousand men. The general rendezvous appointed for these troops was at the Three Rivers. The army was greatly divided. A considerable corps, commanded by General Frazer, had reached the Three Rivers, and the main body was on its way from Quebec. The distance from the Sorel was about fifty miles, and several armed vessels and transports, full of troops, lay about five miles higher up than the Three Rivers, full in the way. *

General Thompson, who commanded the army after the illness of General Thomas, understanding the party at the Three Rivers to consist of about eight hundred men, partly Canadians, had detached Colonel St. Clair with between six and seven hundred men, to attack it, if there should be any probability of doing so

* Annual Register.

with advantage. Colonel St. Clair advanced to Nicolet, where, believing himself not strong enough for the service on which he had been ordered, he waited for further reinforcements, or additional instructions. At this time General Sullivan arrived; and, understanding the enemy to be weak at the Three Rivers, orders General Thompson to join Colonel St. Clair at Nicolet, with a reinforcement of nearly fourteen hundred men, to take command of the whole detachment, and to attack the troops lying at the Three Rivers, provided there was a favourable prospect of success.

General Thompson joined Colonel St. Clair at Nicolet, and, believing himself strong enough to perform the service consigned to him, fell down the river by night, and passed to the other side, with the intention of surprising Frazer. The plan was to attack the village a little before day-break, at the same instant, at each end; whilst two smaller corps were drawn up to cover and support the attack.

The troops passed the armed vessels without being perceived, but arrived at Three Rivers about an hour later than had been intended; in consequence of which they were discovered, and the alarm was given at their landing. To avoid the fire of some ships in the river, they attempted to pass through what appeared to be a point of woods, but was in reality a deep morass three miles in extent. The delays occasioned by their detention in this morass, gave General Frazer full time to land some field pieces, and prepare for their reception; while General Nesbit fell into their rear, and cut off their return to the boats. They advanced to the charge, but were soon repulsed; and finding it impracticable to return the way they came, were driven some miles through a deep swamp, which they traversed with inconceivable toil, and every degree of distress. The British at length gave over the pursuit.

Battle of
the Three
Rivers.

In this unfortunate enterprise, General Thompson and Colonel Irwin, with about two hundred men, were made prisoners; and from twenty to thirty were killed. The loss of the British was inconsiderable.

The whole American force in Canada now amounted to about eight thousand men, not one half of whom were fit for duty. About two thousand five hundred effectives were with General Sullivan at the Sorel. The whole were in a state of total insubordination—much harassed with fatigue—and dispirited by their late losses, by the visible superiority of the enemy, and by the apprehension that their retreat would be entirely cut off. Under all these discouraging circumstances, General Sullivan formed the rash determination of defending the post at Sorel; and was induced only by the unanimous opinion of his officers, and a conviction that the troops would not support him, to abandon it a few

hours before the British took possession of it.
The same causes drew him reluctantly from
Chamblée and St. John's; but he resolved to remain at the Isle Aux Noix, until he should receive orders to retreat.   He had been joined at
St. John's by General Arnold, who had crossed
over at Longueisle just in time to save the garrison of Montreal.

The Isle Aux Noix is a low unhealthy place,
badly supplied with water; where the troops
were so universally seized with fevers, as to compel General Sullivan to retire to the Isle Lamotte.
At that place he received the orders of General
Schuyler to embark on the lakes for Crown Point.

The armed vessels on the Sorel and St. Lawrence were destroyed, and the fortifications of
Chamblée and St. John's set on fire.   All the
baggage of the army, and nearly all the military
stores were saved.

The British army, during this whole retreat,
followed close in the rear, and took possession
of the different posts which the Americans had
occupied, immediately after they were evacuated.

On the Sorel the pursuit stopped.   The Americans had the command of the lake, and the
British general deemed it prudent to wrest it
from them before he advanced farther.   To effect this, it was necessary to construct a number
of vessels, which required time and labour.
Meanwhile, General Gates was ordered to take

command of the northern army, which was directed to be reinforced with six thousand militia.

Thus terminated the enterprise against
Canada. It was a bold, and, at one period, promised to be a successful effort to annex that extensive province to the United Colonies. The
dispositions of the Canadians favoured the measure; and had Quebec fallen, there is reason to
believe the colony would have entered cordially
into the union. Had a few incidents turned out
fortunately; had Arnold been able to reach Quebec a few days sooner, or to cross the St. Lawrence on his first arrival—or had the gallant
Montgomery not fallen in the assault of the 31st
December, it is probable the expedition would
have been crowned with complete success. But
the radical causes of failure, putting fortune
out of the question, were to be found in the
lateness of the season when the troops were assembled, in a defect of the preparations necessary for such a service, and still more in the
shortness of the time for which the men were
enlisted. Had the expedition been successful,
the practicability of maintaining the country is
much to be doubted. Whilst General Montgomery lay before Quebec, and expected to obtain possession of the place, he extended his
views to its preservation. His plan required a
permanent army of ten thousand men; strong
fortifications at Jacques Cartier, and the rapids
of Richelieu; and armed vessels in the river,

above the last place. With this army and these precautions, he thought the country might be defended; but not with an inferior force.

It seems, therefore, to have been an enterprise requiring means beyond the ability of congress; and the strength exhausted on it would have been more judiciously employed in securing the command of the lakes George and Champlain, and the fortified towns upon them.

While General Carleton was making preparations to enter the lakes, General Schuyler was using his utmost exertions to retain the command of them. But, so great was the difficulty of procuring workmen and materials, that he found it impossible to equip a fleet which would be equal to the exigency. It consisted of only fifteen small vessels; the largest of which was a schooner mounting twelve guns, carrying six and four pound balls. The command of this squadron, at the instance of General Washington, was given to General Arnold.

With almost incredible exertions, the British general constructed a powerful fleet; and, afterwards, dragged up the rapids of St. Therese and St. John's, a vast number of long boats and other vessels, among which was a gondola weighing thirty tons. This immense work was completed in little more than three months; and, as if by magic, General Arnold saw on Lake Champlain, early in October, a fleet consisting of near thirty vessels; the largest of which, the Inflexible, car-

General Carleton constructs a fleet.

Enters Lake Champlain.

ried eighteen twelve-pounders. This formidable fleet, having on board General Carleton himself, and navigated by seven hundred prime seamen under the command of Captain Pringle, proceeded immediately in quest of Arnold, who was advantageously posted between the island of Valicour and the western main.

Notwithstanding the disparity of force, a warm action ensued. A wind, unfavourable to the British, kept the Inflexible and some other large vessels at too great a distance to render any service. This circumstance enabled Arnold to keep up the engagement until night, when Captain Pringle discontinued it, and anchored his whole fleet in a line, as near the vessels of his adversary as was practicable. In this engagement, the best schooner belonging to the American flotilla was burnt, and a gondola was sunk.

Defeats the American flotilla.

In the night, Arnold attempted to escape to Ticonderoga; and, the next morning, was out of sight; but, being immediately pursued, was overtaken about noon, and brought to action a few leagues short of Crown Point. He kept up a warm engagement for about two hours, during which the vessels that were most ahead escaped to Ticonderoga. Two gallies and five gondolas, which remained, made a desperate resistance. At length one of them struck; after which Arnold ran the remaining vessels on shore, and blew them up; having first saved his men, though great efforts were made to take them.

On the approach of the British army, a small detachment, which had occupied Crown Point as an out-post, evacuated the place, and retired to Ticonderoga, which Schuyler determined to defend to the last extremity.

CHAP. III

1776

General Carleton took possession of Crown Point, and advanced a part of his fleet into Lake George, within view of Ticonderoga. His army also approached that place, as if designing to invest it; but, after reconnoitring the works, and observing the steady countenance of the garrison, he thought it too late to lay siege to the fortress. Re-embarking his army, he returned to Canada, where he placed it in winter quarters; making the Isle Aux Noix his most advanced post.

Takes possession of Crown Point.

Retires into winter quarters.

CHAPTER IV.

Transactions in Virginia....Action at Great Bridge....
Norfolk evacuated....Burnt....Transactions in North
Carolina....Action at Moore's Creek Bridge....Inva-
sion of South Carolina....British fleet repulsed at Fort
Moultrie....Transactions in New York....Measures
leading to Independence....Independence declared.

1775
July.

Transactions
in Virginia.

WHILST the war was carried on thus vigorously in the north, the southern colonies were not
entirely unemployed. The convention of Virginia determined to raise two regiments of regular troops for one year, and to enlist a part of
the militia as minute-men.

Lord Dunmore, the Governor of the colony,
who was joined by the most active of the disaffected, and by a number of slaves whom he had
encouraged to run away from their masters, was
collecting a naval force, which threatened to be
extremely troublesome in a country so intersected
with large navigable rivers as the colony of Vir-

October.

ginia. With this force he carried on a slight
predatory war, and, at length, attempted to burn
the town of Hampton. The inhabitants, having received intimation of his design, gave notice
of it to the commanding officer at Williamsburg,
where some regulars and minute-men were stationed. Two companies were despatched to
their assistance, who arrived just before the assault was made, and obliged the assailants to
retreat, with some loss, to their vessels.

In consequence of this repulse, his Lordship proclaimed martial law; summoned all persons capable of bearing arms to repair to the royal standard, or be considered as traitors; and offered freedom to all indented servants and slaves who should join him. *

This proclamation made some impression about Norfolk, where the Governor collected such a force of the disaffected and negroes, as gave him an entire ascendancy in that part of the colony.

Intelligence of these transactions being received at Williamsburg, a regiment of regulars and about two hundred minute-men, were ordered down under the command of Colonel Woodford, † for the defence of the inhabitants. Hearing of their approach, Lord Dunmore took a well chosen position on the north side of Elizabeth river, at the Great Bridge, where it was necessary for the provincials to cross in order to reach Norfolk; at which place he had established himself in some force. Here he erected a small fort on a piece of firm ground surrounded by a marsh, which was accessible, on either side, only by a long causeway. Colonel Woodford encamped within cannon-shot of this post, in a small village at the south end of the causeway;

---

* Gazette-Remembrancer.
† The author was in this expedition, and relates the circumstances attending it chiefly from his own observation.

across which, just at its termination, he constructed a breast-work; but, being without artillery, was unable to make any attempt on the fort.

In this position both parties continued for a few days, when Lord Dunmore ordered Captain Fordyce, the commanding officer at the Great Bridge, though inferior in numbers, to storm the works of the provincials. Between daybreak and sunrise, this officer, at the head of about sixty grenadiers of the 14th regiment, who led the column, advanced along the causeway with fixed bayonets, against the breast-work. The alarm was immediately given; and, as is the practice with raw troops, the bravest rushed to the works, where, regardless of order, they kept up a heavy fire on the front of the British column. Captain Fordyce, though received so warmly in front, and taken in flank by a party posted on a small eminence on his right, marched up with great intrepidity, until he fell dead within a few steps of the breast-work. The column immediately broke and retreated; but being covered by the artillery of the fort, was not pursued.

In this ill-judged attack, every grenadier is said to have been killed or wounded; while the Americans did not lose a single man.

The following night, the fort was evacuated. The provincial troops proceeded to Norfolk, under the command of Colonel Howe of North

Carolina, and Lord Dunmore took refuge on board his vessels.

After taking possession of the town, the American soldiers frequently amused themselves by firing into the vessels in the harbour, from the buildings near the water. Irritated by this, Lord Dunmore determined to destroy the houses immediately on the shore; and, on the night of the first of January, under cover of a heavy cannonade, landed a body of troops, and set fire to a number of houses near the river. The provincials, who entertained strong prejudices against this station, saw the flames spread from house to house without making any attempt to extinguish them. After the fire had continued several weeks, in which time it had consumed about four-fifths of the town, Colonel Howe, who had waited on the convention to urge the necessity of destroying the place, returned with orders to burn the remaining houses; which were carried into immediate execution.

Thus was destroyed the most populous and flourishing town in Virginia. Its destruction was one of those ill-judged measures, of which the consequences are felt long after the motives are forgotten.

After Norfolk was laid in ashes, Lord Dunmore continued a predatory war on the rivers—burning houses, and robbing plantations—which served only to distress a few individuals, and to increase the detestation in which he was held

CHAP. IV

1776

February.

Transactions
in North
Carolina.

through the country. At length, his wretched followers, wearied with their miserable condition, were sent to Florida. *

As the war became more serious, the convention deemed it necessary to increase the number of regular regiments from two to nine, which were afterwards taken into the continental service.

In North Carolina, Governor Martin, though obliged to take refuge on board a ship of war, in Cape Fear river, indulged the hope of being able to reduce that colony.

A body of ignorant and disorderly men on the western frontier, styling themselves regulators, had attempted by arms, some time before the existing war, to control and stop the administration of justice. After failing in this attempt, they became as hostile to the colonial, as they had been to the royal government.

The province also contained many families who had lately emigrated from the highlands of Scotland; and who, retaining their attachment to the place of their nativity, transferred it to the government under which they had been bred. From the union of these parties, Governor Martin entertained sanguine hopes of making a successful struggle for North Carolina. His confidence was increased by the assurances he had received, that a considerable land and naval armament was destined for the southern colonies.

---

* Virginia Gazette.

To prepare for co-operating with this force, should it arrive; or, in any event, to make an effort to give the ascendancy in North Carolina to the royal cause, he sent several commissions to the leaders of the highlanders, for raising and commanding regiments; and granted one to a Mr. M'Donald, their chief, to act as their general. He also sent them a proclamation, to be used on a proper occasion, commanding all persons, on their allegiance, to repair to the royal standard. This was erected by General M'Donald at Cross Creek, about the middle of February, and nearly fifteen hundred men arranged themselves under it.

February.

Upon the first advice that the loyalists were assembling, Brigadier General Moore marched at the head of a provincial regiment, with such militia as he could suddenly collect, and some pieces of cannon, and took a strong position within a few miles of them. General M'Donald soon approached, and sent a letter to Moore, enclosing the Governor's proclamation, and recommending to him and his party to join the King's standard by a given hour the next day. The negotiation was protracted by Moore, in the hope that the numerous bodies of militia who were advancing to join him, would soon enable him to surround his adversary. M'Donald, at length, perceived his danger, and, suddenly decamping, endeavoured by forced marches to extricate himself from it, and join Governor

Fifteenth.

Twentieth.

Martin and Lord William Campbell, who were encouraged to commence active operations by the arrival of General Clinton in the colony.

The provincial parties, however, were so alert in every part of the country, that he found himself under the necessity of engaging Colonels Caswell and Lillington, who, with about one thousand minute-men and militia, had entrenched themselves directly in his front, at a place called Moore's Creek Bridge. The royalists were greatly superior in number, but were under the disadvantage of being compelled to cross the bridge, the planks of which were partly taken up, in the face of the intrenchments occupied by the provincials. They commenced the attack, however, with great spirit; but Colonel M'Leod who commanded them, in consequence of the indisposition of M'Donald, and several others of their bravest officers and men, having fallen in the first onset, their courage deserted them, and they fled in great disorder, leaving behind them their general and several others of their leaders, who fell into the hands of the provincials. *

Action at Moore's Creek Bridge.

This victory was of eminent service to the American cause in North Carolina. It broke the spirits of a great body of men, who would have constituted a formidable reinforcement to an invading army; increased the confidence of the provincials in themselves, and attached to

* Annual Register—Gordon—Ramsay—Gazette.

them the timid and wavering, who form a large portion of every community.

General Clinton, who was to command in the south, had left Boston with a force too inconsiderable to attempt any thing until he should be reinforced by the troops expected from Europe. After parting with Governor Tryon in New York, he had proceeded to Virginia, where he passed a few days with Lord Dunmore; but finding himself too weak to effect any thing in that province, he repaired to North Carolina, and remained with Governor Martin until the arrival of Sir Peter Parker. Fortunately for the province, the unsuccessful insurrection of M'Donald had previously broken the strength and spirits of the loyalists, and deprived them of their most active chiefs; in consequence of which, the operations which had been meditated against North Carolina were deferred. Clinton continued in Cape Fear until near the end of May, when, hearing nothing certain from General Howe, he determined to make an attempt on the capital of South Carolina.

Early in the month of April, a letter from the secretary of state to Mr. Eden, the royal governor of Maryland, disclosing the designs of administration against the southern colonies, was intercepted in the Chesapeake; and thus, South Carolina became apprized of the danger which threatened its metropolis. Mr. Rutledge, a gentleman of vigour and talents, who had been

CHAP. IV

1776

May.

June.

Invasion
of South
Carolina.

chosen president of that province on the dissolution of the regal government, adopted the most
energetic means for placing it in a posture of
defence.

In the beginning of June, the British fleet
came to anchor off the harbour of Charleston.
The bar was crossed with some difficulty; after
which, it was determined to commence operations by silencing a fort on Sullivan's island.

During the interval between passing the bar
and attacking the fort, the continental troops of
Virginia and North Carolina arrived in Charleston; and the American force amounted to between five and six thousand men, of whom two
thousand five hundred were regulars.   This army
was commanded by General Lee, whose fortune
it had been to meet General Clinton at New
York, in Virginia, and in North Carolina. Viewing with a military eye the situation of the post
entrusted to his care, Lee was disinclined to hazard his army by engaging it deeply in the defence of the town; but the solicitude of the
South Carolinians to preserve their capital, aided
by his confidence in his own vigilance, prevailed
over a caution which was thought extreme, and
determined him to attempt to maintain the
place.

Two regular regiments of South Carolina,
commanded by Colonels Gadsden and Moultrie,
garrisoned fort Johnson and fort Moultrie.
About five hundred regulars, and three hundred

militia under Colonel Thompson, were stationed in some works which had been thrown up on the north-eastern extremity of Sullivan's island; and the remaining troops were arranged on Hadrell's Point, and along the bay in front of the town. General Lee remained in person with the troops at Hadrell's Point, in the rear of Sullivan's island. His position was chosen in such a manner as to enable him to observe and support the operations in every quarter, and especially to watch and oppose any attempt of the enemy to pass from Long Island to the continent; a movement of which he seems to have been particularly apprehensive.

The British ships, after taking their stations, commenced an incessant and heavy cannonade on the American works. Its effect, however, on the fort, was not such as had been expected. This was attributable to its form, and to its materials. It was very low, with merlons of great thickness; and was constructed of earth, and a species of soft wood common in that country, called the palmetto, which, on being struck with a ball, does not splinter, but closes upon it.

June 28.

British fleet
repulsed at
Fort
Moultrie

The fire from the fort was deliberate; and, being directed with skill, did vast execution. The garrison united the cool determined courage of veterans, with the enthusiastic ardour of youth. General Lee crossed over in a boat, to determine whether he should withdraw them; and was enraptured with the ardour they displayed. They assured him they would lose the fort only with their lives; and the mortally wounded breathed their last, exhorting their fellow soldiers to the most heroic defence of the place.

The engagement continued until night. By that time, the ships were in such a condition, as to be unfit to renew the action on the ensuing day. The Bristol lost one hundred and eleven men, and the Experiment seventy-nine. Captain Scott, of the one, lost his arm; and Captain Morris, of the other, was mortally wounded. Lord Campbell, late Governor of the province, who served as a volunteer on board one of these vessels, was also mortally wounded; and both ships were so shattered, as to inspire hopes that they would be unable to repass the bar. About nine, they slipped their cables and moved off.

A few days afterwards, the troops were re-embarked, and all farther designs against the southern colonies being for the present relinquished, the squadron sailed for New York. *

The attack on fort Moultrie was supported by the British seamen with their accustomed bravery; and the slaughter on board the ships was uncommonly great. The loss of the Americans, in killed and wounded, was only thirty-five men.

Great and well merited praise was bestowed on Colonel Moultrie, who commanded the fort,

---

* Annual Register—Gordon—Ramsay—Letters of General Lee.

and on the garrison, for the resolution displayed in defending it. Nor was the glory acquired on this occasion confined to them. All the troops that had been stationed on the island partook of it: and the thanks of the United Colonies were voted by congress to General Lee, Colonel Moultrie, Colonel Thompson, and the officers and men under their command.

This fortunate event, for such it may well be termed, though not of much magnitude in itself, was, like many other successes attending the American arms in the commencement of the war, of great importance in its consequences. By impressing on the colonists a conviction of their ability to maintain the contest, it increased the number of those who resolved to resist British authority, and assisted in paving the way to a declaration of independence.

Even before the evacuation of Boston, it had been foreseen that New York must become the seat of war; and that most important military operations would be carried on in that colony. The fortifications which had been commenced for the defence of its capital were indefatigably prosecuted; and, after the arrival of General Washington, these works, combined with those to be erected in the passes through the highlands up the Hudson, were the objects of his unremitting attention.

The difficulty which had been experienced in expelling the British from Boston, had demonstrated the importance of preventing their establishment in New York; and had contributed to the determination of contesting with them, very seriously, the possession of that important place. The execution of this determination, however, was difficult and dangerous. The defence of New York, against an enemy commanding the sea, requires an army capable of meeting him in the open field, and of acting offensively both on Long and York Islands. Congress had not adopted measures which might raise such an army. The Commander-in-chief, in his letters to that body, had long and earnestly urged the policy of bringing the whole strength of the country into regular operation. The government was not inattentive to his remonstrances; but many circumstances combined to prevent such a military establishment as the exigency required.

The congress which assembled in 1775 had adjourned with strong hopes that the differences between the Mother Country and the Colonies would soon be adjusted to their mutual satisfaction. When the temper manifested both by the king and his parliament had dissipated these hopes, and the immense preparations of Great Britain for war, evinced the necessity of preparations equally vigorous on the part of America, the resolution to make them was finally taken. But, unaccustomed to the great duties of conducting a war of vast extent, they could not esti-

mate rightly the value of the means employed,
nor calculate the effects which certain causes
would produce. Opinions of the most pernicious
tendency prevailed; from which they receded
slowly, and from which they could be ultimately
forced only by melancholy experience.

The most fatal among these was the theory,
that an army could be created every campaign
for the purposes of that campaign; and that
such temporary means would be adequate to the
defence of the country. They relied confidently
on being able on any emergency, to call out a
force suited to the occasion:—they relied too
much on the competence of such a force to the
purposes of war, and they depended too long
on the spirit of patriotism, which was believed
to animate the mass of the people.

Under these impressions, the determination to
form a permanent army was too long delayed;
and the measures necessary to raise such an army
were deferred, till their efficacy became doubtful. It was not until June, 1776, that the representations of the Commander-in-chief could
obtain a resolution, directing soldiers to be enlisted for three years, and offering a bounty of
ten dollars to each recruit. The time when this
resolution could certainly have been executed,
had passed away. That zeal for the service,
which was manifested in the first moments of
the war, had long since begun to abate; and
though the determination to resist had become

more general, that enthusiasm which prompts individuals to expose themselves to more than an equal share of danger and hardship, was visibly declining. The progress of these sentiments seems to have been unexpected; and the causes producing such effects appear not to have been perceived. The regiments voted by congress were incomplete; and that bounty, which, if offered in time, would have effected its object, came too late to fill them.

It was not in numbers only that the weakness of the American army consisted. In arms, ammunition, tents, and clothes, its deficiency was such as to render it unfit for the great purposes of war, and inferior, in all these respects, to the enemy which it was destined to encounter.

But, however inadequate to the object the regular force might be, both the government and the Commander-in-chief were determined to defend New York; and congress passed a resolution to reinforce the army with thirteen thousand eight hundred militia. For the defence of the middle colonies, and for the purpose of repelling any attempt to land on the Jersey shore, it was resolved to form a flying camp, to be composed of ten thousand men, to be furnished by Pennsylvania, Delaware, and Maryland. The militia, both of the flying camp and of the army at New York, were to be engaged to serve until the first of December; and the Commander-in-chief was empowered to call on the neighbour-

ing colonies for such additional temporary aids
of militia, as the exigencies of his army might
render necessary.

Great and embarrassing as were the difficulties
already noticed, they were augmented by the
disaffection of the city of New York, and of the
adjacent islands. Although Governor Tryon
had found it necessary to take refuge on board
some ships lying in the harbour, he had been
permitted to continue an open intercourse with
the inhabitants, which enabled him to communicate freely with the royalists; and to concert
plans of future co-operation. This intercourse
was broken off by the arrival of the Commander-
in-chief;—yet a plot was formed, through the
agency of the mayor, to rise in favour of the
British on their landing; and, as was understood, to seize and deliver up General Washington himself. This plot had extended to the
American army, and even to the general's guards.
It was fortunately discovered in time to be defeated; and some of the persons concerned were
executed. About the same time a similar plot
was discovered in the neighbourhood of Albany;
and there too, executions were found necessary.

Hitherto, the sole avowed object of the war
had been a redress of grievances. The utmost
horror had been expressed at the idea of attempting independence; and the most anxious
desire of re-establishing the union which had so

long subsisted between the two countries on its ancient principles, was openly and generally declared. But however sincere these declarations might have been at the commencement of the conflict, the operation of hostilities was infallible. To profess allegiance and respect for a monarch with whom they were at open war, was an absurdity too great to be long continued. The human mind, when it receives a strong impulse, does not, like projectiles, stop at the point to which the force originally applied may have been calculated to carry it. Various causes act upon it in its course. When the appeal was made to arms, a great majority of those who guided the councils and led the forces of America, wished only for a repeal of the acts of parliament which had occasioned their resistance to the authority of the crown; and would have been truly unwilling to venture upon the unexplored field of self-government. For some time, prayers were offered for the king, in the performance of divine service; and, in the proclamation of a fast by congress, in June, 1775, one of the motives for recommending it, was, to beseech the Almighty "to bless our rightful sovereign King George III. and inspire him with wisdom."

Measures
leading to
independence.

The prejudices in favour of a connexion with England, and of the English constitution, gradually, but rapidly yielded to republican principles, and a desire for independence. New strength was every day added to the opinions,

Independence Hall, Philadelphia

In this unpretentious brick building, erected in 1729-34, and intimately associated with the birth of the nation, the Continental Congress met. Washington was made Commander-in-Chief of the American army in 1775, and the Declaration of Independence was adopted on July 4, 1776, and read to the people assembled in the street. It is now a museum of Revolutionary and historical relics.

Independence Hall, Philadelphia

In this unpretentious brick building, erected in 1729-34, and intimately associated with the birth of the nation, the Continental Congress met, Washington was made Commander-in-Chief of the American army in 1775, and the Declaration of Independence was adopted on July 4, 1776, and read to the people assembled in the street. It is now a museum of Revolutionary and historical relics.

that a cordial reconciliation with Great Britain
had become impossible; that mutual confidence
could never be restored; that reciprocal jealousy,
suspicion, and hate, would take the place of that
affection, which could alone render such a connexion happy and beneficial; that even the com-
mercial dependence of America upon Britain,
was greatly injurious to the former, and that in-
calculable benefits must be derived from opening to themselves the markets of the world; that
to be governed by a distant nation or sovereign,
unacquainted with, and unmindful of their interests, would, even if reinstated in their former
situation, be an evil too great to be voluntarily
borne. But victory alone could restore them to
that situation—and victory would give them independence. The hazard was the same; and
since the risk of every thing was unavoidable,
the most valuable object ought, in common justice, and common prudence, to be the reward of
success. With such horror, too, did they view
the present war, as to suppose it could not possibly receive the support of a free people. The
alacrity therefore with which the English nation
entered into it, was ascribed to a secret and dangerous influence, which was, with rapid progress, undermining the liberties and the morals of
the Mother Country; and which, it was feared,
would cross the Atlantic, and infect the principles of the colonists likewise, should the ancient
connexion be restored. The intercourse of Amer-

ica with the world, and her own experience, had not then been sufficient to teach her the important truth, that the many, as often as the few, can abuse power, and trample on the weak, without perceiving that they are tyrants; that they too, not unfrequently, close their eyes against the light; and shut their ears against the plainest evidence, and the most conclusive reasoning.

It was also urged, with great effect, that the possibility of obtaining foreign aid would be much increased by holding out the dismemberment of the British empire, to the rivals of that nation, as an inducement to engage in the contest.

American independence became the general theme of conversation; and more and more the general wish. The measures of congress took their complexion from the temper of the people. Their proceedings against the disaffected became more and more vigorous; their language respecting the British government was less the language of subjects, and better calculated to turn the public attention towards congress and the provincial assemblies, as the sole and ultimate rulers of the country. General letters of marque and reprisal were granted; and the American ports were opened to all nations and people, not subject to the British crown.

At length, a measure was adopted, which was considered by congress and by America in general, as deciding the question of independence.

Hitherto, it had been recommended to particular colonies, to establish temporary institutions for the conduct of their affairs during the existence of the contest; but now, a resolution was offered, recommending generally to such colonies as had not already established them, the adoption of governments adequate to the exigency. Mr. John Adams, Mr. Rutledge, and Mr. Richard Henry Lee, all zealous advocates for independence, were appointed a committee, to prepare a proper preamble to the resolution. The report of these gentlemen was accepted, and the resolution passed. *

The provincial assemblies and conventions acted on this recommendation; and governments were generally established. In Connecticut and Rhode Island, it was deemed unnecessary to make any change in their actual situation, because, in those colonies, the executive, as well as the whole legislature, had always been elected by themselves. In Maryland, Pennsylvania, and New York, some hesitation was at first discovered; and the assemblies appeared unwilling to take this decisive step. The public opinion,

---

* Before the vote on the question of independence was taken, congress passed resolutions, declaring that all persons residing within, or passing through any one of the United Colonies, owed allegiance to the government thereof; and that any such person who should levy war against any of the United Colonies, or adhere to the king of Great Britain, or other enemies of the said colonies, or any of them, should be guilty of treason: and recommending it to the several legislatures to pass laws for their punishment.

however, was in favour of it, and finally prevailed.

The several colonies, now contemplating
themselves as sovereign states, and mingling
with the arduous duty of providing means to
repel a powerful enemy, the important and interesting labour of framing governments for
themselves and their posterity, exhibited the
novel spectacle of matured and enlightened so-
cieties, uninfluenced by external or internal
force, devising, according to their own judgments, political systems for their own government.

With the exceptions already stated, of Connecticut and Rhode Island, whose systems had
ever been in a high degree democratic, the hitherto untried principle was adopted, of limiting
the departments of governments by a written
constitution, prescribing bounds not to be tran-
scended by the legislature itself.

The solid foundations of a popular government were already laid in all the colonies. The
institutions received from England were admira-
bly calculated to prepare the way for temperate
and rational republics. No hereditary powers
had ever existed; and every authority had been
derived either from the people or the king. The
crown being no longer acknowledged, the people
remained the only source of legitimate power.
The materials in their possession, as well as
their habits of thinking, were adapted only to

governments in all respects representative; and
such governments were universally adopted.

The provincial assemblies, under the influence
of congress, took up the question of independence; and, in some instances, authorized their
representatives in the great national council, to
enter into foreign alliances. Many declared
themselves in favour of a total and immediate
separation from Great Britain; and gave instructions to their representatives conforming to
this sentiment.

Thus supported by public opinion, congress
determined to take this decisive step; and on the
7th of June, a resolution to that effect was
moved by Richard Henry Lee, and seconded
by John Adams. The resolution was referred to
a committee, who reported it in the following
terms. "Resolved, that these United Colonies
are, and of right ought to be free and independent states; and that all political connexion between them and the state of Great Britain is,
and ought to be, totally dissolved."

This resolution was referred to a committee
of the whole, in which it was debated on Saturday the 8th, and Monday the 10th of June. It
appearing that New York, New Jersey, Pennsylvania, Delaware, Maryland, and South
Carolina were not yet matured for the measure,
but were fast advancing to that state, the debate
was adjourned to the first of July, when it was

resumed. In the mean time, a committee * was appointed to prepare the declaration of independence, which was reported on the 28th of June, and laid on the table. On the first of July the debate on the original resolution was resumed. The question was put in the evening of that day, and carried in the affirmative by the votes of New Hampshire, Connecticut, Massachusetts, Rhode Island, New Jersey, Maryland, Virginia, North Carolina, and Georgia, against Pennsylvania and South Carolina. Delaware was divided; and the delegates from New York, having declared their approbation of the resolution, and their conviction that it was approved by their constituents also, but that their instructions, which had been drawn near twelve months before, enjoined them to do nothing which might impede reconciliation with the mother country, were permitted to withdraw from the question. The report of the committee was put off till the next day at the request of Mr. Rutledge of South Carolina, who expressed the opinion that his colleagues would then concur in the resolution for the sake of unanimity.

The next day South Carolina did concur in it. The votes of Pennsylvania and Delaware were also changed by the arrival of other members.

---

* Mr. Jefferson, Mr. John Adams, Mr. Franklin, and Mr. R. R. Livingston. Mr. R. H. Lee, the mover of the resolution, had been compelled by the illness of Mrs. Lee to leave congress the day on which the committee was appointed.

Congress then proceeded to consider the declaration of independence. After some amendments* it was approved, and signed by every member present except Mr. Dickenson. †

This declaration was immediately communicated to the armies, who received it with enthusiasm. It was also proclaimed throughout the United States, and was generally approved by those who had engaged in the opposition to the claims of the British Parliament. Some few individuals, who had been zealous supporters of all measures which had for their object only a redress of grievances, and in whose bosoms the hope of accommodation still lingered,—either too timid to meet the arduous conflict which this measure rendered inevitable, or, sincerely believing that the happiness of America would be best consulted by preserving their political connexion with Great Britain, viewed the dissolution of that connexion with regret. Others, who afterwards deserted the American cause, attributed their defection to this measure. It was also an unfortunate truth, that in the whole country between New England and the Potowmac, which was now become the great theatre of action, although the majority was in favour of independence, a formidable minority existed, who not only refused to act with their country-

---

* See note No. VI at the end of the volume.
† Mr. Jefferson's Correspondence.

men, but were ready to give to the enemy every aid in their power.

It can not, however, be questioned, that the declaration of independence was wise, and well-timed. The soundest policy required that the war should no longer be a contest between subjects and their acknowledged sovereign.

CHAPTER V.

Lord and Sir William Howe arrive before New York....
Circular letter of Lord Howe....State of the American
Army....The British land in force on Long Island....
Battle of Brooklyn....Evacuation of Long Island....
Fruitless negotiations....New York evacuated....Skir-
mish on the heights of Haerlem....Letter on the state
of the army.

WHILE congress was deliberating in Phila- | 1776
delphia on the great question of independence,
the British fleet appeared before New York.

On evacuating Boston, General Howe had re- | Lord and Sir
tired to Halifax; where he purposed to remain | William Howe ar-
till reinforcements should arrive from England. | rive before New York.
But the situation of his army in that place was
so uncomfortable, and the delays in the arrival
of the troops from Europe were so great, that he
at length resolved to sail for New York, with | June 10.
the forces already under his command.

In the latter end of June, he arrived off Sandy
Hook, in the Grey Hound; and, on the 29th of
that month, the first division of the fleet from
Halifax reached that place. The rear division
soon followed; and the troops were landed on
Staten Island, on the third and fourth of July. | July 3 & 4.
They were received with great demonstrations
of joy by the inhabitants, who took the oaths
of allegiance to the British crown, and embodied
themselves under the authority of the late Governor Tryon, for the defence of the island.

Strong assurances were also received from Long Island, and the neighbouring parts of New Jersey, of the favourable dispositions of a great proportion of the people to the royal cause.

It was foreseen that the provisions remaining on the small islands about New York, must fall into the possession of the invading army, and General Washington had intended to remove them to a place of safety; but, the existing state of public opinion requiring the co-operation of the several committees, this measure of wise precaution could not be completely executed; and General Howe, on his arrival, obtained ample supplies for his army.

The command of the fleet destined for the American service was intrusted to Lord Howe, the brother of the general; and they were both constituted commissioners for restoring peace to the colonies, and granting pardons, with such exceptions as they should think proper to make.

He arrived at Staten Island on the twelfth of July.

The difficulty of closing the Hudson against an enemy possessing a powerful fleet was soon demonstrated. Two frigates passed the batteries without injury, and took a station which enabled them to cut off the communication by water, between the army at New York, and that at Ticonderoga. An attempt to set these frigates on fire failed in its execution, and only a tender was burnt;—soon after which these vessels returned to the fleet.

Lord Howe was not deterred by the declaration of Independence from trying the influence of his powers for pacification. He sent on shore, by a flag, a circular letter, dated off the coast of Massachusetts, addressed severally to the late governors under the crown, enclosing a declaration, which he requested them to make public. This declaration announced his authority to grant pardons to any number or description of persons, who, during the tumult and disorders of the times, might have deviated from their just allegiance, and who might be willing, by a speedy return to their duty, to reap the benefits of the royal favour; and to declare any colony, town, port, or place, in the peace and under the protection of the crown, and excepted from the penal provisions of the act of parliament prohibiting all trade and intercourse with the colonies. Assurances were also given that the meritorious services of all persons who should aid and assist in restoring public tranquillity in the colonies, or in any parts thereof, would be duly considered.

These papers were immediately transmitted by the Commander-in-chief to congress, who resolved that they should "be published in the several gazettes, that the good people of the United States might be informed of what nature were the commissioners, and what the terms, with the expectation of which, the insidious court of Britain had sought to amuse and disarm them; and that the few who still remained suspended by a hope, founded either in the justice or moderation of their late king, might now, at length, be convinced, that the valour alone of their country is to save its liberties."

About the same time, Lord Howe sent, with a flag, a letter addressed to "George Washington, esquire," which the General refused to receive, as "it did not acknowledge the public character with which he was invested by congress, and in no other character could he have any intercourse with his lordship." In a resolution approving this proceeding, congress directed, "that no letter or message be received on any occasion whatever from the enemy, by the Commander-in-chief, or others, the commanders of the American army, but such as shall be directed to them in the characters they respectively sustain."

The commissioners felt some difficulty in recognizing either the civil or military character conferred on individuals by the existing powers in America; and yet it was desirable, either for the purpose of effecting a pacification, or, if that should be impracticable, of increasing the divisions already existing, to open negotiations, and hold out the semblance of restoring peace. They cast about for means to evade this preliminary obstacle to any discussion of the terms they were authorized to propose; and, at length, Colonel Patterson, adjutant general of the British army, was sent on shore by General Howe, with a letter directed to George Washington, &c. &c. &c. He was introduced to the general, whom he addressed by the title of "Excellency;" and, after the usual compliments, opened the subject of his mission, by saying, that General Howe much regretted the difficulties which had arisen respecting the address of the letters; that the mode adopted was deemed consistent with propriety, and was founded on precedent, in cases of ambassadors and plenipotentiaries, where disputes or difficulties had arisen about rank; that General Washington might recollect he had, last summer, addressed a letter to "the honourable William Howe;" that Lord, and General Howe, did not mean to derogate from his rank, or the respect due to him, and that they held his person and character in the highest esteem;—but that the direction, with the addition of &c. &c. &c. implied every thing which ought to follow. Colonel Patterson then produced a letter which he said was the same that had been sent, and which he laid on the table.

The General declined receiving it, and said, that a letter directed to a person in a public character, should have some description or indication of that character; otherwise it would be considered as a mere private letter. It was true the *etceteras* implied every thing, and they also implied any thing; that the letter to General Howe, alluded to, was an answer to one received from him under a like address; which, having been taken by the officer on duty, he did not think proper to return, and therefore answered in the same mode of address; and that he should absolutely decline any letter relating to his public station, directed to him as a private person.

Colonel Patterson then said, that General Howe would not urge his delicacy farther, and repeated his assertions that no failure of respect was intended.

After some conversation relative to the treatment of prisoners, Colonel Patterson said, that the goodness and benevolence of the king had induced him to appoint Lord Howe, and General Howe, his commissioners to accommodate the unhappy dispute at present subsisting: that they had great powers, and would derive much pleasure from effecting the accommodation; and that he wished this visit to be considered as the first advance towards so desirable an object.

General Washington replied, that he was not vested with any powers on this subject; but he would observe that, so far as he could judge from what had yet transpired, Lord Howe and General Howe were only empowered to grant pardons; that those who had committed no fault, wanted no pardon; and that the Americans were only defending what they deemed their indubi-

table rights. This, Colonel Patterson said,
would open a very wide field for argument: and,
after expressing his fears that an adherence to
forms might obstruct business of the greatest
moment and concern, he took his leave.

The substance of this conversation was communicated to congress, who directed its publication.

The reinforcements to the British army, of
whom about four hundred and fifty had been
captured by the American cruisers, were now arriving daily from Europe; and General Howe
had also been joined by the troops from Charleston. His strength was estimated at twenty-four
thousand men.

To this army, alike formidable for its numbers, its discipline, and its equipments,—aided
in its operations by a numerous fleet, and conducted by commanders of skill and experience,
was opposed a force, unstable in its nature,—
incapable, from its structure, of receiving discipline,—and inferior to its enemy, in numbers,
in arms, and in every military equipment. It
consisted, when General Howe landed on Staten
Island, of ten thousand men, who were much enfeebled by sickness. The diseases which always
afflict new troops, were increased by exposure
to the rain and night air, without tents. At the
instance of the General, some regiments, stationed in the different states, were ordered to
join him; and, in addition to the requisitions of

men to serve until December—requisitions not yet complied with—the neighbouring militia were called into service for the exigency of the moment. Yet, in a letter written to congress on the 8th of August, he stated that "for the several posts on New York, Long, and Governor's Island, and Paulus Hook, the army consisted of only seventeen thousand two hundred and twenty-five men, of whom three thousand six hundred and sixty-eight were sick; and that, to repel an immediate attack, he could count certainly on no other addition to his numbers, than a battalion from Maryland under the command of Colonel Smallwood." This force was rendered the more inadequate to its objects by being necessarily divided for the defence of posts, some of which were fifteen miles distant from others, with navigable waters between them.

"These things," continued the letter, "are melancholy, but they are nevertheless true. I hope for better. Under every disadvantage, my utmost exertions shall be employed to bring about the great end we have in view; and, so far as I can judge from the professions and apparent dispositions of my troops, I shall have their support. The superiority of the enemy, and the expected attack, do not seem to have depressed their spirits. These considerations lead me to think that though the appeal may not terminate so happily as I could wish, yet the enemy will not succeed in their views without considerable

loss. Any advantage they may gain, I trust will
cost them dear."

Soon after this letter, the army was reinforced
by Smallwood's regiment, and by two regiments
from Pennsylvania, with a body of New England and New York militia, which increased it
to twenty-seven thousand men, of whom one
fourth were sick.

A part of the army was stationed on Long
Island, under the command of Major General
Sullivan. The residue occupied different stations on York Island, except two small detachments, one on Governor's Island, and the other
at Paulus Hook; and except a part of the New
York militia under General Clinton, who were
stationed on the Sound, towards New Rochelle,
and about East and West Chester, in order to
oppose any sudden attempt which might be made
to land above Kingsbridge, and cut off the communication with the country.

Expecting daily to be attacked, and believing
that the influence of the first battle would be
considerable, the Commander-in-chief employed
every expedient which might act upon that enthusiastic love of liberty, that indignation
against the invaders of their country, and that
native courage, which were believed to animate
the bosoms of his soldiers; and which were relied on as substitutes for discipline and experience. "The time," say his orders issued soon
after the arrival of General Howe, "is now

near at hand, which must determine whether Americans are to be freemen or slaves; whether they are to have any property they can call their own; whether their houses and farms are to be pillaged and destroyed, and themselves consigned to a state of wretchedness from which no human efforts will deliver them. The fate of unborn millions will now depend, under God, on the courage and conduct of this army. Our cruel and unrelenting enemy leaves us only the choice of a brave resistance, or the most abject submission. We have therefore to resolve to conquer or to die. Our own, our country's honour, call upon us for a vigorous and manly exertion; and if we now shamefully fail, we shall become infamous to the whole world. Let us then rely on the goodness of our cause, and the aid of the Supreme Being, in whose hands victory is, to animate and encourage us to great and noble actions. The eyes of all our countrymen are now upon us, and we shall have their blessings and praises, if happily we are the instruments of saving them from the tyranny meditated against them. Let us therefore animate and encourage each other, and show the whole world that a freeman contending for liberty, on his own ground, is superior to any slavish mercenary on earth."

To the officers, he recommended coolness in time of action; and to the soldiers, strict attention and obedience, with a becoming firmness and spirit.

He assured them that any officer, soldier, or corps, distinguished by any acts of extraordinary bravery, should most certainly meet with notice and rewards; whilst, on the other hand, those who should fail in the performance of their duty, would as certainly be exposed and punished.

Whilst preparations were making for the expected engagement, intelligence was received of the repulse of the British squadron which had attacked fort Moultrie. The Commander-in-chief availed himself of the occasion of communicating this success to his army, to add a spirit of emulation to the other motives which should impel them to manly exertions. "This glorious example of our troops," he said, "under the like circumstances with ourselves, the General hopes, will animate every officer and soldier to imitate, and even to out-do them, when the enemy shall make the same attempt on us. With such a bright example before us of what can be done by brave men fighting in defence of their country, we shall be loaded with a double share of shame and infamy, if we do not acquit ourselves with courage, and manifest a determined resolution to conquer or die."

As the crisis approached, his anxiety increased. Endeavouring to breathe into his army his own spirit, and to give them his own feeling, he thus addressed them. "The enemy's whole reinforcement is now arrived; so that an attack must, and will soon be made. The General, therefore, again repeats his earnest request that every officer and soldier will have his arms and ammunition in good order; keep within his quarters and encampments as far as possible; be ready for action at a moment's call; and when called to it, remember, that liberty, property, life, and honour, are all at stake; that upon their courage and conduct rest the hopes of their bleeding and insulted country; that their wives, children, and parents, expect safety from them only; and that we have every reason to believe, that heaven will crown with success so just a cause.

"The enemy will endeavour to intimidate by show and appearance; but remember, they have been repulsed on various occasions by a few brave Americans; their cause is bad; and if opposed with firmness and coolness on their first onset, with our advantage of works, and knowledge of the ground, the victory is most assuredly ours. Every good soldier will be silent and attentive, wait for orders, and reserve his fire until he is sure of doing execution; of this the officers are to be particularly careful."

He directed explicitly that any soldier who should attempt to conceal himself, or retreat without orders, should instantly be shot down; and solemnly promised to notice and reward those who should distinguish themselves. Thus did he, by infusing those sentiments which would

stimulate to the greatest individual exertion,
into every bosom, endeavour to compensate for
the want of arms, of discipline, and of numbers.

As the defence of Long Island was intimately connected with that of New York, a brigade had been stationed at Brooklyn, a post capable of being maintained for a considerable time. An extensive camp had been marked out and fortified at the same place. Brooklyn is a village on a small peninsula made by East river, the Bay, and Gowan's Cove. The encampment fronted the main land of the island, and the works stretched quite across the peninsula, from Whaaleboght Bay in the East river on the left, to a deep marsh on a creek emptying into Gowan's Cove, on the right. The rear was covered and defended against an attack from the ships, by strong batteries on Red Hook and on Governor's Island, which in a great measure commanded that part of the bay, and by other batteries on East river, which kept open the communication with York Island. In front of the camp was a range of hills covered with thick woods, which extended from east to west nearly the length of the island, and across which were three different roads leading to Brooklyn ferry. These hills, though steep, are every where passable by infantry.

The movements of General Howe indicating an intention to make his first attack on Long Island, General Sullivan was strongly reinforced.

Early in the morning of the twenty-second, the principal part of the British army, under the command of General Clinton, landed under cover of the guns of the fleet, and extended from the ferry at the Narrows, through Utrecht and Gravesend, to the village of Flatland.*

Confident that an engagement must soon take place, General Washington made still another effort to inspire his troops with the most deter-

mined courage. "The enemy," said he, in addressing them, "have now landed on Long Island, and the hour is fast approaching, on which the honour and success of this army, and the safety of our bleeding country depend. Remember, officers and soldiers, that you are freemen, fighting for the blessings of liberty—that slavery will be your portion and that of your posterity, if you do not acquit yourselves like men." He repeated his instructions respecting their conduct in action, and concluded with the most animating and encouraging exhortations.

Major General Putnam was now directed to take command at Brooklyn, with a reinforcement of six regiments; and he was charged most earnestly by the Commander-in-chief, to be in constant readiness for an attack, and to guard the woods between the two camps with his best troops.

General Washington had passed the day at Brooklyn, making arrangements for the ap-

---

* General Howe's letter.

proaching action; and, at night, had returned to New York.

The Hessians under General De Heister composed the centre of the British army at Flatbush; Major General Grant commanded the left wing which extended to the coast, and the greater part of the British forces under General Clinton. Earl Percy and Lord Cornwallis turned short to the right, and approached the opposite coast of Flatland.*

The two armies were now separated from each other by the range of hills already mentioned. The British centre at Flatbush was scarcely four miles distant from the American lines at Brooklyn; and a direct road led across the heights from the one to the other. Another road, rather more circuitous than the first, led from Flatbush by the way of Bedford, a small village on the Brooklyn side of the hills. The right and left wings of the British army were nearly equi-distant from the American works, and about five or six miles from them. The road leading from the Narrows along the coast, and by the way of Gowan's Cove, afforded the most direct route to their left; and their right might either return by the way of Flatbush and unite with the centre, or take a more circuitous course, and enter a road leading from Jamaica to Bedford. These several roads unite between

---

* General Howe's letter.

Bedford and Brooklyn, a small distance in front of the American lines.

The direct road from Flatbush to Brooklyn was defended by a fort which the Americans had constructed in the hills; and the coast and Bedford roads were guarded by detachments posted on the hills within view of the British camp. Light parties of volunteers were directed to patrol on the road leading from Jamaica to Bedford; about two miles from which, near Flatbush, Colonel Miles of Pennsylvania was stationed with a regiment of riflemen. The convention of New York had ordered General Woodhull, with the militia of Long Island, to take post on the high grounds, as near the enemy as possible; but he remained at Jamaica, and seemed scarcely to suppose himself under the control of the regular officer commanding on the island.

About nine at night, General Clinton silently drew off the van of the British army across the country, in order to seize a pass in the heights, about three miles east of Bedford, on the Jamaica road.   In the morning, about two hours before day-break, within half a mile of the pass, his patrols fell in with and captured one of the American parties, which had been stationed on this road.   Learning from his prisoners that the pass was unoccupied, General Clinton immediately seized it; and, on the appearance of day, the whole column passed the heights, and advanced into the level country between them and Brooklyn.*

Before Clinton had secured the passes on the road from Jamaica, General Grant advanced along the coast at the head of the left wing, with ten pieces of cannon. As his first object was to draw the attention of the Americans from their left, he moved slowly, skirmishing as he advanced with the light parties stationed on that road.*

This movement was soon communicated to General Putnam, who reinforced the parties which had been advanced in front; and, as General Grant continued to gain ground, still stronger detachments were employed in this service. About three in the morning, Brigadier General Lord Stirling was directed to meet the enemy, with the two nearest regiments, on the road leading from the Narrows. Major General Sullivan, who commanded all the troops without the lines, advanced at the head of a strong detachment on the road leading directly to Flatbush; while another detachment occupied the heights between that place and Bedford.

About the break of day, Lord Stirling reached the summit of the hills, where he was joined by the troops which had been already engaged, and were retiring slowly before the enemy, who almost immediately appeared in sight. A warm cannonade was commenced on both sides, which

* General Howe's letter.

continued for several hours; and some sharp, but not very close skirmishing took place between the infantry. Lord Stirling, being anxious only to defend the pass he guarded, could not descend in force from the heights; and General Grant did not wish to drive him from them until that part of the plan, which had been entrusted to Sir Henry Clinton, should be executed.

In the centre, General De Heister, soon after daylight, began to cannonade the troops under General Sullivan; but did not move from his ground at Flatbush, until the British right had approached the left and rear of the American line. In the mean time, in order the more effectually to draw their attention from the point where the grand attack was intended, the fleet was put in motion, and a heavy cannonade was commenced on the battery at Red Hook.

About half past eight, the British right having then reached Bedford, in the rear of Sullivan's left, General De Heister ordered Colonel Donop's corps to advance to the attack of the hill; following, himself, with the centre of the army. The approach of Clinton was now discovered by the American left, which immediately endeavoured to regain the camp at Brooklyn. While retiring from the woods by regiments, they encountered the front of the British. About the same time, the Hessians advanced from Flatbush, against that part of the detachment which occupied the direct road to Brooklyn.* Here, General Sullivan commanded in person; but he found it difficult to keep his troops together long enough to sustain the first attack. The firing heard towards Bedford had disclosed the alarming fact that the British had turned their left flank, and were getting completely into their rear. Perceiving at once the full danger of their situation, they sought to escape it by regaining the camp with the utmost possible celerity. The sudden rout of this party enabled De Heister to detach a part of his force against those who were engaged near Bedford. In that quarter, too, the Americans were broken, and driven back into the woods; and the front of the column led by General Clinton, continuing to move forward, intercepted and engaged those who were retreating along the direct road from Flatbush. Thus attacked both in front and rear, and alternately driven by the British on the Hessians, and by the Hessians back again on the British, a succession of skirmishes took place in the woods, in the course of which, some parts of corps forced their way through the enemy, and regained the lines of Brooklyn, and several individuals saved themselves under cover of the woods; but a great proportion of the detachment was killed or taken. The fugitives were pursued up to the American works; and such is represented to have been the ardour of the British

* General Howe's letter.

soldiers, that it required the authority of their cautious commander to prevent an immediate assault.

The fire towards Brooklyn gave the first intimation to the American right, that the enemy had gained their rear. Lord Stirling perceived the danger, and that he could only escape it by retreating instantly across the creek. This movement was immediately directed; and, to secure it, his lordship determined to attack, in person, a British corps under Lord Cornwallis, stationed at a house rather above the place at which he intended to cross the creek. About four hundred men of Smallwood's regiment were drawn out for this purpose, and the attack was made with great spirit. This small corps was brought up several times to the charge; and Lord Stirling stated that he was on the point of dislodging Lord Cornwallis from his post; but the force in his front increasing, and General Grant also advancing on his rear, the brave men he commanded were no longer able to oppose the superior numbers which assailed them on every quarter; and those who survived were, with their General, made prisoners of war. This attempt, though unsuccessful, gave an opportunity to a large part of the detachment to save themselves by crossing the creek.

The loss sustained by the American army in this battle could not be accurately ascertained by either party. Numbers were supposed to have been drowned in the creek, or suffocated in the marsh, whose bodies were never found; and exact accounts from the militia are seldom to be obtained, as the list of the missing is always swelled by those who return to their homes. General Washington did not admit it to exceed a thousand men; but in this estimate he must have included only the regular troops. In the letter written by General Howe, the amount of prisoners is stated at one thousand and ninety-seven; among whom were Major General Sullivan, and Brigadiers Lord Stirling and Woodhull, by him named Udell. He computes the loss of the Americans at three thousand three hundred men; but his computation is probably excessive. He supposes, too, that the troops engaged on the heights, amounted to ten thousand; but they could not have much exceeded half that number. His own loss is stated at twenty-one officers, and three hundred and forty-six privates; killed, wounded, and taken.

As the action became warm, General Washington passed over to the camp at Brooklyn, where he saw, with inexpressible anguish, the destruction in which his best troops were involved, and from which it was impossible to extricate them. Should he attempt any thing in their favour with the men remaining within the lines, it was probable the camp itself would be lost, and that whole division of his army destroyed. Should he bring over the remaining battalions from New York, he would still be inferior in point of numbers; and his whole army, perhaps the fate of his country, might be staked on the issue of a single battle thus inauspiciously commenced. Compelled to behold the carnage of his troops, without being able to assist them, his efforts were directed to the preservation of those which remained.

Believing the Americans to be much stronger than they were in reality, and unwilling to commit any thing to hazard, General Howe made no immediate attempt to force their lines. He encamped in front of them; and, on the twenty-eighth at night, broke ground in form, within six hundred yards of a redoubt on the left.

July 28.

In this critical state of things, General Washington determined to withdraw from Long Island. This difficult movement was effected on the night of the twenty-eighth, with such silence, that all the troops and military stores, with the greater part of the provisions, and all the artillery, except such heavy pieces as could not be drawn through the roads, rendered almost impassable by the rains which had fallen, were carried over in safety. Early next morning, the British out-posts perceived the rear guard crossing the East river, out of reach of their fire.

July 29.

From the commencement of the action on the morning of the twenty-seventh, until the American troops had crossed the East river on the morning of the twenty-ninth, the exertions and fatigues of the Commander-in-chief were incessant. Throughout that time, he never closed his eyes, and was almost constantly on horseback.

The manner in which this critical operation was executed, and the circumstances under which it was performed, added greatly to the reputation of the American general, in the opinion of all military men. To withdraw, without loss, a defeated, dispirited, and undisciplined army from the view of an experienced and able officer, and to transport them in safety across a large river, while watched by a numerous and vigilant fleet, require talents of no ordinary kind; and the retreat from Long Island may justly be ranked among those skilful manœuvres which distinguish a master in the art of war.

The attempt to defend Long Island was so perilous in itself, and so disastrous in its issue, that it was condemned by many at the time, and is yet represented as a great error of the Commander-in-chief. But, in deciding on the wisdom of measures, the event will not always lead to a correct judgment. Before a just opinion can be formed, it is necessary to consider the previous state of things—to weigh the motives which induced the decision—and to compare the value of the object, and the probability of securing it, with the hazards attending the attempt.

It was very desirable to preserve New York, if practicable; or, if that could not be done, to consume the campaign in the struggle for that place. The abandonment of Long Island, besides giving the enemy secure and immediate possession of an extensive and fertile country, would certainly facilitate the success of his attempt upon New York. It was therefore to be avoided, if possible.

The impossibility of avoiding it was not evident until the battle was fought. It is true, that the American force on the island could not have been rendered equal, even in point of numbers, to that of the British; but, with the advantage of the defencible country through which the assailants were to pass, and of a fortified camp which could be attacked only on one side, hopes might be entertained, without the imputation of being oversanguine, of maintaining the position for a considerable time; and, ultimately, of selling it at a high price. This opinion is supported by the subsequent movements of General Howe, who, even after the victory of the twenty-seventh, was unwilling to hazard an assault on the American works, without the co-operation of the fleet; but chose rather to carry them by regular approaches. Nor would the situation of the troops on Long Island have been desperate, even in the event of a conjoint attack by land and water, before their strength and spirits were broken by the action of the twenty-seventh. The

East river was guarded by strong batteries on both sides, and the entrance into it from the bay was defended by Governor's Island, which was fortified, and in which two regiments were stationed. The ships could not lie in that river, without first silencing those batteries—a work not easily accomplished. The aid of the fleet, therefore, could be given only at the point of time when a storm of the works should be intended; and when that should appear practicable, the troops might be withdrawn from the island.

There was then considerable hazard in maintaining Long Island; but not so much as to demonstrate the propriety of relinquishing a post of such great importance, without a struggle.

With more appearance of reason, the General has been condemned for not having guarded the road which leads over the hills from Jamaica to Bedford.

The written instructions given to the officer commanding on Long Island, two days previous to the action, directed that the woods should be well guarded, and the approach of the enemy through them rendered as difficult as possible. But his numbers were not sufficient to furnish detachments for all the defiles through the mountains; and if a corps, capable of making an effectual resistance, had been posted on this road, and a feint had been made on it, while the principal attack was by the direct road from Flatbush, or by that along the coast, the events of the day would probably have been not less disastrous. The columns marching directly from Flatbush must, on every reasonable calculation, have been in possession of the plain in the rear of the detachment posted on the road from Jamaica, so as to intercept its retreat to the camp. So great is the advantage of those who attack, in being able to choose the point against which to direct their grand effort.

The most adviseable plan, then, appears to have been, to watch the motions of the enemy so as to be master of his designs; to oppose with a competent force every attempt to seize the heights; and to guard all the passes in such a manner as to receive notice of his approach through any one of them, in sufficient time to recall the troops maintaining the others.

This plan was adopted—and the heavy disasters of the day are attributable, principally, to the failure of those charged with the execution of that very important part of it which related to the Jamaica road. The letter of General Howe states that an American patrolling party was taken on this road; and General Washington, in a private and confidential communication to a friend, says, "This misfortune happened, in a great measure, by two detachments of our people who were posted in two roads leading through a wood, to intercept the enemy in their

march, suffering a surprise, and making a precipitate retreat."

The events of this day, too, exhibited a practical demonstration of a radical defect in the
structure of the army. It did not contain a
single corps of cavalry. That miscalculating
economy which refuses the means essential to the
end, was not sufficiently relaxed to admit of so
expensive an establishment. Had the General
been furnished with a few troops of light-horse,
to serve merely as videts, it is probable that the
movement so decisive of the fate of the day
could not have been made unnoticed. The troops
on the lines do not appear to have observed the
column which was withdrawn, on the evening
of the twenty-sixth, from Flatbush to Flatland.
Had this important manœuvre been communicated, it would, most probably, have turned the
attention of General Putnam, more particularly,
to the Jamaica road. It is to the want of videts,
that a failure to obtain this important intelligence is to be ascribed. The necessity of changing the officer originally intrusted with the command, was also an unfortunate circumstance,
which probably contributed to the event which
happened.

Whatever causes might have led to this defeat, it gave a gloomy aspect to the affairs of
America. Heretofore, her arms had been frequently successful, and her soldiers had always
manifested a great degree of intrepidity. A

confidence in themselves, a persuasion of superiority over the enemy, arising from the goodness of their cause, and their early and habitual use of fire arms, had been carefully encouraged. This sentiment had been nourished by all their experience preceding this event. When they found themselves, by a course of evolutions in which they imagined they perceived a great superiority of military skill, encircled with unexpected dangers, from which no exertions could extricate them, their confidence in themselves and in their leaders was greatly diminished, and the approach of the enemy inspired the apprehension that some stratagem was concealed, from which immediate flight alone could preserve them.

In a letter from General Washington to congress, the state of the army after this event was thus feelingly described: "Our situation is truly distressing. The check our detachment sustained on the 27th ultimo, has dispirited too great a proportion of our troops, and filled their minds with apprehension and despair. The militia, instead of calling forth their utmost efforts to a brave and manly opposition, in order to repair our losses, are dismayed, intractable, and impatient to return. Great numbers of them have gone off; in some instances, almost by whole regiments; in many, by half ones and by companies, at a time. This circumstance, of itself, independent of others, when fronted by a well appointed enemy, superior in number to our whole collected force, would be sufficiently disagreeable; but when it is added, that their example has infected another part of the army; that their want of discipline, and refusal of almost every kind of restraint and government, have rendered a like conduct but too common in the whole; and have produced an entire disregard of that order and subordination necessary for the well doing of an army, and which had been before inculcated as well as the nature of our military establishment would admit of; our condition is still more alarming, and with the deepest concern I am obliged to confess my want of confidence in the generality of the troops.

"All these circumstances fully confirm the opinion I ever entertained, and which I, more than once, in my letters, took the liberty of mentioning to congress, that no dependence could be placed in a militia, or other troops than those enlisted and embodied for a longer period than our regulations have hitherto prescribed. I am persuaded, and am as fully convinced as of any one fact that has happened, that our liberties must, of necessity, be greatly hazarded, if not entirely lost, if their defence be left to any but a permanent army."

The first use made by Lord Howe of the victory of the 27th of August, was to avail himself of the impression it had probably made on congress, by opening a negotiation in conformity

Fruitless negotiations.

with his powers as a commissioner. For this purpose, General Sullivan was sent on parole to Philadelphia, with a verbal message, the import of which was, "that though he could not at present treat with congress as a political body, yet he was very desirous of having a conference with some of its members, whom he would consider, for the present, only as private gentlemen, and meet them as such at any place they would appoint.

"That, in conjunction with General Howe, he had full powers to compromise the dispute between Great Britain and America, on terms advantageous to both; the obtaining of which detained him near two months in England, and prevented his arrival in New York before the declaration of independence took place.

"That he wished a compact might be settled at this time, when no decisive blow was struck, and neither party could allege being compelled to enter into such agreement.

"That in case congress were disposed to treat, many things which they had not as yet asked, might, and ought to be granted them; and that if, upon the conference, they found any probable ground of an accommodation, the authority of congress must be afterwards acknowledged— otherwise the compact would not be complete."

This proposition was not without its embarrassments. Its rejection would give some countenance to the opinion, that, if independence

were waved, a restoration of the ancient connexion between the two countries, on principles
formerly deemed constitutional, was still practicable; an opinion which would have an unfavourable effect on the public sentiment. On
the other hand, to enter into a negotiation under
such circumstances, might excite a suspicion,
that their determination to maintain the independence they had declared, was not immoveable; and that things were in such a situation,
as to admit of some relaxation in the measures
necessary for the defence of the country.

The answer given to Lord Howe, through
General Sullivan, was, "that congress, being the
representatives of the free and independent
States of America, can not, with propriety, send
any of its members to confer with his Lordship
in their private characters; but that, ever desirous of establishing peace on reasonable terms,
they will send a committee of their body to
know whether he has any authority to treat with
persons authorized by congress for that purpose,
on behalf of America; and what that authority
is;—and to hear such propositions as he shall
think proper to make, respecting the same."

The President was, at the same time, directed
to communicate to General Washington the
opinion of congress, that no propositions for
making peace "ought to be received or attended
to, unless the same be made in writing, and
addressed to the representatives of the United

States in congress, or persons authorized by them: And if applications on that subject be made to him by any of the commanders of the British forces, that he inform them, that these United States, who entered into the war only for the defence of their lives and liberties, will cheerfully agree to peace on reasonable terms, whenever such shall be proposed to them in manner aforesaid."

It is worthy of remark, that, in these resolutions, congress preserves the appearance of insisting on the independence of the United States, without declaring it to be the indispensable condition of peace.

Mr. Franklin, Mr. John Adams, and Mr. Edward Rutledge, all zealous supporters of independence, were appointed "to receive the communications of Lord Howe."

They waited on his Lordship; and, on their return, reported, that he had received them on the 11th of September, on Staten Island, opposite to Amboy, with great politeness.

He opened the conversation by acquainting them, that though he could not treat with them as a committee of congress, yet, as his powers enabled him to confer and consult with any private gentlemen of influence in the colonies, on the means of restoring peace between the two countries, he was glad of this opportunity of conferring with them on that subject; if they thought themselves at liberty to enter into a conference with him in that character. The committee observed to his Lordship, that, as their business was to hear, he might consider them in what light he pleased, and communicate to them any propositions he might be authorized to make for the purpose mentioned; but that they could consider themselves in no other character than that in which they were placed by order of congress. His Lordship then proceeded to open his views at some length. He offered peace only on the condition that the colonies should return to their allegiance and obedience to the British crown. He made no explicit propositions as inducements to this measure, but gave assurances that there was a good disposition in the king and his ministers to make the government easy to them, with intimations that, in case of submission, the offensive acts of parliament would be revised, and the instructions to the Governors reconsidered; so that, if any just causes of complaint were found in the acts, or any errors in government were found to have crept into the instructions, they might be amended or withdrawn.

The committee gave it as their opinion to his Lordship, that a return to the domination of Great Britain was not now to be expected. They mentioned the repeated humble petitions of the colonies to the king and parliament, which had been treated with contempt, and answered only by additional injuries; the unexampled patience which had been shown under their tyrannical government; and that it was not until the late act of parliament, which denounced war against them, and put them out of the king's protection, that they declared their independence; that this declaration had been called for by the people of the colonies in general, and that every colony had approved it when made,—and all now considered themselves as independent states, and were settling, or had settled, their governments accordingly; so that it was not in the power of congress to agree for them that they should return to their former dependent state; that there was no doubt of their inclination for peace, and their willingness to enter into a treaty with Britain, that might be advantageous to both countries; that though his Lordship had, at present, no power to treat with them as independent states, he might, if there was the same good disposition in Britain, much sooner obtain fresh powers from his government, for that purpose, than powers could be obtained by congress, from the several colonies, to consent to a submission.

His Lordship then expressed his regret that no accommodation was like to take place, and put an end to the conference.

These fruitless negotiations produced no suspension of hostilities.

The British army, now in full possession of Long Island, was posted from Bedford to Hurlgate; and thus fronted and threatened York

Island from its extreme southern point, to the part opposite the northern boundary of Long Island, a small distance below the heights of Haerlem; comprehending a space of about nine miles.

The two armies were divided only by the East river, which is generally less than a mile wide.

Immediately after the victory at Brooklyn, dispositions were made by the enemy to attack New York, and a part of the fleet sailed round Long Island, and appeared in the Sound. Two frigates passed up the East river, without receiving any injury from the batteries, and anchored behind a small island which protected them from the American artillery. At the same time, the main body of the fleet lay at anchor close in with Governor's Island, from which the American troops had been withdrawn, ready to pass up either the North or East river, or both, and act against any part of York Island.

These movements indicated a disposition, not to make an attack directly on New York, as had been expected, but to land near Kingsbridge, and take a position which would cut off the communication of the American army with the country.

Aware of the danger of his situation, General Washington began to remove such stores as were not immediately necessary; and called a council of general officers for the purpose of deciding, whether New York should be evacuated without delay, or longer defended.

In his letter communicating to congress the result of this council, which was against an immediate evacuation, he manifested a conviction of the necessity of that measure, though he yielded to that necessity with reluctance. Speaking of the enemy, he observed, "It is now extremely obvious from their movements, from our intelligence, and from every other circumstance, that, having their whole army upon Long Island, except about four thousand men who remain on Staten Island, they mean to enclose us in this island, by taking post in our rear, while their ships effectually secure the front; and thus, by cutting off our communication with the country, oblige us to fight them on their own terms, or surrender at discretion; or, if that shall be deemed more adviseable, by a brilliant stroke endeavour to cut this army to pieces, and secure the possession of arms and stores, which they well know our inability to replace.

"Having their system unfolded to us, it becomes an important consideration how it could be most successfully opposed. On every side there is a choice of difficulties, and experience teaches us, that every measure on our part (however painful the reflection) must be taken with some apprehension, that all our troops will not do their duty.

"In deliberating upon this great question," he added, "it was impossible to forget that history, our own experience, the advice of our ablest friends in Europe, the fears of the enemy, and even the declarations of congress, demonstrate that, on our side, the war should be defensive;— (it has ever been called a war of posts;)—that we should, on all occasions, avoid a general action, nor put any thing to the risk, unless compelled by necessity, into which we ought never to be drawn."

After communicating the decision which had been made by the council of officers, he stated the opinion of those who were in favour of an immediate evacuation with such force, as to confirm the belief that it remained his own.

The majority, who overruled this opinion, did not expect to be able to defend the city, permanently, but to defer the time of losing it, in the hope of wasting so much of the campaign, before General Howe could obtain possession of it, as to prevent his undertaking any thing farther until the following year. They therefore advised a middle course between abandoning the town absolutely, and concentrating their whole strength for its defence. This was, to form the army into three divisions; one of which should remain in New York; the second be stationed at Kingsbridge, and the third occupy the intermediate space, so as to support either extreme. The sick were to be immediately removed to

Orange Town. A belief that congress was inclined to maintain New York at every hazard, and a dread of the unfavourable impression which its evacuation might make on the people, seem to have had great influence in producing the determination to defend the place yet a short time longer.

September 10.

This opinion was soon changed. The movements of the British general indicated clearly an intention either to break their line of communication, or to enclose the whole army in York Island. His dispositions were alike calculated to favour the one or the other of those objects. The general, who had continued to employ himself assiduously in the removal of the military stores to a place of safety,* called a second council to deliberate on the farther defence of the city, which determined, by a

September 12.

large majority, that it had become not only prudent, but absolutely necessary to withdraw the army from New York.

In consequence of this determination, Brigadier General Mercer, who commanded the flying camp on the Jersey shore, was directed to move up the North river, to the post opposite fort Washington; and every effort was used to expedite the removal of the stores.

---

* He had, on the first appearance of the enemy in force before New York urged the removal of the women and children, with their most valuable effects, to a place of safety.

On the morning of the fifteenth, three ships of war proceeded up the North river as high as Bloomingdale; a movement which entirely stopped the farther removal of stores by water. About eleven on the same day, Sir Henry Clinton, with a division of four thousand men who had embarked at the head of New Town bay, where they had lain concealed from the view of the troops posted on York Island, proceeded through that bay into the East river, which he crossed; and, under cover of the fire of five men of war, landed at a place called Kipp's bay, about three miles above New York.

The works thrown up to oppose a landing at this place, were of considerable strength, and capable of being defended for some time; but the troops stationed in them abandoned them without waiting to be attacked, and fled with precipitation. On the commencement of the cannonade, General Washington ordered the brigades of Parsons and Fellowes to the support of the troops posted in the lines, and rode himself towards the scene of action. The panic of those who had fled from the works was communicated to the troops ordered to sustain them; and the Commander-in-chief had the extreme mortification to meet the whole party retreating in the utmost disorder, totally regardless of the great efforts made by their generals to stop their disgraceful flight. Whilst General Washington was exerting himself to rally them, a small corps of the enemy appeared; and they again broke and fled in confusion. The only part to be taken was immediately to withdraw the few remaining troops from New York, and to secure the posts on the heights. For this latter purpose, the lines were instantly manned; but no attempt was made to force them. The retreat from New York was effected with an inconsiderable loss of men, sustained in a skirmish at Bloomingdale; but all the heavy artillery, and a large portion of the baggage, provisions, and military stores, much of which might have been saved had the post at Kipp's bay been properly defended, were unavoidably abandoned. In this shameful day, one colonel, one captain, three subalterns, and ten privates were killed: one lieutenant colonel, one captain, and one hundred and fifty-seven privates were missing.

The unsoldierly conduct displayed on this occasion was not attributable to a want of personal courage, but to other causes. The apprehensions excited by the defeat on Long Island had not yet subsided; nor had the American troops recovered their confidence either in themselves or in their commanders. Their situation appeared to themselves to be perilous; and they had not yet acquired that temper which teaches the veteran to do his duty wherever he may be placed; to assure himself that others will do their duty likewise; and to rely that those, who take into view the situation of the whole, will not expose him to useless hazard; or neglect those precautions which the safety and advantage of the whole may require.

Unfortunately, there existed in a great part of the army, several causes, in addition to the shortness of enlistments and reliance on militia, which were but too operative in obstructing the progress of these military sentiments. In New England, whence the supplies of men had been principally drawn, the zeal excited by the revolution had taken such a direction, as in a great degree to abolish those distinctions between the platoon officers and the soldiers, which are indispensable to the formation of an army suited to all the purposes of war. It has been already said that these officers, who constitute an important part of every army, were, in many companies, elected by the privates. Of consequence, a disposition to associate with them on the footing of equality, was a recommendation of more weight, and frequently conduced more to the choice, than individual merit. Gentlemen of high rank have stated that, in some instances, men were elected, who agreed to put their pay in a common stock with that of the soldiers, and divide equally with them. It is not cause of wonder, that among such officers, the most disgraceful and unmilitary practices should frequently prevail; and that the privates should not respect them sufficiently, to acquire habits of obedience and subordination. This vital defect

had been in some degree remedied, in new model-
ling the army before Boston; but it still existed
to a fatal extent.

Having taken possession of New York, General Howe stationed a few troops in the town;
and, with the main body of his army, encamped
on the island near the American lines. His right
was at Horen's Hook on the East river, and
his left reached the North river near Bloomingdale; so that his encampment extended quite
across the island, which is, in this place, scarcely
two miles wide; and both his flanks were covered
by his ships.

The strongest point of the American lines was
at Kingsbridge, both sides of which had been
carefully fortified. M'Gowan's Pass, and Morris's Heights were also occupied in considerable
force, and rendered capable of being defended
against superior numbers. A strong detachment
was posted in an intrenched camp on the heights
of Haerlem, within about a mile and a half of
the British lines.

The present position of the armies favoured
the views of the American General. He wished
to habituate his soldiers, by a series of successful
skirmishes, to meet the enemy in the field; and
he persuaded himself that his detachments, knowing a strong intrenched camp to be immediately
in their rear, would engage without apprehension, would soon display their native courage,

and would speedily regain the confidence they

had lost.

Opportunities to make the experiments he wished were soon afforded. The day after the retreat from New York, the British appeared in considerable force in the plains between the two camps; and the General immediately rode to his advanced posts, in order to make in person such arrangements as this movement might require. Soon after his arrival, Lieutenant Colonel Knowlton of Connecticut, who, at the head of a corps of rangers, had been skirmishing with this party, came in, and stated their numbers on conjecture at about three hundred men; the main body being concealed in a wood.

The General ordered Colonel Knowlton with his rangers, and Major Leitch with three companies of the third Virginia regiment, which had joined the army only the preceding day, to gain their rear, while he amused them with the appearance of making dispositions to attack their front.

This plan succeeded. The British ran eagerly down a hill, in order to possess themselves of some fences and bushes, which presented an advantageous position against the party expected in front; and a firing commenced—but at too great a distance to do any execution. In the mean time, Colonel Knowlton, not being precisely acquainted with their new position, made his attack rather on their flank than rear; and a warm action ensued.

In a short time, Major Leitch, who had led the detachment with great intrepidity, was brought off the ground mortally wounded, having received three balls through his body; and soon afterwards the gallant Colonel Knowlton also fell. Not discouraged by the loss of their field officers, the captains maintained their ground, and continued the action with great animation. The British were reinforced; and General Washington ordered some detachments from the adjacent regiments of New England and Maryland, to the support of the Americans. Thus reinforced, they made a gallant charge, drove the enemy out of the wood into the plain, and were pressing him still farther, when the General, content with the present advantage, called back his troops to their intrenchments.*

In this sharp conflict, the loss of the Americans, in killed and wounded, did not exceed fifty men. The British lost more than double that number. But the real importance of the affair was derived from its operation on the spirits of the whole army. It was the first success they had obtained during this campaign; and its influence was very discernible. To give it the more effect, the parole the next day was Leitch; and the General, in his orders, publicly

---

* The author received the account of this skirmish from the Colonel of the third Virginia Regiment, and from the Captains commanding the companies that were engaged.

thanked the troops under the command of that officer, who had first advanced on the enemy, and the others who had so resolutely supported them. He contrasted their conduct with that which had been exhibited the day before; and the result, he said, evidenced what might be done where officers and soldiers would exert themselves. Once more, therefore, he called upon them so to act, as not to disgrace the noble cause in which they were engaged. He appointed a successor to "the gallant and brave Colonel Knowlton, who would," he said, "have been an honour to any country, and who had fallen gloriously, fighting at his post."

In this active part of the campaign, when the utmost stretch of every faculty was required, to watch and counteract the plans of a skilful and powerful enemy, the effects of the original errors committed by the government, in its military establishment, were beginning to be so seriously felt, as to compel the Commander-in-chief to devote a portion of his time and attention to the complete removal of the causes which produced them.

The situation of America was becoming extremely critical. The almost entire dissolution of the existing army, by the expiration of the time for which the greater number of the troops had been engaged, was fast approaching. No steps had been taken to recruit the new regiments which congress had resolved to raise for

the ensuing campaign; and there was much reason to apprehend, that in the actual state of
things, the terms offered would not hold forth
sufficient inducements to fill them.

With so unpromising a prospect before him,
the General found himself pressed by an army,
permanent in its establishment, supplied with
every requisite of war, formidable for its discipline and the experience of its leaders, and
superior to him in numbers. These circumstances, and the impressions they created, will
be best exhibited by an extract from a letter
written at the time to congress. It is in these

words: "From the hours allotted to sleep, I

will borrow a few moments to convey my
thoughts, on sundry important matters, to congress. I shall offer them with that sincerity
which ought to characterize a man of candour;
and with the freedom which may be used in giving useful information, without incurring the
imputation of presumption.

"We are now, as it were, upon the eve of
another dissolution of our army. The remembrance of the difficulties which happened upon
that occasion last year; the consequences which
might have followed the change, if proper advantages had been taken by the enemy; added
to a knowledge of the present temper and disposition of the troops; reflect but a very gloomy
prospect upon the appearance of things now,
and satisfy me, beyond the possibility of doubt,

that unless some speedy and effectual measures are adopted by congress, our cause will be lost.

"It is in vain to expect that any, or more than a trifling part of this army, will engage again in the service, on the encouragement offered by congress. When men find that their townsmen and companions are receiving twenty, thirty, and more dollars, for a few months service, (which is truly the case,) this can not be expected, without using compulsion; and to force them into the service would answer no valuable purpose. When men are irritated, and their passions inflamed, they fly hastily and cheerfully to arms; but after the first emotions are over, to expect among such people as compose the bulk of an army, that they are influenced by any other motives than those of interest, is to look for what never did, and I fear never will happen; the congress will deceive themselves therefore if they expect it.

"A soldier, reasoned with upon the goodness of the cause he is engaged in, and the inestimable rights he is contending for, hears you with patience, and acknowledges the truth of your observations; but adds, that it is of no more consequence to him than to others. The officer makes you the same reply, with this further remark, that his pay will not support him, and he can not ruin himself and family to serve his country, when every member of the community is equally benefited and interested by his labours. The few, therefore, who act upon principles of disinterestedness, are, comparatively speaking, no more than a drop in the ocean. It becomes evidently clear, then, that as this contest is not likely to become the work of a day; as the war must be carried on systematically; and to do it, you must have good officers; there is, in my judgment, no other possible means to obtain them, but by establishing your army upon a permanent footing, and giving your officers good pay. This will induce gentlemen, and men of character, to engage; and, until the bulk of your officers are composed of such persons as are actuated by principles of honour and a spirit of enterprise, you have little to expect from them. They ought to have such allowances as will enable them to live like, and support the character of gentlemen; and not be driven by a scanty pittance to the low and dirty arts which many of them practise, to filch the public of more than the difference of pay would amount to, upon an ample allowance. Besides, something is due to the man who puts his life in your hands, hazards his health, and forsakes the sweets of domestic enjoyments. Why a captain in the continental service should receive no more than five shillings currency per day, for performing the same duties that an officer of the same rank in the British service receives ten shillings sterling for, I never could conceive; especially, when the latter is provided with every necessary he requires, upon the best terms, and the former can scarcely procure them at any rate. There is nothing that gives a man consequence, and renders him fit for command, like a support that renders him independent of every body but the state he serves.

"With respect to the men, nothing but a good bounty can obtain them upon a permanent establishment, and for no shorter time than the continuance of the war ought they to be engaged; as facts incontestably prove that the difficulty and cost of enlistments increase with time. When the army was first raised at Cambridge, I am persuaded the men might have been got, without a bounty, for the war: after that, they began to see that the contest was not likely to end so speedily as was imagined, and to feel their consequence, by remarking, that to get their militia, in the course of the last year, many towns were induced to give them a bounty. Foreseeing the evils resulting from this, and the destructive consequences which would unavoidably follow short enlistments, I took the liberty, in a long letter, (date not now recollected, as my letter book is not here,) to recommend the enlistments for and during the war, assigning such reasons for it, as experience has since convinced me, were well founded. At that time, twenty dollars would, I am persuaded, have engaged the men for this term: but it will not do to look back—and if the present opportunity is slipped, I am persuaded that twelve months more will increase our difficulties four fold. I shall therefore take the liberty of giving it as my opinion, that a good bounty be immediately offered, aided by the proffer of at least a hundred, or a hundred and fifty acres of land, and a suit of clothes, and a blanket, to each non-commissioned officer and soldier, as I have good authority for saying, that however high the men's pay may appear, it is barely sufficient, in the present scarcity and dearness of all kinds of goods, to keep them in clothes, much less to afford support to their families. If this encouragement, then, is given to the men, and such pay allowed to the officers, as will induce gentlemen of liberal character and liberal sentiments to engage; and proper care and caution be used in the nomination, (having more regard to the characters of persons than the number of men they can enlist,) we should, in a little time, have an army able to cope with any that can be opposed to it, as there are excellent materials to form one out of: but whilst the only merit an officer possesses is his ability to raise men; whilst those men consider and treat him as an equal, and in the character of an officer, regard him no more than a broomstick, being mixed together as one common herd; no order nor discipline can prevail, nor will the officer ever meet with that respect which is essentially necessary to due subordination.

"To place any dependence upon militia, is assuredly resting upon a broken staff. Men just dragged from the tender scenes of domestic life; unaccustomed to the din of arms; totally unacquainted with every kind of military skill, which, being followed by a want of confidence in themselves, when opposed to troops regularly trained, disciplined, and appointed—superior in knowledge, and superior in arms—makes them timid, and ready to fly from their own shadows. Besides, the sudden change in their manner of living, particularly in their lodging, brings on sickness in many, impatience in all; and such an unconquerable desire of returning to their respective homes, that it not only produces shameful and scandalous desertions among themselves, but infuses the like spirit into others. Again, men accustomed to unbounded freedom and no control, can not brook the restraint which is indispensably necessary to the good order and government of an army; without which, licentiousness, and every kind of disorder, triumphantly reign. To bring men to a proper degree of subordination, is not the work of a day, a month, or a year; and unhappily for us, and the cause we are engaged in, the little discipline I have been labouring to establish in the army under my immediate command, is in a manner done away by having such a mixture of troops as have been called together within these few months."

The frequent remonstrances of the Command-er-in-chief; the opinions of all military men; and the severe, but correcting hand of experience, had at length produced some effect on the government of the union;—and soon after the defeat on Long Island, congress had directed the committee composing the board of war, to prepare a plan of operations for the next succeeding campaign. Their report proposed a permanent army, to be enlisted for the war, and to be raised by the several states, in proportion to their ability. A bounty of twenty dollars was offered to each recruit; and small portions of land to every officer and soldier.

The resolutions adopting this report were received by the Commander-in-chief soon after the transmission of the foregoing letter. Believing the inducements they held forth for the completion of the army to be still insufficient, he, in his letter acknowledging the receipt of them, urged in the most serious terms, the necessity of raising the pay of the officers, and the bounty

offered to recruits. "Give me leave to say, sir," he observed, "I say it with due deference and respect, (and my knowledge of the facts, added to the importance of the cause, and the stake I hold it in, must justify the freedom,) that your affairs are in a more unpromising way than you seem to apprehend.

"Your army, as mentioned in my last, is upon the eve of political dissolution. True it is, you have voted a larger one in lieu of it; but the season is late, and there is a material difference between voting battalions, and raising men. In the latter, there are more difficulties than Congress seem aware of; which makes it my duty (as I have been informed of the prevailing sentiments of this army) to inform them, that unless the pay of the officers (especially that of the field officers) is raised, the chief part of those that are worth retaining will leave the service at the expiration of the present term; as the soldiers will also, if some greater encouragement is not offered them, than twenty dollars and one hundred acres of land."

After urging in strong terms the necessity of a more liberal compensation to the army, and stating that the British were actually raising a regiment with a bounty of ten pounds sterling for each recruit, he added, "when the pay and establishment of an officer once become objects of interested attention, the sloth, negligence, and even disobedience of orders, which at this time but too generally prevail, will be purged off;—but while the service is viewed with indifference; while the officer conceives that he is rather conferring than receiving an obligation: there will be a total relaxation of all order and discipline; and every thing will move heavily on, to the great detriment of the service, and inexpressible trouble and vexation of the general.

"The critical situation of our affairs at this time will justify my saying, that no time is to be lost in making fruitless experiments. An unavailing trial of a month, to get an army upon the terms proposed, may render it impracticable to do it at all, and prove fatal to our cause; as I am not sure whether any rubs in the way of our enlistments, or unfavourable turn in our affairs, may not prove the means of the enemy's recruiting men faster than we do."

After stating at large the confusion and delay, inseparable from the circumstance that the appointments for the new army were to be made by the states, the letter proceeds, "upon the present plan, I plainly foresee an intervention of time between the old and new army, which must be filled with militia, if to be had, with whom no man, who has any regard for his own reputation, can undertake to be answerable for consequences. I shall also be mistaken in my conjectures, if we do not lose the most valuable officers in this army, under the present mode of appointing them; consequently, if we have an army at all, it will be composed of materials not only entirely raw, but, if uncommon pains are not taken, entirely unfit: and I see such a distrust and jealousy of military power, that the Commander-in-chief has not an opportunity, even by recommendation, to give the least assurance of reward for the most essential services.

"In a word, such a cloud of perplexing circumstances appears before me, without one flattering hope, that I am thoroughly convinced, unless the most vigorous and decisive exertions are immediately adopted to remedy these evils, the certain and absolute loss of our liberties will be the inevitable consequence: as one unhappy stroke will throw a powerful weight into the scale against us, and enable General Howe to recruit his army, as fast as we shall ours; numbers being disposed, and many actually doing so already. Some of the most probable remedies, and such as experience has brought to my more intimate knowledge, I have taken the liberty to point out; the rest I beg leave to submit to the consideration of congress.

"I ask pardon for taking up so much of their time with my opinions, but I should betray that trust which they and my country have reposed in me, were I to be silent upon matters so extremely interesting."

On receiving this very serious letter, congress passed resolutions conforming to many of its suggestions. The pay of the officers was raised, and a suit of clothes allowed annually to each soldier: The legislatures of the states having troops in the continental service, either at New York, Ticonderoga, or New Jersey, were requested to depute committees to those places in order to officer the regiments on the new estab-

CHAP. V lishment: and it was recommended to the com-

1776   mittees to consult the General on the subject of
appointments.

Washington's Headquarters at White Plains

Here, twenty-two miles northeast of New York City, Washington made his headquarters in October, 1776, and directed the Battle of White Plains or Chatterton Hill. Opposed to the American forces was a British army, greatly superior in numbers, under General Howe, whose delay in attacking the Americans enabled Washington to take up an unassailable position at North Castle, preparatory to his subsequent masterly retreat across New Jersey.

Washington's Headquarters at White Plains

Here, twenty-two miles northeast of New York City, Washington made his headquarters in October, 1776, and directed the Battle of White Plains or Chatterton Hill. Opposed to the American forces was a British army, greatly superior in numbers, under General Howe, whose delay in attacking the Americans enabled Washington to take up an unassailable position at North Castle, preparatory to his subsequent masterly retreat across New Jersey.

CHAPTER VI.

The British land at Frog's Neck....The American army evacuates York Island, except fort Washington....Both armies move towards the White Plains....Battle of the White Plains....The British army returns to Kingsbridge....General Washington crosses the North river....The lines of fort Washington carried by the British, and the garrison made prisoners....Evacuation of fort Lee....Weakness of the American army....Ineffectual attempts to raise the militia....General Washington retreats through Jersey....General Washington crosses the Delaware....Danger of Philadelphia....Capture of General Lee....The British go into winter quarters....Battle of Trenton....Of Princeton....Firmness of congress.

THE armies did not long retain their position on York Island. General Howe was sensible of the strength of the American camp, and was not disposed to force it. His plan was to compel General Washington to abandon it, or to give battle in a situation in which a defeat must be attended with the total destruction of his army. With this view, after throwing up entrenchments on M'Gowan's hill for the protection of New York, he determined to gain the rear of the American camp, by the New England road, and also to possess himself of the North river above Kingsbridge. To assure himself of the practicability of acquiring the command of the river, three frigates passed up it under the fire from fort Washington, and from the opposite

1776

post on the Jersey shore, afterwards called fort Lee, without sustaining any injury from the batteries, or being impeded by the chevaux-de-frise which had been sunk in the channel between those forts.

This point being ascertained, he embarked a great part of his army on board flat bottomed boats, and, passing through Hurl Gate into the Sound, landed at Frog's Neck, about nine miles from the camp on the heights of Haerlem.

In consequence of this movement, Washington strengthened the post at Kingsbridge, and detached some regiments to West Chester for the purpose of skirmishing with the enemy, so soon as he should march from the ground he occupied. The road from Frog's Point to Kingsbridge leads through a strong country, intersected by numerous stone fences, so as to render it difficult to move artillery, or even infantry, in compact columns, except along the main road, which had been broken up in several places. The General, therefore, entertained sanguine hopes of the event, should a direct attack be made on his camp.

General Howe continued some days waiting for his artillery, military stores, and reinforcements from Staten Island, which were detained by unfavourable winds.

In the mean time, as the habits of thinking in America required that every important measure should be the result of consultation, and should receive the approbation of a majority, the propriety of removing the American army from its present situation was submitted to a council of the general officers. After much investigation, it was declared to be impracticable, without a change of position, to keep up their communication with the country, and avoid being compelled to fight under great disadvantages, or to surrender themselves prisoners of war. General Lee, who had just arrived from the south, and whose experience as well as late success gave great weight to his opinions, urged the necessity of this movement with much earnestness. It was, at the same time, determined to hold fort Washington, and to defend it as long as possible. A resolution of congress of the 11th of October, desiring General Washington, by every art and expense, to obstruct, if possible, the navigation of the river, contributed, not inconsiderably, to this determination.

The American army evacuates York island except Fort Washington

In pursuance of this opinion of the military council, measures were taken for moving the army up the North River, so as to extend its front, or left, towards the White Plains, beyond the British right, and thus keep open its communication with the country. The right, or rear division, remained a few days longer about Kingsbridge under the command of General Lee, for the security of the heavy baggage and military stores, which, in consequence of the difficulty of obtaining wagons, could be but slowly removed.

General Howe, after uniting his forces at Pell's Point, moved forward his whole army, except four brigades destined for the defence of New York, through Pelham's manor, towards New Rochelle. Some skirmishes took place on the march with a part of Glover's brigade, in which the conduct of the Americans was mentioned with satisfaction by the Commander-in-chief; and, as General Howe took post at New

Rochelle, a village on the Sound, General Washington occupied the heights between that place and the North River.

At New Rochelle, the British army was joined by the second division of Germans, under the command of General Knyphausen, and by an incomplete regiment of cavalry from Ireland; some of whom had been captured on their pas-

sage. Both armies now moved towards the White Plains, a strong piece of ground already occupied by a detachment of militia. The main body of the American troops formed a long line of entrenched camps, extending from twelve to thirteen miles, on the different heights from Valentine's Hill, near Kingsbridge, to the White Plains, fronting the British line of march, and the Brunx, which divided the two armies. The motions of General Howe were anxiously watched, not only for the purposes of security, and of avoiding a general action, but in order to seize any occasion which might present itself of engaging his out-posts with advantage. While the British army lay at New Rochelle, the position of a corps of American loyalists commanded by Major Rogers was supposed to furnish such an occasion. He was advanced, farther eastward, to Mamaraneck, on the Sound, where he was believed to be covered by the other troops. An attempt was made to surprise him in the night, by a detachment which should pass between him and the main body of the British army, and, by a coup de main, bear off his whole corps. Major Rogers was surprised, and about sixty of his regiment killed and taken. The loss of the Americans was only two killed, and eight or ten wounded; among the latter was Major Green of Virginia, a brave officer, who led the detachment, and who received a ball through his body.

Not long afterwards, a regiment of Pennsylvania riflemen, under Colonel Hand, engaged an equal number of Hessian chasseurs, with some advantage.

The caution of the English general was increased by these evidences of enterprise in his adversary. His object seems to have been to avoid skirmishes, and to bring on a general action, if that could be effected under favourable circumstances; if not, he calculated on nearly all the advantages of a victory from the approaching dissolution of the American army.

He proceeded therefore slowly. His march was in close order, his encampments compact, and well guarded with artillery; and the utmost circumspection was used to leave no vulnerable point.

As the sick and baggage reached a place of safety, General Washington gradually drew in his out-posts, and took possession of the heights on the east side of the Brunx, fronting the head of the British columns, at the distance of seven or eight miles from them. The next day, he was joined by General Lee, who, after securing the sick and the baggage, had, with considerable address, brought up the rear division of the army; an operation the more difficult as the deficiency of teams was such that a large portion of the labour usually performed by horses or oxen, devolved on men.

General Washington was encamped on high broken ground, with his right flank on the Brunx. This stream meandered so as also to cover the front of his right wing, which extended along the road leading towards New Rochelle, as far as the brow of the hill where his centre was posted. His left, which formed almost a right angle with his centre, and was nearly parallel to his right, extended along the hills northward, so as to keep possession of the commanding ground, and secure a retreat, should it be necessary, to a still stronger position in his rear.

On the right of the army, and on the west side of the Brunx, about one mile from camp, on a road leading from the North River, was a hill, of which General M'Dougal was ordered to take possession, for the purpose of covering the right flank. His detachment consisted of about sixteen hundred men, principally militia; and his communication with the main army was open, that part of the Brunx being passable without difficulty.

Intrenchments were thrown up to strengthen the lines.

General Howe, having made arrangements to attack Washington in his camp, advanced early in the morning in two columns, the right commanded by Sir Henry Clinton, and the left by General Knyphausen; and, about ten, his van appeared in full view, on which a cannonade commenced without much execution on either side.

The British right formed behind a rising ground, about a mile in front of the American camp, and extending from the road leading from Mamaraneck towards the Brunx, stood opposed to the American centre.

On viewing Washington's situation, Howe, who accompanied Knyphausen, determined to carry the hill occupied by M'Dougal, as preliminary to an attack on the centre and right of the American camp. He therefore directed Colonel Rawle, with a brigade of Hessians, to cross the

Brunx and make a circuit so as to turn M'Dougal's right flank, while Brigadier General Leslie, with a strong corps of British and Hessian
troops should attack him in front. When Rawle
had gained his position, the detachment commanded by Leslie also crossed the Brunx, and
commenced a vigorous attack. * The militia
in the front line immediately fled; but the regulars maintained their ground with great gallantry. Colonel Smallwood's regiment of Maryland, and Colonel Reitzimer's of New York,
advanced boldly towards the foot of the hill to
meet Leslie, but, after a sharp encounter, were
overpowered by numbers, and compelled to retreat. General Leslie then attacked the remaining part of M'Dougal's forces, who were soon
driven from the hill, but kept up for some time
an irregular fire from the stone walls about the
scene of action. General Putnam, with Real's
brigade, was ordered to support them; but not
having arrived till the hill was lost, the attempt
to regain it was deemed unadviseable, and the
troops retreated to the main army.

In this animated engagement, the loss was
supposed to be nearly equal. That of the Americans was between three and four hundred in
killed, wounded, and taken. Colonel Smallwood
was among the wounded.

General Washington continued in his lines expecting an assault. But a considerable part of

* General Howe's letter.

the day having been exhausted in gaining the
hill which had been occupied by M'Dougal, the
meditated attempt on his intrenchments was
postponed until the next morning; and the British army lay on their arms the following night,
in order of battle, on the ground taken during
the day.

This interval was employed by General Washington in strengthening his works, removing his
sick and baggage, and preparing for the expected
attack by adopting the arrangement of his
troops to the existing state of things. His left
maintained its position; but his right was drawn
back to stronger ground. Perceiving this, and
being unwilling to leave any thing to hazard,
Howe resolved to postpone farther offensive operations, until Lord Percy should arrive with
four battalions from New York, and two from
Mamaraneck. This reinforcement was received   October 30.
on the evening of the thirtieth, and preparations
were then made to force the American intrenchments the next morning. In the night, and during the early part of the succeeding day, a violent rain still farther postponed the assault.

Having now removed his provisions and heavy
baggage to much stronger ground, and apprehending that the British general, whose left wing
extended along the height, taken from M'Dougal, to his rear, might turn his camp, and occupy
the strong ground to which he designed to
retreat, should an attempt on his lines prove

successful, General Washington changed his position in the night, and withdrew to the heights of North Castle, about five miles from the White Plains.

Deeming this position too strong to be attempted with prudence, General Howe determined to change his plan of operations, and to give a new direction to his efforts.*

While forts Washington and Lee were held by the Americans, his movements were checked, and York Island insecure. With a view to the acquisition of these posts, he directed General Knyphausen to take possession of Kingsbridge, which was defended by a small party of Americans placed in fort Independence. On his approach, this party retreated to fort Washington; and Knyphausen encamped between that place and Kingsbridge.

In the mean time, General Howe retired slowly down the North River. His designs were immediately penetrated by the American general, who perceived the necessity of passing a part of his army into Jersey, but was restrained from immediately leaving the strong ground he occupied by the apprehension that his adversary might, in that event, return suddenly and gain his rear. A council of war was called, which de-

termined unanimously, that, should General Howe continue his march towards New York, all the troops raised on the west side of the Hud-

* General Howe's letter.

son should cross that river, to be afterwards followed by those raised in the eastern part of the continent, leaving three thousand men for the defence of the Highlands about the North river.

In a letter to congress communicating this movement of the British army, and this determination of the council, the general said, "I can not indulge the idea that General Howe, supposing him to be going to New York, means to close the campaign, and to sit down without attempting something more. I think it highly probable, and almost certain, that he will make a descent with part of his troops into the Jerseys; and, as soon as I am satisfied that the present manœuvre is real, and not a feint, I shall use all the means in my power to forward a part of our force to counteract his designs.

"I expect the enemy will bend their force against fort Washington, and invest it immediately. From some advices, it is an object that will attract their earliest attention."

He also addressed a letter to the governor of New Jersey, expressing a decided opinion that General Howe would not content himself with investing fort Washington, but would invade the Jerseys; and urging him to put the militia in the best possible condition to reinforce the army, and to take the place of the new levies, who could not, he suggested, be depended on to continue in service one day longer than the first of December, the time for which they were engaged.

Immediate intelligence of this movement was likewise given to General Greene, who commanded in the Jerseys; and his attention was particularly pointed to fort Washington.

As the British army approached Kingsbridge, three ships of war passed up the North River, notwithstanding the fire from forts Washington and Lee, and notwithstanding the additional obstructions which had been placed in the channel.

November 8.
On being informed of this, another letter was addressed to General Greene, stating that this fact was so plain a proof of the inefficacy of all the obstructions thrown in the river, as to justify a change in the dispositions which had been made. "If," continued the letter, "we can not prevent vessels from passing up, and the enemy are possessed of the surrounding country, what valuable purpose can it answer to attempt to hold a post from which the expected benefit can not be derived? I am therefore inclined to think it will not be prudent to hazard the men and stores at Mount Washington; but as you are on the spot, I leave it to you to give such orders respecting the evacuation of the place, as you may think most adviseable; and so far revoke the orders given to Colonel Magaw to defend it to the last."

Measures were now taken to cross the North River with the troops which had been raised on its western side, and General Washington determined to accompany that division of the army. The eastern regiments remained on the eastern side of the river, under the command of General Lee, with orders to join the Commander-in-chief, should the British army cross the Hudson.

After visiting the posts about Peekskill, and making all the arrangements in his power for their defence, General Washington passed the North River in the rear of the troops designed to act in the Jerseys, and proceeded to the quarters of General Greene, near fort Lee.

From too great a confidence * in the strength of fort Washington, and a conviction of its importance, General Greene had not withdrawn its garrison under the discretionary orders he had received, but still indulged a hope that the post might be maintained, or, should its situation become desperate, that means might be found to transport the troops across the river to the Jersey shore, which was defended by fort Lee.

Mount Washington is a high piece of rocky ground, near the North River, very difficult of ascent, especially towards the north, or Kingsbridge. The fort was capable of containing

---

* Extract of a letter from General Greene, dated September 11th, 1778.

"Remember the effect that the loss of the garrison of fort Washington had; there were men enough to have defended themselves against all the army had they not been struck with a panic; but, being most of them irregular troops, they lost their confidence when the danger began to grow pressing, and so fell a prey to their own fears."—*Life of Greene,* v. 1, p. 121.

about one thousand men; but the lines and out-works, which were chiefly on the southern side, towards New York, were drawn quite across the island. The ground was naturally strong, the approaches difficult, and the fortifications, though not sufficient to resist heavy artillery, were believed to be in a condition to resist any attempt to carry them by storm The garrison consisted of troops, some of whom were among the best in the American army; and the command had been given to Colonel Magaw, a brave and intelligent officer, in whom great confidence was placed.

General Howe, after retiring from the White Plains, encamped at a small distance from Kingsbridge, on the heights of Fordham; and, having made the necessary preparations for an

assault, summoned the garrison to surrender, on pain of being put to the sword. Colonel Magaw replied, that he should defend the place to the last extremity, and communicated the summons

to General Greene at fort Lee, who transmitted it to the Commander-in-chief, then at Hacken-sack He immediately rode to fort Lee, and, though it was late in the night, was proceeding to fort Washington, where he expected to find Generals Putnam and Greene, when, in crossing the river, he met those officers returning from a visit to that fort. They reported that the garrison was in high spirits, and would make a good defence; on which he returned with them to fort Lee.

Early next morning, Colonel Magaw posted his troops, partly on a commanding hill north of the fort, partly in the outermost of the lines drawn across the island on the south of the fort, and partly between those lines, on the woody and rocky heights fronting Haerlem River, where the ground being extremely difficult of ascent, the works were not closed. Colonel Rawlings, of Maryland, commanded on the hill towards Kingsbridge; Colonel Cadwallader, of Pennsylvania, in the lines, and Colonel Magaw himself continued in the fort.

The strength of the place had not deterred the British general from resolving to carry it by storm; and, on receiving the answer of Colonel Magaw, arrangements were made for a vigorous attack next day. About ten, the assailants appeared before the works, and moved to the assault in four different quarters. Their first division consisting of Hessians and Waldeckers, amounting to about five thousand men, under the command of General Knyphausen, advanced on the north side of the fort, against the hill occupied by Colonel Rawlings, who received them with great gallantry. The second, on the east, consisting of the British light infantry and guards, was led by Brigadier General Matthews, supported by Lord Cornwallis, at the head of the grenadiers and the thirty-third regiment.

These troops crossed Haerlem River in boats, under cover of the artillery planted in the works, which had been erected on the opposite side of the river, and landed within the third line of defence which crossed the island. The third division was conducted by Lieutenant Colonel Stirling, who passed the river higher up; and the fourth by Lord Percy, accompanied by General Howe in person. This division was to attack the lines in front, on the south side.*

The attacks on the north and south by General Knyphausen and Lord Percy, were made about the same instant, on Colonels Rawlings and Cadwallader, who maintained their ground for a considerable time; but, while Colonel Cadwallader was engaged in the first line against Lord Percy, the second and third divisions which had crossed Haerlem River made good their landing, and dispersed the troops fronting that river, as well as a detachment sent by Colonel Cadwallader to support them. Thus being overpowered, and the British advancing between the fort and the lines, it became necessary to abandon them. In retreating to the fort, some of the men were intercepted by the division under Colonel Stirling, and made prisoners.

The resistance on the north was of longer duration. Rawlings maintained his ground with firmness, and his riflemen did vast execution. A

---

* General Howe's letter.

three gun battery also played on Knyphausen with great effect. At length, the Hessian columns gained the summit of the hill; after which, Colonel Rawlings, who perceived the danger which threatened his rear, retreated under the guns of the fort.

Having carried the lines, and all the strong ground adjoining them, the British general again summoned Colonel Magaw to surrender. While the capitulation was in a course of arrangement, General Washington sent him a billet, requesting him to hold out until the evening, when means should be attempted to bring off the garrison. But Magaw had proceeded too far to retreat; and it is probable the place could not have resisted an assault from so formidable a force as threatened it. The greatest difficulties had been overcome; the fort was too small to contain all the men; and their ammunition was nearly exhausted. Under these circumstances the garrison became prisoners of war.

The lines of Fort Washington carried by the enemy, and the garrison made prisoners.

The loss on this occasion was the greatest the Americans had ever sustained. The garrison was stated by General Washington at about two thousand men. Yet, in a report published as from General Howe, the number of prisoners is said to be two thousand and six hundred, exclusive of officers. Either General Howe must have included in his report persons who were not soldiers, or General Washington must have comprehended the regulars only in his letter. The last conjecture is most probably correct. The loss of the assailants, according to Mr. Stedman, amounted to eight hundred men. This loss fell heaviest on the Germans.

Evacuation
of
Fort Lee.

On the surrender of fort Washington, it was determined to evacuate fort Lee; and a removal of the stores was immediately commenced. Before this operation could be completed, a detachment commanded by Lord Cornwallis, amounting to about six thousand men, crossed

November 18.

the North River below Dobb's ferry, and endeavoured, by a rapid march, to enclose the garrison between the North and Hackensack Rivers. An immediate retreat from that narrow neck of land had become indispensable, and was with difficulty effected. All the heavy cannon at fort Lee, except two twelve-pounders, with a considerable quantity of provisions and military stores, including three hundred tents, were lost.

After crossing the Hackensack, General Washington posted his troops along the western bank of that river, but was unable to dispute its passage at the head of about three thousand effectives, exposed, without tents, in an inclement season; he was in a level country, without a single intrenching tool, among people far from being zealous in the American cause. In other respects this situation was dangerous. The Passaic, in his rear, after running several miles nearly parallel to the Hackensack, unites with

that river below the ground occupied by the
Americans, who were consequently still exposed
to the hazard of being inclosed between two
rivers.

This gloomy state of things was not bright-
ened by the prospect before him. In casting his
eyes around, no cheering object presented itself. No confidence could be placed on receiving reinforcements from any quarter. But, in
no situation could Washington despond. His
exertions to collect an army, and to impede the
progress of his enemy, were perseveringly continued. Understanding that Sir Guy Carleton
no longer threatened Ticonderoga, he directed
General Schuyler to hasten the troops of Pennsylvania and Jersey to his assistance, and ordered * General Lee to cross the North River,
and be in readiness to join him, should the enemy
continue the campaign. But, under the influence
of the same fatal cause which had acted elsewhere, these armies too were melting away, and
would soon be almost totally dissolved. General Mercer, who commanded a part of the flying camp stationed about Bergen, was also
called in; but these troops had engaged to serve
only till the 1st of December, and, like the other
six months men, had already abandoned the
army in great numbers. No hope existed of retaining the remnant after they should possess a
legal right to be discharged; and there was not

November 21.

Weakness
of the
American
army.

* See note No. VII. at the end of the volume.

much probability of supplying their places with other militia. To New England he looked with anxious hope; and his requisitions on those states received prompt attention. Six thousand militia from Massachusetts, and a considerable body from Connecticut, were ordered to his assistance; but some delay in assembling them was unavoidable, and their march was arrested by the appearance of the enemy in their immediate neighbourhood.

Three thousand men, conducted by Sir Henry Clinton, who were embarked on board a fleet commanded by Sir Peter Parker, sailed late in November from New York, and, without much opposition, took possession of Newport. This invasion excited serious alarm in Massachusetts and Connecticut, and these states retained for their own defence, the militia who had been embodied at the instance of the Commander-in-chief.

Not intending to maintain his present position, General Washington had placed some regiments along the Hackensack to afford the semblance of defending its passage until his stores could be removed; and, with the residue of the troops, crossed the Passaic, and took post at Newark. Soon after he had marched, Major General Vaughan appeared before the new bridge over Hackensack. The American detachment which had been left in the rear, being unable to defend it, broke it down, and retired before him over the Passaic.

Having entered the open country, General Washington determined to halt a few days on the south side of this river, make some show of resistance, and endeavour to collect such a force as would keep up the semblance of an army. His letters, not having produced such exertions as the public exigencies required, he deputed General Mifflin to the government of Pennsylvania, and Colonel Reid, his Adjutant General, to the government of New Jersey, with orders to represent the real situation of the army, and the certainty that, without great reinforcements, Philadelphia must fall into the hands of the enemy, and the state of Jersey be overrun.

Ineffectual
attempts
to raise
the militia.

While thus endeavouring to strengthen himself with militia, he pressed General Lee to hasten his march, and cautioned him to keep high enough up the country to avoid the enemy, who, having got possession of the mail containing one of his late letters, would certainly endeavour to prevent the junction of the two armies.

This perilous state of things was rendered still more critical by indications of an insurrection in the county of Monmouth, in Jersey, where great numbers favoured the royal cause. In other places, too, a hostile temper was displayed, and an indisposition to farther resistance began to be manifested throughout that state. These appearances obliged him to make detachments from the militia of his army, to overawe the disaffected of Monmouth, who were on the point of assembling in force.

General Washington retreats through Jersey.

As the British army crossed the Passaic, General Washington abandoned his position behind that river; and the day Lord Cornwallis entered Newark, he retreated to Brunswick, a small village on the Raritan.

November 23.

At this place, the levies drawn from Maryland and Jersey to compose the flying camp, became

December 1.

entitled to their discharge. No remonstrances could detain them; and he sustained the mortification of seeing his feeble army still more enfeebled by being entirely abandoned by these troops, in the face of an advancing enemy. The Pennsylvania militia belonging to the flying camp were engaged to serve till the 1st of January. So many of them deserted, that it was deemed necessary to place guards on the roads, and ferries over the Delaware, to apprehend and send them back to camp. The Governor of New Jersey was again pressed for assistance, but it was not in his power to furnish the aid required. The well affected part of the lower country was overawed by the British army; and the militia of Morris and Sussex came out slowly and reluctantly.

While at Brunswick, attempts were made to retard the advance of the British army by movements indicating an intention to act on the offensive; but this feint was unavailing. Lord

Cornwallis continued to press forward; and, as his advanced guards showed themselves on the opposite side of the bridge, General Washington evacuated the town, and marched through Princeton to Trenton. Directions had already been given to collect all the boats on the Delaware, from Philadelphia upwards for seventy miles, in the hope that the progress of the enemy might be stopped at this river; and that, in the mean time, reinforcements might arrive which would enable him to dispute its passage.

Having, with great labour, transported the few remaining military stores and baggage over the Delaware, he determined to remain as long as possible on the northern banks of that river.

The army which was thus pressed slowly through the Jerseys, was aided by no other cavalry than a small corps of badly mounted Connecticut militia, commanded by Major Shelden; and was almost equally destitute of artillery. Its numbers, at no time during the retreat, exceeded four thousand men, and on reaching the Delaware, was reduced to less than three thousand; of whom, not quite one thousand were militia of New Jersey. Even among the continental troops there were many whose term of service was about to expire.

Its defectiveness of numbers did not constitute its only weakness. The regulars were badly armed, worse clad, and almost destitute of tents, blankets, or utensils for dressing their food. They were composed chiefly of the garrison of fort Lee, and had been obliged to evacuate that place with too much precipitation to bring with them even those few articles of comfort and accommodation with which they had been furnished. The Commander-in-chief found himself at the head of this small band of soldiers, dispirited by their losses and fatigues, retreating almost naked and barefooted, in the cold of November and December, before a numerous, well appointed, and victorious army, through a desponding country, much more disposed to obtain safety by submission, than to seek it by a manly resistance.

In this crisis of American affairs, a proclamation was issued by Lord and General Howe, as commissioners appointed on the part of the crown for restoring peace to America, commanding all persons assembled in arms against his majesty's government, to disband and return to their homes; and all civil officers to desist from their treasonable practices, and relinquish their usurped authority. A full pardon was offered to every person who would, within sixty days, appear before certain civil or military officers of the crown, claim the benefit of that proclamation, and testify his obedience to the laws by subscribing a declaration of his submission to the royal authority. Copies of it were dispersed through the country, after which numbers flocked in daily, to make their peace and obtain protection. The contrast between the splendid appearance of the pursuing army, and that of the ragged Americans who were flying before them, could not fail to nourish the general opinion that the contest was approaching its termination.

Among the many valuable traits in the character of Washington, was that unyielding firmness of mind which resisted these accumulated circumstances of depression, and supported him under them. Undismayed by the dangers which surrounded him, he did not for an instant relax his exertions, nor omit any thing which could obstruct the progress of the enemy, or improve his own condition. He did not appear to despair of the public safety, but struggled against adverse fortune with the hope of yet vanquishing the difficulties which surrounded him; and constantly showed himself to his harassed and enfeebled army, with a serene, unembarrassed countenance, betraying no fears in himself, and invigorating and inspiring with confidence the bosoms of others. To this unconquerable firmness, to this perfect self-possession under the most desperate circumstances, is America, in a great degree, indebted for her independence.

After removing his baggage and stores over the Delaware, and sending his sick to Philadelphia, the American General, finding that Lord Cornwallis still continued in Brunswick, detached twelve hundred men to Princeton in the hope that this appearance of advancing on the British might not only retard their progress, but cover a part of the country, and reanimate the people of Jersey.

Some portion of this short respite from laborious service was devoted to the predominant wish of his heart,—preparations for the next campaign,—by impressing on congress a conviction of the real causes of the present calamitous state of things. However the human mind may resist the clearest theoretic reasoning, it is scarcely possible not to discern obvious and radical errors, while smarting under their destructive consequences. The abandonment of the army by whole regiments of the flying camp, in the face of an advancing and superior enemy; the impracticability of calling out the militia of Jersey and Pennsylvania in sufficient force to prevent Lord Cornwallis from overrunning the first state, or restrain him from entering the last, had it not been saved by other causes, were practical lessons on the subjects of enlistments for a short time, and a reliance on militia, which no prejudice could disregard, and which could not fail to add great weight to the remonstrances formerly made by the Commander-in-chief, which were now repeated.

The exertions of General Mifflin to raise the militia of Pennsylvania, though unavailing in the country, were successful in Philadelphia. A large proportion of the inhabitants of that city capable of bearing arms, had associated for the general defence; and, on this occasion, fifteen hundred of them marched to Trenton; to which place a German battalion was also ordered by congress. On the arrival of these troops, General Washington commenced his march to Princeton, but was stopped by the intelligence that Lord Cornwallis, having received large reinforcements, was advancing rapidly from Brunswick by different routes, and endeavouring to gain his rear.

On receiving this intelligence, he crossed the Delaware, and posted his army in such a manner as to guard the fords. As his rear passed the river, the van of the British army appeared in sight. The main body took post at Trenton, and detachments were placed both above and below, while small parties, without interruption from the people of the country, reconnoitred the Delaware for a considerable distance. From Bordentown below Trenton the course of the river turns westward, and forms an acute angle with its course from Philadelphia to that place; so that Lord Cornwallis might cross a considerable distance above, and be not much, if any, farther from that city than the American army.

The British general made some unsuccessful attempts to seize a number of boats guarded by Lord Stirling, about Coryell's Ferry; and, in order to facilitate his movements down the river, on the Jersey shore, repaired the bridges below Trenton, which had been broken down by order of General Washington. He then advanced

CHAP. VI

1776

December 6.

Seventh.

Eighth.

General Washington crosses the Delaware.

Danger of Philadelphia.

a strong detachment to Bordentown, giving indications of an intention to cross the Delaware at the same time above and below; and either to march in two columns to Philadelphia, or completely to envelop the American army in the angle of the river. To counteract this plan, the American General stationed a few gallies to watch the movements of his enemy below, and aid in repelling any effort to pass over to the Pennsylvania shore; and made such a disposition of his little army as to guard against any attempt to force a passage above, which he believed to be the real design.

Having made his arrangements, he waited anxiously for reinforcements; and, in the meantime, sent daily parties over the river to harass the enemy, and to observe his situation.

The utmost exertions were made by government to raise the militia. In the hope that a respectable body of continental troops would aid these exertions, General Washington had directed General Gates, with the regulars of the northern army, and General Heath, with those at Peekskill, to march to his assistance.

Although General Lee had been repeatedly urged to join the Commander-in-chief, he proceeded slowly in the execution of these orders, manifesting a strong disposition to retain his separate command, and rather to hang on, and threaten the rear of the British army, than to strengthen that in its front. With this view he

proposed establishing himself at Morristown.
On receiving a letter from General Washington
disapproving this proposition, and urging him
to hasten his march, Lee still avowed a prefer-
ence for his own plan, and proceeded reluctantly
towards the Delaware. While passing through
Morris county, at the distance of twenty miles
from the British encampment, he, very incau-
tiously, quartered under a slight guard, in a
house about three miles from his army. Information of this circumstance was given by a
countryman to Colonel Harcourt, at that time
detached with a body of cavalry to watch his
movements, who immediately formed and executed the design of seizing him. Early in the
morning of the 12th of December, this officer
reached Lee's quarters, who received no intimation of his danger until the house was sur- Capture of
rounded, and he found himself a prisoner. He General Lee.
was carried off in triumph to the British army,
where he was, for some time, treated as a deserter from the British service.

This misfortune made a serious impression on
all America. The confidence originally placed
in General Lee had been increased by his success in the southern department, and by a belief
that his opinions, during the military operations
in New York, had contributed to the adoption
of those judicious movements which had, in
some measure, defeated the plans of General
Howe in that quarter. It was also believed that

he had dissented from the resolution of the council of war for maintaining forts Washington and Lee. No officer, except the Commander-in-chief, possessed, at that time, in so eminent a degree, the confidence of the army, or of the country; and his loss was, almost universally, bewailed as one of the greatest calamities which had befallen the American arms. It was regretted by no person more than by General Washington himself. He respected the merit of that eccentric veteran, and sincerely lamented his captivity.

General Sullivan, on whom the command of that division devolved after the capture of Lee, promptly obeyed the orders which had been directed to that officer; and, crossing the Delaware at Philipsburg, joined the Commander-in-chief. On the same day General Gates arrived with a few northern troops. By these and other reinforcements, the army was augmented to about seven thousand effective men.

The attempts of the British general to get possession of boats for the transportation of his army over the Delaware having failed, he gave indications of an intention to close the campaign, and to retire into winter quarters. About four thousand men were cantoned on the Delaware at Trenton, Bordentown, the White Horse, and Mount Holly; and the remaining part of the army of Jersey was distributed from that river to the Hackensack. Strong corps were

The British go into winter quarters.

posted at Princeton, Brunswick, and Elizabeth-town.

To intimidate the people, and thereby impede the recruiting service, was believed to be no inconsiderable inducement with General Howe, for covering so large a portion of Jersey. To counteract these views, General Washington ordered three of the regiments from Peekskill to halt at Morristown, and to unite with about eight hundred militia assembled at that place under Colonel Ford. General Maxwell was sent to take command of these troops, with orders to watch the motions of the enemy, to harass him in his marches, to give intelligence of all his movements, to keep up the spirits of the militia, and to prevent the inhabitants from going within the British lines, and taking protection.

The short interval between this cantonment of the British troops, and the recommencement of active operations, was employed by General Washington in repeating the representations he had so often made to congress, respecting preparations for the ensuing campaign. The dangers resulting from a reliance on temporary armies had been fully exemplified; and his remonstrances on that subject were supported by that severe experience which corrects while it chastises. In the course of the campaign, he had suffered greatly from the want of cavalry, of artillery, and of engineers. His ideas on these im-

December 20.

portant subjects had been already stated to congress, and were now reurged. With respect to the additional expense to be incurred by the measures recommended, he observed, "that our funds were not the only object now to be taken into consideration. The enemy, it was found, were daily gathering strength from the disaffected. This strength, like a snow ball by rolling, would increase, unless some means should be devised to check effectually the progress of their arms. Militia might possibly do it for a little while; but in a little while also, the militia of those states which were frequently called upon would not turn out at all, or would turn out with so much reluctance and sloth, as to amount to the same thing. Instance New Jersey! Witness Pennsylvania! Could any thing but the river Delaware have saved Philadelphia?

"Could any thing," he asked, "be more destructive of the recruiting business than giving ten dollars bounty for six weeks service in the militia, who come in, you can not tell how; go, you can not tell when; and act, you can not tell where; who consume your provisions, exhaust your stores, and leave you at last in a critical moment.

"These, sir," he added, "are the men I am to depend upon ten days hence. This is the basis upon which your cause will rest, and must for ever depend, until you get a large standing army sufficient of itself to oppose the enemy."

Washington Crossing the Delaware

From the painting by Emanuel Leutze, in the Metropolitan Museum of Art, New York City.

On December 8, 1776, following his retreat across New Jersey, with the British army under Cornwallis pressing him closely, Washington transported his army of 6,000 men across the Delaware into Pennsylvania and to safety. He had seized all the boats within seventy miles, leaving Cornwallis to wait until the river froze over before he could follow.

In recrossing the Delaware (as here depicted) to strike the British at Trenton, Washington executed the most brilliant military maneuver of his career.

In his sesquicentennial address delivered at Cambridge, Massachusetts, July 3, 1925, President Coolidge related this incident which gives us Cornwallis's estimate of the importance of the Trenton victory.

"It is recorded that a few evenings after the surrender of Lord Cornwallis at Yorktown a banquet was given by Washington and his staff to the British commander and his staff. One likes to contemplate the sportsmanship of that function. Amiabilities and good wishes were duly exchanged, and finally Lord Cornwallis rose to present his compliments to Washington. There had been much talk of past campaigning experiences, and Cornwallis, turning to Washington, expressed the judgment that when history's verdict was made up, 'the brightest garlands for your Excellency will be gathered, not from the shores of the Chesapeake, but from the banks of the Delaware.'"

Washington Crossing the Delaware

From the painting by Emanuel Leutze, in the Metropolitan Museum of Art, New York City.

On December 8, 1776, following his retreat across New Jersey, with the British army under Cornwallis pressing him closely, Washington transported his army of 6,000 men across the Delaware into Pennsylvania and to safety. He had seized all the boats within seventy miles, leaving Cornwallis to wait until the river froze over before he could follow.

In recrossing the Delaware (as here depicted) to strike the British at Trenton, Washington executed the most brilliant military maneuver of his career.

In his sesquicentennial address delivered at Cambridge, Massachusetts, July 3, 1925, President Coolidge related this incident which gives us Cornwallis's estimate of the importance of the Trenton victory:

"It is recorded that a few evenings after the surrender of Lord Cornwallis at Yorktown a banquet was given by Washington and his staff to the British commander and his staff. One likes to contemplate the sportsmanship of that function. Amiabilities and good wishes were duly exchanged, and finally Lord Cornwallis rose to present his compliments to Washington. There had been much talk of past campaigning experiences, and Cornwallis, turning to Washington, expressed the judgment that when history's verdict was made up 'the brightest garlands for your Excellency will be gathered, not from the shores of the Chesapeake, but from the banks of the Delaware.' "

He also hinted the idea, extremely delicate in itself, of enlarging his powers so as to enable him to act, without constant applications to congress for their sanction of measures, the immediate adoption of which was essential to the public interests. "This might," he said, "be termed an application for powers too dangerous to be trusted." He could only answer, "that desperate diseases required desperate remedies. He could with truth declare that he felt no lust for power, but wished with as much fervency as any man upon this wide extended continent, for an opportunity of turning the sword into a ploughshare; but his feelings as an officer and a man had been such as to force him to say, that no person ever had a greater choice of difficulties to contend with than himself."

After recapitulating the measures he had adopted, which were not within his power, and urging many other necessary arrangements, he added, "it may be thought I am going a good deal out of the line of my duty to adopt these measures, or to advise thus freely. A character to lose; an estate to forfeit; the inestimable blessing of liberty at stake; and a life devoted, must be my excuse."

The present aspect of American affairs was gloomy in the extreme. The existing army, except a few regiments, affording an effective force of about fifteen hundred men, would dissolve in a few days. New Jersey had, in a great measure, submitted; and the militia of Pennsylvania had not displayed the alacrity expected from them. General Howe would, most probably, avail himself of the ice which would soon form, and of the dissolution of the American army, to pass the Delaware and seize Philadelphia. This event was dreaded, not only on account of its intrinsic importance, but of its peculiar effect at this time, when an army was to be recruited on which the future hopes of America were to rest. It was feared, and with reason, that it would make such an impression on the public mind as to deter the American youth from engaging in a contest becoming desperate.

Impelled by these considerations, General Washington meditated a blow on the British army, while dispersed in its cantonments, which might retrieve the affairs of America in the opinion of the public, and recover the ground that had been lost.

He formed the daring plan of attacking all the British posts on the Delaware at the same instant. If successful in all, or any of these attacks, he hoped not only to wipe off the impression made by his losses, and by his retreat, but also to relieve Philadelphia from immediate danger, and to compel his adversary to compress himself in such a manner as no longer to cover the Jerseys.

The positions taken to guard the river were equally well adapted to offensive operations.

The regulars were posted above Trenton from Yardley's up to Coryell's Ferry. The Pennsylvania flying camp, and Jersey militia, under the command of General Irvine, extended from Yardley's to the ferry opposite Bordentown; and General Cadwallader with the Pennsylvania militia lay still lower down the river.

In the plan of attack which had been digested, it was proposed to cross in the night at M'Konkey's Ferry, about nine miles above Trenton; to march down in two divisions, the one taking the river road, and the other the Pennington road, both which lead into the town; the first, towards that part of the western side which approaches the river, and the last towards the north. This part of the plan was to be executed by the General in person, at the head of about two thousand four hundred continental troops. It was thought practicable to pass them over the river by twelve, and to reach the point of destination by five in the morning of the next day, when the attack was to be made. General Irvine was directed to cross at the Trenton Ferry, and to secure the bridge below the town, in order to prevent the escape of the enemy by that road. General Cadwallader was to pass over at Dunk's Ferry, and carry the post at Mount Holly. It had been in contemplation to unite the troops employed in fortifying Philadelphia, to those at Bristol, and to place the whole under General Putnam; but such indications were given in that city of an insurrection of the royal cause, that this part of the plan was abandoned. The cold on the night of the 25th was very severe. Snow, mingled with hail and rain, fell in great quantities, and so much ice was made in the river that, with every possible exertion, the division conducted by the General in person could not effect its passage until three, nor commence its march down the river till near four. As the distance to Trenton by either road is nearly the same, orders were given to attack at the instant of arrival, and, after driving in the out-guards, to press rapidly after them into the town, and prevent the main body from forming.

Battle of
Trenton.

December 26.

General Washington accompanied the upper column, and arriving at the out-post on that road, precisely at eight, drove it in, and, in three minutes, heard the fire from the column which had taken the river road. The picket guard attempted to keep up a fire while retreating, but was pursued with such ardour as to be unable to make a stand. Colonel Rawle, who commanded in the town, paraded his men, and met the assailants. In the commencement of the action, he was mortally wounded, upon which the troops, in apparent confusion, attempted to gain the road to Princeton. General Washington threw a detachment into their front, while he advanced rapidly on them in person. Finding themselves surrounded, and their artillery already seized, they laid down their arms, and surrendered themselves prisoners of war. About twenty of the enemy were killed, and about one thousand made prisoners. Six field pieces, and a thousand stand of small arms were also taken. On the part of the Americans, two privates were killed; two frozen to death; and one officer, Lieutenant Monroe, * of the third Virginia regiment, and three or four privates wounded.

Unfortunately, the ice rendered it impracticable for General Irvine to execute that part of the plan which was allotted to him. With his utmost efforts, he was unable to cross the river; and the road towards Bordentown remained open. About five hundred men, among whom was a troop of cavalry, stationed in the lower end of Trenton, availed themselves of this circumstance, and crossing the bridge in the commencement of the action, escaped down the river. The same cause prevented General Cadwallader from attacking the post at Mount Holly. With great difficulty a part of his infantry passed the river, but returned on its being found absolutely impracticable to cross with the artillery.

Although this plan failed in so many of its parts, the success attending that which was conducted by General Washington in person was followed by the happiest effects.

Had it been practicable for the divisions under Generals Irvine and Cadwallader to cross

---

* Since President of the United States.

the river, it was intended to proceed from Trenton to the posts at and about Bordentown, to
sweep the British from the banks of the Delaware, * and to maintain a position in the Jerseys. But finding that those parts of the plan
had failed, and supposing the British to remain
in force below, while a strong corps was posted
at Princeton, General Washington thought it
unadviseable to hazard the loss of the very important advantage already gained, by attempting to increase it, and recrossed the river with
his prisoners and military stores. Lieutenant
Colonel Baylor, his aid-de-camp, who carried the
intelligence of this success to congress, was presented with a horse completely caparisoned for
service, and recommended to the command of a
regiment of cavalry.

Nothing could surpass the astonishment of
the British commander at this unexpected display of vigour on the part of the American General. His condition, and that of his country,
had been thought desperate. He had been deserted by all the troops having a legal right to

---

* A fact has been stated to the author which shows to
what an extent the plan might have been executed had it
been possible to cross the river. Colonel Reed, who was
with the division of Cadwallader, passed the ferry with
the van of the infantry, and immediately despatched some
trusty persons to examine the situation of the troops at
Mount Holly. The report made by his messengers was,
that they had looked into several houses in which the soldiers were quartered, and had found them generally fast
asleep, under the influence, as was supposed, of the spirituous
liquors they had drunk the preceding day, which was Christ-
mas-day. That there appeared to be no apprehension of
danger, nor precaution against it.

leave him; and, to render his situation completely ruinous, nearly two-thirds of the continental soldiers still remaining with him, would be entitled to their discharge on the first day of January. There appeared to be no probability of prevailing on them to continue longer in the service, and the recruiting business was absolutely at an end. The spirits of a large proportion of the people were sunk to the lowest point of depression. New Jersey appeared to be completely subdued; and some of the best judges of the public sentiment were of opinion that immense numbers in Pennsylvania, also, were determined not to permit the sixty days allowed in the proclamation of Lord and Sir William Howe, to elapse, without availing themselves of the pardon it proffered. Instead of offensive operations, the total dispersion of the small remnant of the American army was to be expected, since it would be rendered too feeble by the discharge of those engaged only until the last day of December, to attempt, any longer, the defence of the Delaware, which would by that time, in all probability, be passable on the ice. While every appearance supported these opinions, and the British General, without being sanguine, might well consider the war as approaching its termination, this bold and fortunate enterprise announced to him, that he was contending with an adversary who could never cease to be formidable while the possibility of resistance remained. Finding the conquest of America more distant than had been supposed, he determined, in the depth of winter to recommence active operations; and Lord Cornwallis, who had retired to New York with the intention of embarking for Europe, suspended his departure, and returned to the Jerseys in great force, for the purpose of regaining the ground which had been lost.

Meanwhile, Count Donop, who commanded the troops below Trenton, on hearing the disaster which had befallen Colonel Rawle, retreated by the road leading to Amboy, and joined General Leslie at Princeton. The next day, General Cadwallader crossed the Delaware, with orders to harass the enemy, but to put nothing to hazard until he should be joined by the continental battalions, who were allowed a day or two of repose, after the fatigues of the enterprise against Trenton. General Mifflin joined General Irvine with about fifteen hundred Pennsylvania militia, and those troops also crossed the river.

Finding himself once more at the head of a force with which it seemed practicable to act offensively, the General determined to employ the winter in endeavouring to recover Jersey.

With this view, he ordered General Heath to leave a small detachment at Peekskill, and with the main body of the New England militia, to enter Jersey, and approach the British cantonments on that side. General Maxwell was or-

dered, with all the militia he could collect, to
harass their flank and rear, and to attack their
out-posts on every favourable occasion, while
the continental troops, led by himself, recrossed
the Delaware, and took post at Trenton. On
the last day of December, the regulars of New
England were entitled to a discharge. With
great difficulty, and a bounty of ten dollars,
many of them were induced to renew their engagements for six weeks.

The British were now collected in force at
Princeton under Lord Cornwallis; and appearances confirmed the intelligence, secretly * obtained, that he intended to attack the American
army.

Generals Mifflin and Cadwallader, who lay
at Bordentown and Crosswix, with three thousand six hundred militia, were therefore ordered
to join the Commander-in-chief, whose whole
effective force, with this addition, did not exceed five thousand men.

Lord Cornwallis advanced upon him the next
morning; and about four in the afternoon, the
van of the British army reached Trenton. On
its approach, General Washington retired across
the Assumpinck, a creek which runs through the
town. The British attempted to cross the creek

CHAP. VI

1776

December 30.

1777
January 1.

January 2.

---

* In this critical moment, when correct intelligence was so
all important, Mr. Robert Morris raised on his private credit
in Philadelphia, five hundred pounds in specie, which he
transmitted to the Commander-in-chief, who employed it in
procuring information not otherwise to have been obtained.

at several places, but finding all the fords guarded, they desisted from the attempt, and kindled their fires. The Americans kindled their fires likewise; and a cannonade was kept up on both sides till dark.

The situation of General Washington was again extremely critical. Should he maintain his position, he would certainly be attacked next morning, by a force so very superior, as to render the destruction of his little army inevitable. Should he attempt to retreat over the Delaware, the passage of that river had been rendered so difficult by a few mild and foggy days which had softened the ice, that a total defeat would be hazarded. In any event, the Jerseys would, once more, be entirely in possession of the enemy; the public mind again be depressed; recruiting discouraged; and Philadelphia, a second time, in the grasp of General Howe.

In this embarrassing state of things, he formed the bold design of abandoning the Delaware, and marching, by a circuitous route, along the left flank of the British army, into its rear, at Princeton, where its strength could not be great; and, after beating the troops at that place, to move rapidly to Brunswick, where the baggage and principal magazines of the army lay under a weak guard. He indulged the hope that this manœuvre would call the attention of the British general to his own defence. Should Lord Cornwallis, contrary to every reasonable calculation, proceed to Philadelphia, nothing worse could happen in that quarter, than must happen should the American army be driven before him; and some compensation for that calamity would be obtained by expelling the enemy completely from Jersey, and cutting up, in detail, all his parties in that state.

This plan being approved by a council of war, preparations were made for its immediate execution. As soon as it was dark, the baggage was removed silently to Burlington; and, about one in the morning, after renewing their fires, and leaving their guards to go the rounds as usual; the army decamped with perfect silence, and took a circuitous route along the Quaker road to Princeton, where three British regiments had encamped the preceding night, two of which commenced their march early in the morning to join the rear of their army at Maidenhead. At sunrise, when they had proceeded about two miles, they saw the Americans on their left, advancing in a direction which would enter the road in their rear. They immediately faced about, and, repassing Stony Brook, moved under cover of a copse of wood towards the American van, which was conducted by General Mercer. A sharp action ensued, which, however, was not of long duration. The militia, of which the advanced party was principally composed, soon gave way; and the few regulars attached to them were not strong enough to maintain

January 3.

Of Princeton.

their ground. While exerting himself gallantly to rally his broken troops, General Mercer was mortally wounded, and the van was entirely routed. But the fortune of the day was soon changed. The main body, led by General Washington in person, followed close in the rear, and attacked the British with great spirit. Persuaded that defeat would irretrievably ruin the affairs of America, he advanced in the very front of danger, and exposed himself to the hottest fire of the enemy. He was so well supported by the same troops who, a few days before, had saved their country at Trenton, that the British, in turn, were compelled to give way. Their line was broken, and the two regiments separated from each other. Colonel Mawhood, who commanded that in front, and was, consequently, nearest the rear division of the army, under Lord Cornwallis, retired to the main road, and continued his march to Maidenhead. The fifty-fifth regiment, which was on the left, being hard pressed, fled in confusion across the fields into a back road, leading between Hillsborough and Kingston towards Brunswick. The vicinity of the British forces at Maidenhead secured Colonel Mawhood, and General Washington pressed forward to Princeton. The regiment remaining in that place took post in the college, and made a show of resistance; but some pieces of artillery being brought up to play upon that building, it was abandoned, and the greater part of them became prisoners. A few saved themselves by a precipitate flight to Brunswick.

In this engagement, rather more than one hundred British were killed in the field, and near three hundred were taken prisoners. The loss of the Americans, in killed, was somewhat less, but in their number was included General Mercer, a valuable officer, who had served with the Commander-in-chief during his early campaigns in Virginia, and was greatly esteemed by him. Colonels Haslet and Potter, Captain Neal of the artillery, Captain Fleming, and five other valuable officers, were also among the slain.

On the return of day-light, Lord Cornwallis discovered that the American army had decamped in the night; and immediately conceived the whole plan. Alarmed at the danger which threatened Brunswick, he marched with the utmost expedition for that place, and was close in the rear of the American army before it could leave Princeton.

The situation of General Washington was again perilous in the extreme. His small army was exhausted with fatigue. His troops had been without sleep, all of them one night, and some of them, two. They were without blankets, many of them were bare-footed and otherwise thinly clad, and were eighteen miles from his place of destination. He was closely pursued by a superior enemy who must necessarily come up with him before he could accomplish his designs on Brunswick. Under these circumstances he abandoned the remaining part of his original plan, and took the road leading up the country to Pluckemin, where his troops were permitted to refresh themselves. Lord Cornwallis continued his march to Brunswick, which he reached in the course of that night.

The sufferings of the American soldiers had been so great from the severity of the season, and the very active service in which they had been engaged; their complaints, especially on the part of the militia, were so loud; their numbers were reducing so fast by returning home, and by sickness; that General Washington found it impracticable to continue offensive operations. He retired to Morristown, in order to put his men under cover, and to give them some repose.

The bold, judicious, and unexpected attacks made at Trenton and Princeton, had a much more extensive influence than would be supposed from a mere estimate of the killed and taken. They saved Philadelphia for the winter; recovered the state of Jersey; and, which was of still more importance, revived the drooping spirits of the people, and gave a perceptible impulse to the recruiting service throughout the United States.

The problem, that a nation can be defended against a permanent force, by temporary armies, by occasional calls of the husbandman from his plough to the field, was completely disproved;

and, in demonstrating its fallacy, the independence of America had nearly perished in its cradle. The utmost efforts were now directed to the creation of an army for the ensuing campaign, as the only solid basis on which the hopes of the patriot could rest. During the retreat through the Jerseys, and while the expectation prevailed that no effectual resistance could be made to the British armies, some spirited men indeed were animated to greater and more determined exertions; but this state of things produced a very different effect on the great mass, which can alone furnish the solid force of armies. In the middle states especially, the panic of distrust was perceived. Doubts concerning the issue of the contest became extensive; and the recruiting service proceeded so heavily and slowly as to excite the most anxious solicitude for the future.

The affairs of Trenton and Princeton were magnified into great victories; and were believed by the body of the people to evidence the superiority of their army and of their general. The opinion that they were engaged in hopeless contest, yielded to a confidence that proper exertions would ensure ultimate success.

This change of opinion was accompanied with an essential change of conduct; and, although the regiments required by congress were not completed, they were made much stronger than was believed to be possible before this happy revolution in the aspect of public affairs.

Firmness
of Congress.

The firmness of congress throughout the gloomy and trying period which intervened between the loss of fort Washington and the battle of Princeton, gives the members of that time a just claim to the admiration of the world, and to the gratitude of their fellow citizens. Undismayed by impending dangers, they did not, for an instant, admit the idea of surrendering the independence they had declared, and purchasing peace by returning to their colonial situation. As the British army advanced through Jersey, and the consequent insecurity of Philadelphia rendered an adjournment from that place a necessary measure of precaution, their exertions seemed to increase with their difficulties. They sought to remove the despondence which was seizing and paralyzing the public mind, by an address to the states, in which every argument was suggested which could rouse them to vigorous action. They made the most strenuous efforts to animate the militia, and impel them to the field, by the agency of those whose popular eloquence best fitted them for such a service.

1776
December 20.

When reassembled at Baltimore, the place to which they had adjourned, their resolutions exhibited no evidence of confusion or dismay; and the most judicious efforts were made to repair the mischief produced by past errors.

Declaring that, in the present state of things, the very existence of civil liberty depended on the right execution of military powers, to a vigorous direction of which, distant, numerous, and deliberative bodies were unequal, they authorized General Washington to raise sixteen additional regiments, and conferred upon him, for six months, almost unlimited powers for the conduct of the war.

Towards the close of 1776, while the tide of fortune was running strongest against them, some few members, distrusting their ability to make a successful resistance, proposed to authorize their commissioners at the court of Versailles to transfer to France the same monopoly of their trade which Great Britain had possessed. * This proposition is stated to have been relinquished, because it was believed that concessions of this kind would impair many arguments which had been used in favour of independence, and disunite the people. It was next proposed to offer a monopoly of certain enumerated articles; but the unequal operation of this measure gave to the proposition a speedy negative. Some proposed offering to France an offensive and defensive league; but this also was rejected. The more enlightened members argued that, though the friendship of small states might be purchased, that of France could not. They alleged that, if she would risk a war with Great Britain by openly espousing their cause, she

* Ramsay.

would not be induced to that measure by the prospect of direct advantages, so much as by a desire to lessen the overgrown power of a dangerous rival. * It was therefore urged that the most certain means of influencing France to interfere, was an assurance that the United States were determined to persevere in refusing to resume their former allegiance. Under the influence of this better opinion, resolutions were again entered into, directing their commissioners in Europe to give explicit assurances of their determination at all events to maintain their independence. Copies of these resolutions were sent to the principal courts of Europe; and agents were appointed to solicit their friendship to the new formed states. † These despatches fell into the hands of the British, and were published by them; a circumstance which promoted the views of congress, who were persuaded that an apprehension of their coming to an accommodation with Great Britain constituted a material objection to the interference of foreign courts, in what was represented as merely a domestic quarrel. A resolution adopted in the deepest distress, to listen to no terms of reunion with their parent state, would, it was believed, convince those who wished for the dismemberment of the British empire, that sound policy required their interference so far as to prevent the conquest of the United States.

---

* Ramsay.
† Secret Journals of Congress, vol. ii. p. 38, and post.

CHAPTER VII.

American army inoculated....General Heath moves to
  Kingsbridge....Returns to Peekskill....Destruction of
  stores at Peekskill....At Danbury....Expedition to
  Sagg Harbour....Camp formed at Middlebrook....Sir
  William Howe moves out to Somerset Court House
  ....Returns to Amboy....Attempts to cut off the retreat
  of the American army to Middlebrook....Lord Cornwallis skirmishes with Lord Stirling....General Prescot
  surprised and taken....The British army embarks.

THE effect of the proclamation published by
Lord and General Howe on taking possession of
New Jersey, was, in a great degree, counteracted
by the conduct of the invading army. Fortunately for the United States, the hope that security was attainable by submission, was soon
dissipated. Whatever may have been the exertions of their General to restrain his soldiers, they
still considered and treated the inhabitants
rather as conquered rebels than returning friends.
Indulging in every species of licentiousness, the
plunder and destruction of property were among
the least offensive of the injuries they inflicted.
The persons, not only of the men, but of that
sex through which indignities least to be for-
given, and longest to be remembered, are received, were exposed to the most irritating out-
rage. Nor were these excesses confined to those
who had been active in the American cause. The

1777

lukewarm, and even the loyalists, were the victims of this indiscriminating spirit of rapine and
violence.

The effect of such proceedings on a people
whose country had never before been the seat of
war, and whose non-resistance had been occasioned solely by the expectation of that security
which had been promised as the reward of submission to the royal authority, could not fail to
equal the most sanguine hopes of the friends of
the revolution. A sense of personal wrongs produced a temper which national considerations
had proved too weak to excite; and, when the
battles of Trenton and Princeton relieved the
inhabitants from fears inspired by the presence
of their invaders, the great body of the people
flew to arms; and numbers who could not be
brought into the field to check the advancing
enemy, and prevent the ravages which uniformly
afflict a country that becomes the seat of war,
were prompt in avenging those ravages. Small
bodies of militia scoured the country, seized on
stragglers, behaved unexceptionably well in several slight skirmishes, and were collecting in
such numbers as to threaten the weaker British
posts with the fate which had befallen Trenton
and Princeton.

To guard against that spirit of enterprise
which his adversary had displayed to such advantage, General Howe determined to strengthen
his posts by contracting them. The position

taken for the purpose of covering the country were abandoned; and the British force in New Jersey was collected at New Brunswick, on the Raritan, and at Amboy, a small town at the mouth of that river.

Feeble as was the American army, this move-ment was not effected without some loss. On the evacuation of Elizabethtown, General Max-well attacked the British rear, and captured about seventy men with a part of their baggage.

The American troops had been so diminished by the extreme severity of the service, that it was with much difficulty the appearance of an army could be maintained. Fresh militia and volunteers arrived in camp, whose numbers were exaggerated by report. These additions to his small remaining regular force enabled the Gen-eral to take different positions near the lines of the enemy, to harass him perpetually, restrain his foraging parties, and produce considerable distress in his camp.

While, with little more than an imaginary army, General Washington thus harassed and confined his adversary, he came to the hazardous resolution of freeing himself and his troops from the fear of a calamity which he found it im-possible to elude, and which had proved more fatal in his camp than the sword of the enemy.

January 12.

Inoculation having been rarely practised in the western world, the American youth remained liable to the small pox. Notwithstanding the efforts to guard against this disease, it had found its way into both the northern and middle army, and had impaired the strength of both to an alarming degree. To avoid the return of the same evil, the General determined to inoculate all the soldiers in the American service. With the utmost secrecy, preparations were made to give the infection in camp; and the hospital physicians in Philadelphia were ordered to carry all the southern troops, as they should arrive, through the disease. Similar orders were also given to the physicians at other places; and thus an army exempt from the fear of a calamity which had, at all times, endangered the most important operations, was prepared for the ensuing campaign. This example was followed through the country; and this alarming disease was no longer the terror of America.

As the main body of the British army was cantoned in Jersey, and a strong detachment occupied Rhode Island, General Washington believed that New York could not be perfectly secure. His intelligence strengthened this opinion; and, as an army, respectable in point of numbers, had been assembled about Peekskill, he ordered General Heath to approach New York for the purpose of foraging, and, should appearances favour the attempt, of attacking the forts which guarded the entrance into the island. The hope was entertained that General Howe, alarmed for New York, might either withdraw his troops from Jersey, or so weaken his posts in that state as to endanger them. Should this hope be disappointed, it was believed that something handsome might be done, either on York or Long Island.

In pursuance of this plan, General Heath marched down to West Chester, and summoned fort Independence to surrender; but, the garrison determining to hold the place, a council of war deemed it unadviseable to risk an assault. An embarkation of troops which took place, about that time, at Rhode Island, alarmed General Heath for his rear, and induced him to resume his ground in the Highlands.

General Heath moves down to Kingsbridge, but returns to Peekskill without effecting anything.

Though this attempt entirely failed, the Commander-in-chief still meditated important operations during the winter. All the intelligence from Europe demonstrated the necessity of these operations, and the fallacy of the hope, still extensively cherished, that the war would be abandoned by Great Britain. The administration was still supported by great majorities in parliament; and the nation seemed well disposed to employ all its means to reannex to the empire, what were still denominated, revolted colonies. It was not to be doubted that large reinforcements would arrive in the spring; and the safety of the nation would be in hazard should General Howe remain in full force till they should be received. The utmost efforts were made by the Commander-in-chief to collect a sufficient number of troops to enable him to give a decisive blow to some one of the positions of his enemy. The state sovereignties, where the real energies of government resided, were incessantly urged to fill their regiments, and to bring their quotas into the field; and congress, at his instance, passed resolutions authorizing him to draw the troops from Peekskill, and to call out the militia of the neighbouring states. "It being," these resolutions proceed to say, "the earnest desire of congress, to make the army under the immediate command of General Washington sufficiently strong, not only to curb and confine the enemy within their present quarters, and prevent their drawing support of any kind from the country, but, by the divine blessing, totally to subdue them before they can be reinforced."

These resolves were communicated to the general, in a letter, manifesting the confident expectation of congress that the desire expressed in them would soon be realized. But the energy displayed in their passage could not be maintained in their execution.

Many causes concurred to prevent the collection of a force competent to those vigorous operations which the enterprising genius of the Commander-in-chief had provisionally planned, and the sanguine temper of congress had anticipated. Some of the state assemblies did not even complete the appointment of officers till the spring; and then, bitter contests concerning

rank remained to be adjusted when the troops
should join the army. After these arrangements
were made, the difficulty of enlisting men was
unexpectedly great. The immense hardships to
which the naked soldiers had been exposed, during a winter campaign, in the face of a superior
enemy; the mortality resulting from those hardships, and probably from an injudicious arrangement of the hospital department which
was found to be the tomb of the sick; had excited a general disgust to the service; and a consequent unwillingness to engage in it.

From these causes the army continued so
feeble that the general, instead of being able to
execute the great designs he had meditated, entertained serious fears that Sir William Howe
would take the field during the winter, force his
positions, cross the Delaware on the ice, and proceed to Philadelphia. In the apprehension of
this attempt, and to avoid that confusion which
would result from the removal of stores in the
crisis of military operations, he had taken the
precaution, as soon as the armies were in winter
quarters, to convey those which were most valuable, to a distance from the route which it was
supposed the British army would pursue.

The real condition of the army is exhibited in
a letter from the Commander-in-chief to congress, in answer to that which enclosed the resolutions already mentioned, and which expressed
the brilliant schemes of victory formed by the

government. "Could I," said the general, "accomplish the important objects so eagerly wished
by congress; confining the enemy within their
present quarters, preventing their getting supplies from the country, and totally subduing
them before they are reinforced, I should be
happy indeed. But what prospect or hope can
there be of my effecting so desirable a work at
this time? The enclosed return,* to which I
solicit the most serious attention of congress,
comprehends the whole force I have in Jersey.
It is but a handful, and bears no proportion on
the scale of numbers to that of the enemy.
Added to this, the major part is made up of
militia. The most sanguine in speculation can
not deem it more than adequate to the least valuable purposes of war."

Skirmishes.

Though unable to act with the vigour he
wished, the American general kept up a war of
skirmishes through the winter. In the course of
it, the British loss was believed to be considerable; and hopes were entertained that, from the
scarcity of forage, neither their cavalry nor draft
horses would be in a condition to take the field
when the campaign should open. Their foraging parties were often attacked to advantage.
Frequent small successes, the details of which
filled the papers throughout the United States,
not only increased the confidence of the Ameri-

---

* See note No. VIII. at the end of the volume.

can soldiers, but served greatly to animate the people.

The hope of collecting a sufficient force during the winter to make any valuable impression on the British army being disappointed, the views of the General were directed to the next campaign.

As the new army was to be raised by the authority of the state governments, he urged on them the necessity of bringing a respectable force into the field early in the spring, with all the earnestness which was suggested by his situation, and zeal for the service.

In Connecticut and Massachusetts, the country was laid off into districts, each of which was required, by a given day, to furnish a soldier enlisted for three years, or during the war; in default of which, one person, from those capable of bearing arms, was to be drafted to serve until the first of the ensuing January. The Commander-in-chief, though still deprecating the introduction of men into the army whose terms of service would be of short duration, felt the necessity of submitting to this expedient, as the most eligible which could now be adopted.

In Virginia, where the same difficulty attended enlistments, it was proposed by the executive to fill the regiments with volunteers, who should engage to serve for six months. This plan was submitted to General Washington by Governor Henry, and his opinion asked upon it. "I am under the necessity of observing," said the General in reply, "that the volunteer plan which you mention will never answer any valuable purpose, and that I can not but disapprove the measure. To the short engagements of our troops may be fairly and justly ascribed almost every misfortune that we have experienced."

In a subsequent letter to the same gentleman, enforcing earnestly the necessity of bringing a sufficient army into the field, though coercive measures should be adopted, some alternatives were suggested, which, in a later period of the war, constituted the basis of various experiments to furnish the quota of troops required from that state.

As the season for active operations approached, fresh difficulties, growing out of the organization of the American system, unfolded themselves. As every state was exposed to invasion, and the command of the ocean enabled the British general to transfer the war, at pleasure, to any part of the Union, the attention of each was directed exclusively to its particular situation. Each state in the neighbourhood of the great theatre of action, contemplating its own danger, claimed the protection which is due from the whole to its parts. Although the object of the confederation was the same with that pursued by each of its members, the spirit incident to every league could not be controlled in an

empire where, notwithstanding the existence of
a head, the essentials of government resided in
the members. It was displayed in repeated efforts to give to the energies of the army such
various directions, as would leave it unable to
effect any great object, or to obstruct any one
plan the enemy might form. The patriotism of
the day, however, and the unexampled confidence placed by all the state governments in the
Commander-in-chief, prevented the mischiefs
this spirit is so well calculated to generate. His
representations made their proper impression;
and the intention of retaining continental troops
for local defence was abandoned, though with
some reluctance. The burden, however, of calling militia from their domestic avocations, at
every threat of invasion, to watch every military
post in each state, became so intolerable, that the
people cast about for other expedients to relieve
themselves from its weight. The plan of raising regular corps, to be exclusively under state
authority, and thus be a perpetual substitute for
the yeomanry of the country, presented itself
as the most effectual and convenient mode of
protecting the coasts from insult.

During the winter, General Howe kept his
troops in their quarters, attending to their comfort. As the season for more active operations
approached, his first attention was directed to
the destruction of the scanty supplies prepared
by the Americans for the ensuing campaign. A

small place on the Hudson called Peekskill, about fifty miles above New York, was generally the residence of the officer commanding in the Highlands, and was used for the reception of stores, to be distributed into the neighbouring posts as occasion might require. Its strength, like that of all others depending for defence on militia, was subject to great fluctuation. As soon as the ice was out of the river, General Howe took advantage of its occasional weakness, to carry on an expedition against it, for the purpose of destroying the stores there deposited, or of bringing them away.

March 23.

Colonel Bird was detached up the river on this service, with about five hundred men, under convoy of a frigate and some armed vessels. General M'Dougal, whose numbers did not at that time exceed two hundred and fifty men, received timely notice of his approach, and exerted himself for the removal of the stores into the strong country in his rear. Before this could be effected, Colonel Bird appeared; and M'Dougal,

Destruction
of stores at
Peekskill.

after setting fire to the remaining stores and barracks, retired into the strong grounds in the rear of Peekskill. The British detachment completed the conflagration, and returned to New York. During their short stay, a piquet guard was attacked by Colonel Willet, and driven in with the loss of a few men; a circumstance, believed by General M'Dougal, to have hastened the re-embarkation of the detachment.

Military stores to a considerable amount had likewise been deposited at Danbury, on the western frontier of Connecticut. Although this place is not more than twenty miles from the Sound, yet the roughness of the intervening country, the frequent passage of troops from the eastward through the town, and the well known zeal of the neighbouring militia, were believed sufficient to secure the magazines collected at it. Against Danbury an expedition was projected; and two thousand men under the command of Governor Tryon, major general of the provincials in the British service, assisted by Brigadiers Agnew and Sir William Erskine, were employed in it.

On the 25th of April the fleet appeared off the coast of Connecticut; and in the evening the troops were landed without opposition between Fairfield and Norwalk. General Silliman, then casually in that part of the country, immediately despatched expresses to assemble the militia. In the mean time Tryon proceeded to Danbury, which he reached about two the next day. On his approach, Colonel Huntingdon, who had occupied the town with about one hundred and fifty men, retired to a neighbouring height, and Danbury, with the magazines it contained, was consumed by fire. General Arnold, who was also in the state superintending the recruiting service, joined General Silliman at Reading, where that officer had collected about five hundred militia. General Wooster, who had resigned his commission in the continental service, and been appointed major general of the militia, fell in with them at the same place, and they proceeded in the night through a heavy rain to Bethel, about eight miles from Danbury. Having heard next morning that Tryon, after destroying the town and magazines, was returning, they divided their troops; and General Wooster, with about three hundred men, fell in his rear, while Arnold, with about five hundred, crossing the country, took post in his front at Ridgefield. Wooster came up with his rear about eleven in the morning, attacked it with great gallantry, and a sharp skirmish ensued, in which he was mortally wounded,* and his troops were repulsed. Tryon then proceeded to Ridgefield, where he found Arnold already intrenched on a strong piece of ground, and prepared to dispute his passage. A warm skirmish ensued, which continued nearly an hour. Arnold was at length driven from the field; after which he retreated to Paugatuck, about three miles east of Norwalk. At break of day next morning, after setting Ridgefield on fire, the British resumed their march. About

eleven in the forenoon, they were again met by Arnold, whose numbers increased during the day to rather more than one thousand men; among whom were some continental troops. A continued skirmishing was kept up until five in the afternoon, when the British formed on a hill

---

* Congress voted a monument to his memory.

near their ships. The Americans attacked them with intrepidity, but were repulsed and broken. Tryon, availing himself of this respite, re-embarked his troops, and returned to New York.

The loss of the British amounted to about one hundred and seventy men. That of the Americans, was represented by Tryon, as being much more considerable. By themselves, it was not admitted to exceed one hundred. In this number, however, were comprehended General Wooster, Lieutenant Colonel Gould, and another field officer, killed; and Colonel Lamb wounded. Several other officers and volunteers were killed.

Military and hospital stores to a considerable amount, which were greatly needed by the army, were destroyed in the magazines at Danbury; but the loss most severely felt was rather more than one thousand tents, which had been provided for the campaign about to open.

Not long afterwards this enterprise was successfully retaliated. A British detachment had been for some time employed in collecting forage and provisions on the eastern end of Long Island. Howe supposed this part of the country to be so completely secured by the armed vessels which incessantly traversed the Sound, that he confided the protection of the stores, deposited at a small port called Sagg Harbour, to a schooner with twelve guns, and a company of infantry.

General Parsons, who commanded a few recruits at New Haven, thinking it practicable to elude the cruisers in the bay, formed the design of surprising this party, and other adjacent posts, the execution of which was entrusted to Lieutenant Colonel Meigs, a gallant officer, who had accompanied Arnold in his memorable march to Quebec. He embarked with about two hundred and thirty men, on board thirteen whale boats, and proceeded along the coast to Guilford, where he was to cross the Sound. With about one hundred and seventy of his detachment, under convoy of two armed sloops, he proceeded across the Sound to the north division of the island near South Hold, in the neighbourhood of which a small foraging party, against which the expedition was in part directed, was supposed to lie; but they had marched two days before to New York. The boats were conveyed across the land, a distance of about fifteen miles, into a bay which deeply intersects the eastern end of Long Island, where the troops re-embarked. Crossing the bay, they landed at two in the morning, about four miles from Sagg Harbour, which place they completely surprised, and carried with charged bayonets. At the same time, a division of the detachment secured the armed schooner, and the vessels laden with forage, which were set on fire, and entirely consumed. Six of the enemy were killed, and

Expedition
of Colonel
Meigs to
Sagg
Harbour.

May.

May 24.

ninety taken prisoners. A very few escaped under cover of the night.

The object of his expedition being effected without the loss of a man, Colonel Meigs returned to Guilford with his prisoners. "Having," as was stated in the letter to General Parsons, "moved with such uncommon celerity, as to have transported his men, by land and water, ninety miles in twenty-five hours." Congress directed a sword to be presented to him, and passed a resolution expressing the high sense entertained of his merit, and of the prudence, activity, and valour, displayed by himself and his party.

The exertions made by the Commander-in-chief through the winter to raise a powerful army for the ensuing campaign, had not been successful. The hopes respecting its strength which the flattering reports made from every quarter had authorized him to form, were cruelly disappointed; and he found himself not only unable to carry into effect the offensive operations he had meditated, but unequal even to defensive war. That steady and persevering courage, however, which had supported himself and the American cause through the gloomy scenes of the preceding year, did not forsake him; and that sound judgment which applies to the best advantage those means which are attainable, however inadequate they may be, still remained.

His plan of operations was adapted to that which he believed his enemy had formed. He was persuaded either that General Burgoyne would endeavour to take Ticonderoga, and to penetrate to the Hudson, in which event General Howe would co-operate with him by moving up that river, and attempting to possess himself of the forts and high grounds commanding its passage; or that Burgoyne would join the grand army at New York by sea; after which the combined armies would proceed against Philadelphia.

To counteract the designs of the enemy, whatever they might be, to defend the three great points, Ticonderoga, the Highlands of New York, and Philadelphia, against two powerful armies so much superior to him, in arms, in numbers, and in discipline, it was necessary to make such an arrangement of his troops as would enable the parts reciprocally to aid each other, without neglecting objects of great, and almost equal magnitude which were alike threatened, and were far asunder. To effect these purposes, the troops of New England and New York were divided between Ticonderoga and Peekskill, while those from Jersey to North Carolina inclusive, were directed to assemble at the camp to be formed in Jersey. The more southern troops remained in that weak quarter of the union for its protection.

These arrangements being made, and the recruits collected, the camp at Morristown was broken up, the detachments called in, and the army assembled at Middlebrook, just behind a connected ridge of strong and commanding heights, north of the road leading to Philadelphia, and about ten miles from Brunswick.

Camp formed at Middlebrook.

This camp, the approaches to which were naturally difficult, was rendered still more defensible by intrenchments. The heights in front commanded a prospect of the course of the Raritan, the road to Philadelphia, the hills about Brunswick, and a considerable part of the country between that place and Amboy; so as to afford a full view of the most interesting movements of the enemy.

The force brought into the field by America required all the aid which could be derived from strong positions, and unremitting vigilance. On the 20th of May, the total of the army in Jersey, excluding cavalry and artillery, amounted to only eight thousand three hundred and seventy-eight men, of whom upwards of two thousand were sick. The effective rank and file were only five thousand seven hundred and thirty-eight.

Had this army been composed of the best disciplined troops, its inferiority, in point of numbers, must have limited its operations to defensive war; and have rendered it incompetent to the protection of any place, whose defence would require a battle in the open field. But more than half the troops* were unacquainted with the first rudiments of military duty, and had never looked an enemy in the face. As an additional cause of apprehension, a large proportion of the soldiers, especially from the middle states, were foreigners, many of them servants, in whose attachment to the American cause full confidence could not be placed.

General Washington, anticipating a movement by land towards Philadelphia, had taken the precaution to give orders for assembling on the western bank of the Delaware, an army of militia, strengthened by a few continental troops, the command of which was given to General Arnold, who was then in Philadelphia, employed in the settlement of his accounts.

The first and real object of the campaign, on the part of General Howe, was the acquisition of Philadelphia. He intended to march through Jersey; and, after securing the submission of that state, to cross the Delaware on a portable bridge constructed in the winter for the purpose, and proceed by land to that city. If, in the execution of this plan, the Americans could be brought to a general action on equal ground, the advantages of the royal army must insure a victory. But should Washington decline an engagement, and be again pressed over the Dela-

---

* The extreme severity of the service, aided perhaps by the state of the hospitals, had carried to the grave more than two-thirds of the soldiers who had served the preceding campaign, and been engaged for more than one year.

ware, the object would be as certainly obtained.

Had Sir William Howe taken the field before the continental troops were assembled, this plan might probably have been executed without any serious obstruction; but the tents and camp equipage expected from Europe did not arrive until General Washington had collected his forces, and taken possession of the strong post on the heights of Middlebrook. It would be dangerous to attack him on such advantageous ground; for, although his camp might be forced, victory would probably be attended with such loss, as to disable the victor from reaping its fruits.

If it was deemed too hazardous to attack the strong camp at Middlebrook, an attempt to cross the Delaware, in the face of an army collected on its western bank, while that under General Washington remained unbroken in his rear, was an experiment of equal danger. It comported with the cautious temper of Sir William Howe to devise some other plan of operation to which he might resort, should he be unable to seduce the American general from his advantageous position.

The two great bays of Delaware and Chesapeake suggested the alternative of proceeding by water, should he be unable to manœuvre General Washington out of his present encampment.

The plan of the campaign being settled, and some small reinforcements with the expected camp equipage being received from Europe, General Howe, leaving a garrison in New York, and a guard in Amboy, assembled his army at Brunswick, and gave strong indications of an intention

to penetrate through the country to the Delaware, and reach Philadelphia by land.

Believing this to be his real design, Washington placed a select corps of riflemen under the command of Colonel Morgan, an officer who had distinguished himself in the unfortunate attempt to storm Quebec, and in whom those peculiar qualities which fit a man for the command of a partisan corps, designed to act on the lines of a formidable enemy, were eminently united.

He was ordered to take post at Vanvighton's Bridge on the Raritan, just above its confluence with the Millstone River, to watch the left flank of the British army, and seize every occasion to harass it.

Early in the morning of the 14th, Sir William Howe, leaving two thousand men under the command of General Matthews at Brunswick, advanced in two columns towards the Delaware.

Sir William
Howe moves
out to
Somerset
Court House
in great
force.

The front of the first, under Lord Cornwallis, reached Somerset Court House, nine miles from Brunswick, by the appearance of day; and the second, commanded by General de Heister, reached Middlebush about the same time.

This movement was made with the view of inducing General Washington to quit his fortified camp, and approach the Delaware,* in which event, the British general expected to bring on an engagement on ground less disadvantageous than that now occupied by the American army. But that officer understood the importance of his position too well to abandon it. On the first intelligence that the enemy was in motion, he drew out his whole army, and formed it, to great advantage, on the heights in front of his camp. This position was constantly maintained. The troops remained in order of battle during the day; and, in the night, slept on the ground to be defended. In the mean time the Jersey militia, with an alacrity theretofore unexampled in that state, took the field in great numbers. They principally joined General Sullivan, who had retired from Princeton, behind the Sourland hills towards Flemingtown, where an army of some respectability was forming, which could readily co-operate with that under the immediate inspection of the Commander-in-chief.

The settled purpose of General Washington was to defend his camp, but not to hazard a general action on other ground. He had therefore determined not to advance from the heights he occupied, into the open country, either towards the enemy, or the Delaware.

The object of General Howe seems to have been, by acting on his anxiety for Philadelphia, to seduce him from the strong ground about

* General Howe's letter.

Middlebrook, and tempt him to approach the
Delaware, in the hope of defending its passage.
Should he succeed in this, he had little doubt of
being able to bring on an engagement, in which
he counted with certainty on victory. The considerations which restrained General Howe from
attempting to march through Jersey, leaving the
American army in full force in his rear, had determined Washington to allow him to proceed
to the Delaware, if such should be his intention.
In that event, he had determined to throw those
impediments only in the way of the hostile army
which might harass and retard its march; and,
maintaining the high and secure grounds north
of the road to be taken by the enemy, to watch
for an opportunity of striking some important
blow with manifest advantage.

He was not long in penetrating the designs
of his adversary. "The views of the enemy,"
he writes to General Arnold in a letter of the
17th, "must be to destroy this army, and get
possession of Philadelphia. I am, however,
clearly of opinion, that they will not move that
way until they have endeavoured to give a severe
blow to this army. The risk would be too great
to attempt to cross a river, when they must expect to meet a formidable opposition in front,
and would have such a force as ours in their rear.
They might possibly be successful, but the probability would be infinitely against them. Should
they be imprudent enough to make the attempt,

I shall keep close upon their heels, and will do every thing in my power to make the project fatal to them.

"But, besides the argument in favour of their intending, in the first place, a stroke at this army, drawn from the policy of the measure, every appearance contributes to confirm the opinion. Had their design been for the Delaware in the first instance, they would probably have made a secret, rapid march for it, and not have halted so as to awaken our attention, and give us time to prepare for obstructing them. Instead of that they have only advanced to a position necessary to facilitate an attack on our right, the part in which we are most exposed. In addition to this circumstance, they have come out as light as possible, leaving all their baggage, provisions, boats, and bridges, at Brunswick. This plainly contradicts the idea of their intending to push for the Delaware."

Finding the American army could not be drawn from its strong position, General Howe determined to waste no more time in threatening Philadelphia by land, but to withdraw from Jersey, and to embark his army as expeditiously as possible for the Chesapeake or the Delaware. On the night of the 19th he returned to Brunswick, and on the 22d to Amboy, from which place, the heavy baggage and a few of his troops passed into Staten Island, on the bridge which had been designed for the Delaware.

Returns to Amboy.

General Washington had expected this movement from Brunswick, and had made arrangements to derive some advantage from it. General Greene was detached with three brigades to annoy the British rear; and Sullivan and Maxwell were ordered to co-operate with him. In the mean time the army paraded on the heights of Middlebrook, ready to act as circumstances might require.

About sunrise, Colonel Morgan drove in a piquet guard, soon after which that division commenced its march to Amboy. Some sharp skirmishing took place between this party and Morgan's regiment, but the hope of gaining any important advantage was entirely disappointed; and the retreat to Amboy was effected with inconsiderable loss.

In order to cover his light parties, which still hung on the British flank and rear, General Washington advanced six or seven miles, to Quibbletown on the road to Amboy; and Lord Stirling's division was pushed still farther, to the neighbourhood of the Metucking Meeting House, for the purpose of co-operating with the light parties, should the retreat to Staten Island afford an opportunity of striking at the rear.

Believing it now practicable to bring on an engagement, and probably hoping to turn the left of the American army, and gain the heights in its rear, General Howe, in the night of the 25th, recalled the troops from Staten Island; and, early next morning, made a rapid movement, in two columns, towards Westfield. The right, under the command of Lord Cornwallis, took the route by Woodbridge to the Scotch Plains; and the left, led by Sir William Howe in person, marched by Metucking Meeting House, to fall into the rear of the right column. It was intended that the left should take a separate road, soon after this junction, and attack the left flank of the American army at Quibbletown; while Lord Cornwallis should gain the heights on the left of the camp at Middlebrook. Four battalions with six pieces of cannon were detached to Bonhamtown.*

About Woodbridge, the right column fell in with one of the American parties of observation which gave notice of this movement. General Washington discerned his danger, put the whole army instantly in motion, and regained the camp at Middlebrook. Lord Cornwallis fell in with Lord Stirling, and a sharp skirmish ensued, in which the Americans were driven from their ground with the loss of three field pieces, and a few men. They retreated to the hills about the Scotch Plains, and were pursued as far as Westfield. Perceiving the passes in the mountains on the left of the American camp to be guarded, and the object of this skilful manœuvre to be, consequently, unattainable, his lordship

Lord Cornwallis skirmishes near the Scotch Plains with Lord Stirling.

June 30.

* General Howe's letter.

returned through Rahway to Amboy; and the whole army crossed over to Staten Island.

General Washington was now again left to his conjectures respecting the plan of the campaign. Before Sir William Howe had, in any degree disclosed his views, intelligence was received of the appearance of Burgoyne on Lake Champlain, and that Ticonderoga was threatened. This intelligence strengthened the opinion that the design of Howe must be to seize the passes in the mountains on the Hudson, secure the command of that river, and effect a junction between the two armies. Yet he could not permit himself to yield so entirely to this impression, as to make a movement which might open the way by land to Philadelphia. His army therefore maintained its station at Middlebrook; but arrangements were made to repel any sudden attack on the posts which defended the Hudson.

Some changes made in the stations of the British ships and troops having relieved the American general from his apprehensions of a sudden march to Philadelphia, he advanced Sullivan's division to Pompton Plains, on the way to Peekskill; and proceeded with the main body of his army, to Morristown;—thus approaching the highlands of New York, without removing so far from Middlebrook as to be unable to regain that camp should General Howe indicate an intention to seize it.

Meanwhile, the British General prosecuted, diligently, his plan of embarkation, which was, necessarily, attended with circumstances indicating a much longer voyage than that up the North River. These circumstances were immediately communicated to the eastern states, and congress was earnestly pressed to strengthen the fortifications on the Delaware, and to increase the obstructions in that river.

In the midst of these appearances, certain intelligence was received that Burgoyne was in great force on the lakes, and was advancing against Ticonderoga. This intelligence confirmed the opinion that the main object of Howe must be to effect a junction with Burgoyne on the North River. Under this impression, General Washington ordered Sullivan to Peekskill, and advanced, himself, first to Pompton Plains, and afterwards to the Clove, where he determined to remain until the views of the enemy should be disclosed.

While the General thus anxiously watched the movements of his adversary, an agreeable and unexpected piece of intelligence was received from New England. The command of the British troops in Rhode Island had devolved on General Prescot. Thinking himself perfectly secure in an island, the water surrounding which was believed to be entirely guarded by his cruisers, and at the head of an army greatly superior to any force then collected in that department, he

July 16.

indulged himself in convenient quarters, rather distant from camp; and was remiss with respect to the guards about his person. Information of this negligence was communicated to the main, and a plan was formed to surprise him. This spirited enterprise was executed, with equal courage and address, by Lieutenant Colonel Barton of the Rhole Island militia.

General Prescot surprised and taken.

On the night of the 10th, he embarked on board four whale boats, at Warwick Neck, with a party consisting of about forty persons, including Captains Adams and Philips, and several other officers. After proceeding about ten miles by water, unobserved by the British guard-boats, although several ships of war lay in that quarter, he landed on the west of the island, about midway between Newport and Bristol ferry, and marching a mile to the quarters of Prescot, dexterously seized the sentinel at his door, and one of his aids. The general himself was taken out of bed, and conveyed to a place of safety.

The success of this intrepid enterprise diffused the more joy throughout America, because it was supposed to secure the liberation of General Lee, by enabling General Washington to offer an officer of equal rank in exchange for him.

Congress expressed a high sense of the gallant conduct of Colonel Barton, and his party; and presented him with a sword as a mark of approbation.

As the fleet fell down towards Sandy Hook, General Washington withdrew slowly from the Clove, and disposed his army in different divisions, so as to march to any point which might be attacked.

At length, the embarkation was completed, and the fleet put to sea.

The British army embarks.

CHAPTER VIII.

General Washington commences his march to the Delaware....Takes measures for checking Burgoyne.... British army lands at Elk River....General Washington advances to Brandywine....Retreat of Maxwell.... Defeat at Brandywine....Slight skirmish near the White Horse, and retreat to French Creek....General Wayne surprised....General Howe takes possession of Philadelphia....Removal of Congress to Lancaster.

1777
July.

General
Washington
commences
his march
to the
Delaware.

ON receiving intelligence that the British fleet had sailed from New York, the American army commenced its march to the Delaware. About the time of its departure, a letter from Sir William Howe, directed to General Burgoyne at Quebec, was delivered to General Putnam by the person who had received it, as was said, for the purpose of carrying it to Quebec, and was transmitted by Putnam to the Commander-in-chief. In this letter, General Howe said that "he was exhibiting the appearance of moving to the southward, while his real intent was against Boston, from whence he would co-operate with the army of Canada." This stratagem entirely failed. General Washington, at once, perceived that the letter was written with a design that it should fall into his hands, and mislead him with respect to the views of the writer.

While the utmost vigilance and judgment were required to conduct the operations of the army under the immediate command of General Washington, the transactions in the north were too vitally interesting not to engage a large share of his attention. He not only hastened the march of those generals who were designed to act in that department, and pressed the governors of the eastern states to reinforce the retreating army with all their militia, but made large detachments of choice troops from his own; —thus weakening himself in order to strengthen other generals whose strength would be more useful. The fame of being himself the leader of the victorious army did not, with false glare, dazzle his judgment, or conceal the superior public advantage to be derived from defeating the plans of Burgoyne.

On the 30th of July, all doubts respecting the destination of the British fleet were supposed to be removed by its appearance off the capes of Delaware; and orders were immediately given for assembling the detached parts of the army in the neighbourhood of Philadelphia. Scarcely were these orders given, when the aspect of affairs was changed, and they were countermanded. An express from Cape May brought the information that the fleet had sailed out of the bay of Delaware, and was proceeding eastward. From this time, no intelligence respecting it was received until about the 7th of August, when it appeared a few leagues south of the capes of Delaware, after which it disappeared, and was not again seen until late in that month. The fact was, that on entering the capes of Delaware, the difficulties attending an attempt to carry his fleet up that bay and river, determined General Howe to relinquish his original design, and to transport his army to the Chesapeake. Contrary winds prevented his gaining the mouth of that bay until the 16th of August.

The several divisions of the army were immediately ordered* to unite in the neighbourhood of Philadelphia, and the militia of Pennsylvania, Maryland, Delaware, and the northern counties of Virginia, were directed to take the field.

The British fleet, after entering the Chesapeake, sailed up it with favourable winds, and entered Elk River, up which the admiral proceeded as high as it was safely navigable; and on

---

* These orders were received by General Sullivan, who had been encamped about Hanover, in Jersey, on his return from an expedition to Staten Island. The British force on that island amounted to between two and three thousand men, of whom nearly one thuusand were provincials, who were distributed along the coast, opposite the Jersey shore. The Europeans occupied a fortified camp near the watering place; and General Sullivan thought it practicable to surprise the provincials, and bring them off before they could be supported by the Europeans. Only six boats had been procured for the conveyance of his troops; yet they crossed over into the island before day undiscovered, and completely surprised two of the provincial parties, commanded by Colonels Lawrence and Barton, both of whom, with several officers and men were taken. The alarm being given, Sullivan attempted to withdraw from the island. The number of boats not being sufficient for the embarkation of all his troops

the 25th of August the troops were landed at CHAP. VIII
the ferry.

1777

The British army, at its disembarkation, has
been generally computed at eighteen thousand
men. They were in good health and spirits, ad-
mirably supplied with all the implements of
war, and led by an experienced general, of unquestionable military talents.

The day before Sir William Howe landed, the

General
Washington
advances to
Brandywine.

American army marched through Philadelphia,
and proceeded to the Brandywine. The divisions of Greene and Stephen were advanced
nearer to the Head of Elk, and encamped behind
White Clay creek.

Congress had directed General Smallwood
and Colonel Girt to take command of the militia
of Maryland, who had been ordered by General
Washington to assemble near the head of the
bay. The militia of the lower counties of Delaware, commanded by General Rodney, were di-

---

at the same time, some confusion obtained among them.
General Campbell advanced in force on the rear guard while
waiting for the return of the boats, which was captured after
making a gallant resistance.

This enterprise was well planned, and in its commencement, happily executed; but ought not to have been undertaken without a number of boats sufficient to secure the
retreat.

The loss of the British in prisoners amounted to eleven
officers, and one hundred and thirty privates. That of the
Americans, is stated by Sullivan, at one major, one captain,
one lieutenant, and ten privates killed, and fifteen wounded,
and nine officers, and one hundred and twenty-seven privates
prisoners. General Campbell, in his account of the action
says, that he made two hundred and fifty-nine prisoners,
among whom were one lieutenant colonel, three majors, two
captains, and fifteen inferior officers.

rected also to assemble in the British rear, and
to co-operate with those of Maryland. Colonel
Richardson's continental regiment, which had
been stationed on the Eastern shore, was ordered
to join this corps.

The militia of Pennsylvania, commanded by
Major General Armstrong, were united with the
main body of the army. Great exertions were
used to bring them promptly into the field, and
they came forward generally with some degree
of alacrity. Although the numbers required by
congress did not assemble, more appeared than
could be armed.

The real strength of the American army can
not be accurately stated. It was estimated by
Sir William Howe at fifteen thousand, including militia; and this estimate did not far exceed
their real total, as exhibited by the returns. But
it is a fact, attributable in some degree to the
badness of their clothing, and scarcity of tents,
and in some degree to the neglect of the commissary department, to provide those articles of
food which contribute to the preservation of
health, that the effective force was always far
below the total number. The effectives, including militia, did not exceed eleven thousand.

Morgan's regiment of riflemen having been
detached to the northern army, a corps of light
infantry was formed for the occasion, the command of which was given to General Maxwell.
This corps was advanced to Iron Hill, about

three miles in front of White Clay creek. The

cavalry, consisting of four regiments, amounting
to about nine hundred men, including persons of
every description, were employed principally on
the lines.

One division of the British army, commanded
by Sir William Howe in person, had taken post
at Elkton, with its van advanced to Gray's Hill.
General Knyphausen, with a second division,
had crossed the ferry and encamped at Cecil
Court House. He was directed to march up on
the eastern side of the river, and to join Sir
William Howe seven or eight miles south of
Christiana. The intention to make this movement being disclosed by the preparatory arrangements, General Washington advised Maxwell to post a choice body of men in the night
on an advantageous part of the road, in order
to annoy him on his march. In the morning
of the third of September, the two divisions
under Lord Cornwallis and General Knyphausen, moved forward and formed a junction
at Pencader, or Atkins' tavern, where they encamped. In their way, the column led by Lord
Cornwallis fell in with and attacked Maxwell,
who retreated over White Clay creek, with the
loss of about forty killed and wounded.

Lord Cornwallis attacks Maxwell's corps, and compels them to retreat.

The whole American army, except the light
infantry, took a position behind Red Clay creek,
on the road leading from the camp of Sir
William Howe to Philadelphia. On this ground,

September 5.

the General thought it probable that the fate of Philadelphia, and of the campaign, might be decided; and he resorted to all the means in his power to encourage his troops, and stimulate them to the greatest exertions.

On the 8th of September, the British army was again put in motion. The main body advanced by Newark, upon the right of the Americans, and encamped within four miles of that place, extending its left still farther up the country. Meanwhile, a strong column made a show of attacking in front, and, after manœuvring some time, halted at Milton, within two miles of the centre.

General Washington was soon convinced that the column in front was designed only to amuse, while the left should effect the principal and real object. Believing that object to be to turn his right, and cut off his communication with Philadelphia, he changed his ground, and, crossing the Brandywine early in the night, took post behind that river, at Chadd's Ford. General Maxwell was advanced in front, and placed, advantageously, on the hills south of the river, on the road leading over the ford. The militia, under General Armstrong, were posted at a ford two miles below Chadd's; and the right extended some miles above, with a view to other passes deemed less practicable. In this position, General Washington attended the movements of the adverse army.

In the evening, Howe marched forward in two columns, which united, early the next morning, at Kennet's Square; after which he advanced parties on the roads leading to Lancaster, to Chadd's Ford, and to Wilmington.

The armies were now within seven miles of each other, with only the Brandywine between them, which opposed no obstacle to a general engagement. This was sought by Howe, and not avoided by Washington. It was impossible to protect Philadelphia without a victory, and this object was deemed throughout America, and especially by congress, of such magnitude as to require that an action should be hazarded for its attainment.

In the morning of the 11th, soon after day, information was received that the whole British army was in motion, advancing on the direct road leading over Chadd's Ford. The Americans were immediately under arms, and placed in order of battle, for the purpose of contesting the passage of the river. Skirmishing soon commenced between the advanced parties; and, by ten, Maxwell's corps, with little loss on either side, was driven over the Brandywine below the ford. Knyphausen, who commanded this column, paraded on the heights, reconnoitred the American army, and appeared to be making dispositions to force the passage of the river. A skirt of woods, with the river, divided him from Maxwell's corps, small parties of whom occasionally crossed over, and kept up a scattering fire, by which not much execution was done. At length one of these parties, led by Captains Waggoner and Porterfield, engaged the British flank guard very closely, killed a captain with ten or fifteen privates, drove them out of the wood, and were on the point of taking a field piece. The sharpness of the skirmish soon drew a large body of the British to that quarter, and the Americans were again driven over the Brandywine.*

About eleven in the morning, information reached General Washington that a large column with many field pieces, had taken a road leading from Kennet's Square, directly up the country, and had entered the great valley road, down which they were marching to the upper fords of the Brandywine. This information was given by Colonel Ross of Pennsylvania, who was in their rear, and estimated their numbers at five thousand men.

On receiving this information, Washington is said to have determined to detach Sullivan and Lord Stirling to engage the left division of the British army, and with the residue of his troops, to cross Chadd's Ford in person, and attack Knyphausen. Before this plan could be executed, counter intelligence was received inducing an opinion that the movement of the British on their left was a feint, and that the column

---

* The author was an eye-witness of this skirmish.

under Lord Cornwallis, after making demonstrations of crossing the Brandywine above its forks, had marched down the southern side of that river to reunite itself with Knyphausen.

Not long after the first communication was made by Colonel Ross, information was received from Colonel Bland of the cavalry, which produced some doubt respecting the strength of this column. He saw only two brigades; but the dust appeared to rise in their rear for a considerable distance. A major of the militia came in, who alleged that he left the forks of the Brandywine so late in the day that it was supposed Lord Cornwallis must have passed them by that time, had he continued his march in that direction, and who asserted that no enemy had appeared in that quarter. Some light horsemen who had been sent to reconnoitre the road, returned with the same information.

The uncertainty produced by this contradictory intelligence was at length removed; and about two in the afternoon, it was ascertained that the column led by Lord Cornwallis, after making a circuit of about seventeen miles, had crossed the river above its forks, and was advancing in great force.

A change of disposition was immediately made. The divisions commanded by Sullivan, Stirling, and Stephen, took new ground, advanced farther up the Brandywine, and fronted the British column marching down that river.

The division commanded by Wayne remained at
Chadd's Ford, to keep Knyphausen in check; in
which service Maxwell was to co-operate.
Greene's division, accompanied by General
Washington in person, formed a reserve, and
took a central position between the right and left
wings.

The divisions detached against Lord Cornwallis formed hastily on an advantageous piece
of ground, above Birmingham Meeting House,
with their left near the Brandywine, and having both flanks covered by a thick wood. The
artillery was judiciously posted, and the disposition of the whole was well made. Unfortunately, Sullivan's division, in taking its ground,
made too large a circuit, and was scarcely
formed when the attack commenced.

The
American
army
defeated at
Brandywine,
and retreat
to Chester.

On perceiving the Americans, the British army
was formed in order of battle; and, about half
past four, the action began. It was kept up
warmly for some time. The American right first
gave way, and by its flight exposed the flank of
the remaining divisions to a galling fire. The
line continued to break from the right, and, in
a short time, was completely routed. The right
wing made some attempts to rally, but, being
briskly charged, again broke, and the flight became general.

On the commencement of the action on the
right, General Washington pressed forward with
Greene, to the support of that wing; but, before

his arrival, its rout was complete, and he could
only check the pursuit. For this purpose, the
10th Virginia regiment commanded by Colonel
Stevens, and a regiment of Pennsylvania commanded by Colonel Stewart, neither of which
had been in action, were posted advantageously
on the road taken by the defeated army. The
impression made by the fire of these regiments,
and the approach of night, induced Sir William
Howe, after dispersing them, to give over the
pursuit.

When the American right was found to be
fully engaged with Lord Cornwallis, Knyphausen made real dispositions for crossing the
river. Chadd's Ford was defended by an intrenchment and battery, with three field pieces,
and a howitzer. After some resistance, the work
was forced; and, the defeat of the right being
known, the left wing also withdrew from its
ground. The whole army retreated that night
to Chester, and the next day to Philadelphia.

The loss sustained by the Americans in this
action has been estimated at three hundred
killed, and six hundred wounded. Between
three and four hundred, principally the
wounded, were made prisoners.

As must ever be the case in new raised armies,
unused to danger, and from which undeserving
officers have not been expelled, their conduct
was not uniform. Some regiments, especially
those which had served the preceding campaign,

maintained their ground with the firmness and intrepidity of veterans, while others gave way as soon as they were pressed. The authors of a very correct history of the war,* speaking of this action, say, "a part of their troops, among whom were particularly numbered some Virginia† regiments, and the whole corps of artillery, behaved exceedingly well in some of the actions of this day, exhibiting a degree of order, firmness, and resolution, and preserving such a countenance in extremely sharp service, as would not have discredited veterans. Some other bodies of their troops behaved very badly."‡

The official letter of Sir William Howe stated his loss at rather less than one hundred killed, and four hundred wounded. As the Americans sustained very little injury in the retreat, this inequality of loss can be ascribed only to the inferiority of their arms. Many of their muskets were scarcely fit for service; and, being of

---

* Annual Register.

† The third Virginia regiment commanded by Colonel Marshall, which had performed extremely severe duty in the campaign of 1776, was placed in a wood on the right, and in front of Woodford's brigade, and Stephen's division. Though attacked by much superior numbers, it maintained its position without losing an inch of ground, until both its flanks were turned, its ammunition nearly expended, and more than half the officers, and one third of the soldiers were killed and wounded. Colonel Marshall, whose horse had received two balls, then retired in good order to resume his position on the right of his division; but it had already retreated.

‡ Deboore's brigade broke first; and, on an inquiry into his conduct being directed, he resigned. A misunderstanding existed between him and Sullivan, on whose right he was stationed.

unequal calibre, their cartridges could not be so well fitted, and, consequently, their fire could not do as much execution as that of the enemy. This radical defect was felt in all the operations of the army.

From the ardour with which the Commander-in-chief had inspired his troops before this action, it is probable that the conflict would have been more severe, had the intelligence respecting the movement on the left of the British army been less contradictory. Raw troops, changing their ground in the moment of action, and attacked in the agitation of moving, are easily thrown into confusion. This was the critical situation of a part of Sullivan's division, and was the cause of the right's breaking before Greene could be brought up to support it; after which, it was impossible to retrieve the fortune of the day.

But had the best disposition of the troops been made at the time, which subsequent intelligence would suggest, the action could not have terminated in favour of the Americans. Their inferiority in numbers, in discipline, and in arms, was too great to leave them a probable prospect of victory. A battle, however, was not to be avoided. The opinion of the public, and of congress, demanded it. The loss of Philadelphia, without an attempt to preserve it, would have excited discontents which, in the United States, might be productive of serious mischief; and action, though attended with defeat, provided the loss be not too great, must improve an army in which, not only the military talents, but even the courage, of officers, some of them of high rank, remained to be ascertained.

Among the wounded was the Marquis de la Fayette, and Brigadier General Woodford.

The battle of Brandywine was not considered as decisive by congress, the General, or the army. The opinion was carefully cherished that the British had gained only the ground; and that their loss was still more considerable than had been sustained by the Americans. Congress appeared determined to risk another battle for the metropolis of America. Far from discovering any intention to change their place of session, they passed vigorous resolutions for reinforcing the army, and directed General Washington to give the necessary orders for completing the defences of the Delaware.

From Chester, the army marched through Darby, over the Schuylkill bridge, to its former ground, near the falls of that river. General Greene's division, which, having been less in action, was more entire than any other, covered the rear; and the corps of Maxwell remained at Chester until the next day, as a rallying point for the small parties, and straggling soldiers, who might yet be in the neighbourhood.

Having allowed his army one day for repose and refreshment, General Washington recrossed the Schuylkill, and proceeded on the Lancaster road, with the intention of risking another engagement.

Sir William Howe passed the night of the 11th on the field of battle. On the succeeding day, he detached Major General Grant with two brigades to Concord meeting-house; and on the 13th, Lord Cornwallis joined General Grant, and marched towards Chester. Another detachment took possession of Wilmington; to which place the sick and wounded were conveyed.

To prevent a sudden movement to Philadelphia by the lower road, the bridge over the Schuylkill was loosened from its moorings, and General Armstrong was directed, with the Pennsylvania militia to guard the passes over that river.

On the 15th, the American army, intending to gain the left of the British, reached the Warren tavern, on the Lancaster road, twenty-three miles from Philadelphia. Intelligence was received, early next morning, that Howe was approaching in two columns. It being too late to reach the ground he had intended to occupy, Washington resolved to meet and engage him in front.

Both armies prepared, with great alacrity, for battle. The advanced parties had met, and were beginning to skirmish, when they were separated by a heavy rain, which, becoming more and more violent, rendered the retreat of the Americans a measure of absolute necessity. The inferiority of their arms never brought them into such imminent peril as on this occasion. Their gunlocks not being well secured, their muskets soon became unfit for use. Their cartridge-boxes had been so inartificially constructed, as not to protect their ammunition from the tempest. Their cartridges were soon damaged; and this mischief was the more serious, because very many of the soldiers were without bayonets.

After a slight skirmish compelled again to retire, cross the Schuylkill, and proceed to French Creek.

The army being thus rendered unfit for action, the design of giving battle was reluctantly abandoned, and a retreat commenced. It was continued all the day, and great part of the night, through a cold and most distressing rain, and very deep roads. A few hours before day, the troops halted at the Yellow Springs, where their arms and ammunition were examined, and the alarming fact was disclosed, that scarcely a musket in a regiment could be discharged, and scarcely one cartridge in a box was fit for use. This state of things suggested the precaution of moving to a still greater distance, in order to refit their arms, obtain a fresh supply of ammunition, and revive the spirits of the army. The General therefore retired to Warwick furnace, on the south branch of French Creek, where ammunition and a few muskets might be obtained in time to dispute the passage of the Schuylkill, and make yet another effort to save Philadelphia.

The extreme severity of the weather had entirely stopped the British army. During two
days, General Howe made no other movement
than to unite his columns.

From French Creek, General Wayne was detached with his division, into the rear of the
British, with orders to join General Smallwood;
and, carefully concealing himself and his movements, to seize every occasion which this march
might offer, of engaging them to advantage.
Meanwhile, General Washington crossed the
Schuylkill at Parker's ferry, and encamped on
both sides of Perkyomy Creek.

Septem-
ber 19.

General Wayne lay in the woods near the entrance of the road from Darby into that leading
to Lancaster, about three miles in the rear of
the left wing of the British troops encamped at
Trydruffin, where he believed himself to be perfectly secure. But the country was so extensively disaffected that Sir William Howe received accurate accounts of his position and of
his force. Major General Gray was detached
to surprise him, and effectually accomplished his
purpose. About eleven, in the night of the 20th,
his pickets, driven in with charged bayonets,
gave the first intimation of Gray's approach.
Wayne instantly formed his division; and while
his right sustained a fierce assault, directed a retreat by the left, under cover of a few regiments
who, for a short time, withstood the violence of
the shock. In his letter to the Commander-in-

General
Wayne
surprised,
and after
a sharp
action
compelled
to retreat.

chief, he says that they gave the assailants some well-directed fires which must have done considerable execution; and that, after retreating from the ground on which the engagement commenced, they formed again, at a small distance from the scene of action; but that both parties drew off without renewing the conflict. He states his loss at about one hundred and fifty * killed and wounded. The British accounts admit, on their part, a loss of only seven.

When the attack commenced, General Smallwood, who was on his march to join Wayne, a circumstance entirely unexpected by General Gray, was within less than a mile of him; and, had he commanded regulars, might have given a very different turn to the night. But his militia thought only of their own safety; and, having fallen in with a party returning from the pursuit of Wayne, fled in confusion with the loss of only one man.

Some severe animadversions on this unfortunate affair having been made in the army, General Wayne demanded a court martial, which, after investigating his conduct, was unanimously of opinion, "that he had done every thing to be expected from an active, brave, and vigilant officer;" and acquitted him with honour.

Having secured his rear, by compelling Wayne to take a greater distance, Sir William Howe

---

* The British accounts represent the American loss to have been much more considerable. It probably amounted to at least three hundred men.

marched along the valley road to the Schuykill,
and encamped on the bank of that river, from
the Fatland ford up to French Creek, along
the front of the American army. To secure his
right from being turned, General Washington
again changed his position, and encamped with
his left near, but above the British right.

General Howe now relinquished his plan of
bringing Washington to another battle; and,
thinking it adviseable, perhaps, to transfer the
seat of war to the neighbourhood of his ships,
determined to cross the Schuylkill, and take possession of Philadelphia. In the afternoon, he
ordered one detachment to cross at Fatland ford
which was on his right, and another to cross at
Gordon's ford, on his left, and to take possession
of the heights commanding them. These orders
were executed without much difficulty, and the
American troops placed to defend these fords
were easily dispersed.

This service being effected, the whole army
marched by its right, about midnight, and crossing at Fatland without opposition, proceeded a
considerable distance towards Philadelphia, and
encamped, with its left near Sweed's ford, and
its right on the Manatawny road, having Stony
run in its front.

It was now apparent that only immediate victory could save Philadelphia from the grasp of
the British general, whose situation gave him
the option of either taking possession of that

place, or endeavouring to bring on another engagement. If, therefore, a battle must certainly be risked to save the capital, it would be necessary to attack the enemy.

Public opinion, which a military chief finds too much difficulty in resisting, and the opinion of congress required a battle; but, on a temperate consideration of circumstances, Washington came to the wise decision of avoiding one for the present.

His reasons for this decision were conclusive. Wayne and Smallwood had not yet joined the army. The continental troops ordered from Peekskill, who had been detained for a time by an incursion from New York, were approaching; and a reinforcement of Jersey militia, under General Dickenson, was also expected.

To these powerful motives against risking an engagement, other considerations of great weight were added, founded on the condition of his soldiers. An army, manœuvring in an open country, in the face of a very superior enemy, is unavoidably exposed to excessive fatigue, and extreme hardship. The effect of these hardships was much increased by the privations under which the American troops suffered. While in almost continual motion, wading deep rivers, and encountering every vicissitude of the seasons, they were without tents, nearly without shoes, or winter clothes, and often without food.

A council of war concurred in the opinion the Commander-in-chief had formed, not to march against the enemy, but to allow his harassed troops a few days for repose, and to remain on his present ground until the expected reinforcements should arrive.

Immediately after the battle of Brandywine, the distressed situation of the army had been represented to congress, who had recommended it to the executive of Pennsylvania to seize the cloths and other military stores in the ware houses of Philadelphia, and, after granting certificates expressing their value, to convey them to a place of safety. The executive, being unwilling to encounter the odium of this strong measure, advised that the extraordinary powers of the Commander-in-chief should be used on the occasion. Lieutenant Colonel Hamilton, one of the General's aids, a young gentleman already in high estimation for his talents and zeal, was employed on this delicate business. "Your own prudence," said the General, in a letter to him while in Philadelphia, "will point out the least exceptionable means to be pursued; but remember, delicacy and a strict adherence to the ordinary mode of application must give place to our necessities. We must, if possible, accommodate the soldiers with such articles as they stand in need of, or we shall have just reason to apprehend the most injurious and alarming consequences from the approaching season."

All the efforts, however, of this very active officer could not obtain a supply, in any degree, adequate to the pressing and increasing wants of the army.

Colonel Hamilton was also directed to cause the military stores which had been previously collected to a large amount in Philadelphia, and the vessels which were lying at the wharves, to be removed up the Delaware. This duty was executed with so much vigilance, that very little public property fell, with the city, into the hands of the British general, who entered it on the 26th of September. The members of congress separated on the eighteenth, in the evening, and reassembled at Lancaster on the twenty-seventh of the same month.

General Howe takes possession of Philadelphia.

Congress removes to Lancaster.

From the 25th of August, when the British army landed at the Head of Elk, until the 26th of September when it entered Philadelphia, the campaign had been active, and the duties of the American general uncommonly arduous. The best English writers bestow high encomiums on Sir William Howe for his military skill, and masterly movements during this period. At Brandywine especially, Washington is supposed to have been "outgeneraled, more outgeneraled than in any action during the war." If all the operations of this trying period be examined, and the means in possession of both be considered, the American chief will appear, in no respect, inferior to his adversary, or unworthy of the high place assigned to him in the opinions of his countrymen. With an army decidedly inferior, not only in numbers, but in every military requisite except courage, in an open country, he employed his enemy near thirty days in advancing about sixty miles. In this time he fought one general action; and, though defeated, was able to reassemble the same undisciplined, unclothed, and almost unfed army; and, the fifth day afterwards, again to offer battle. When the armies were separated by a storm which involved him in the most distressing circumstances, he extricated himself from them, and still maintained a respectable and imposing countenance.

The only advantage he is supposed to have given was at the battle of Brandywine; and that was produced by the contrariety and uncertainty of the intelligence received. A general must be governed by his intelligence, and must regulate his measures by his information. It is his duty to obtain correct information; and among the most valuable traits of a military character, is the skill to select those means which will obtain it. Yet the best selected means are not always successful; and, in a new army, where military talent has not been well tried by the standard of experience, the general is peculiarly exposed to the chance of employing not the best instruments. In a country, too, which is covered with wood, precise information of the numbers composing different columns is to be gained with difficulty.

It has been said "that the Americans do not appear to have made all the use that might be expected of the advantages which the country afforded for harassing and impeding the British army."

In estimating this objection, it ought to be recollected that General Smallwood was directed, with the militia of Maryland and Delaware, supported by a regiment of continental troops, to hang on and harass the rear of the enemy: that General Maxwell, with a select corps consisting of a thousand men, was ordered to seize every occasion to annoy him on his march: that General Wayne, with his division, was afterwards detached to unite with Smallwood, and command the whole force collected in the rear, which would have been very respectable.

If the militia did not assemble in the numbers expected, or effect the service allotted to them, their failure is not attributable to General Washington. His calls on them had been early and energetic; and the state of his army did not admit of his making larger detachments from it to supply the place they had been designed to fill.

Loud complaints had been made against General Maxwell by the officers of his corps; and a court was ordered to inquire into his conduct, by whom he was acquitted. Whether that officer omitted to seize the proper occasions to annoy the enemy, or the cautious and compact movements of Sir William Howe afforded none, can not be easily ascertained. General Washington felt the loss of Morgan, and wrote pressingly to Gates, after his success against Burgoyne, to restore him that officer, with his regiment, as soon as possible.

CHAPTER IX.

Measures to cut off the communication between the
British army and fleet....Battle of Germantown....
Measures to intercept supplies to Philadelphia....At-
tack on fort Mifflin....On Red Bank....The Augusta
blows up....Fort Mifflin evacuated....Fort Mercer
evacuated....The British open the communication with
their fleet....Washington urged to attack Philadelphia
....General Howe marches out to Chestnut Hill....
Returns to Philadelphia....General Washington goes
into winter quarters.

1777
September.

Measures
taken to
prevent a
communi-
cation be-
tween the
British
army in
Philadelphia
and their
fleet.

PHILADELPHIA being lost, General Washington sought to make its occupation inconvenient and insecure, by rendering it inaccessible to
the British fleet. With this design, works had
been erected on a low marshy island in the Delaware, near the junction of the Schuylkill, which,
from the nature of its soil, was called Mud
Island. On the opposite shore of Jersey, at a
place called Red Bank, a fort had also been constructed which was defended with heavy artillery. In the deep channel between, or under
cover of these batteries, several ranges of frames
had been sunk, to which, from their resemblance
to that machine, the name of chevaux-de-frise
had been given. These frames were so strong
and heavy as to be destructive of any ship which
might strike against them, and were sunk in such
a depth of water as rendered it equally difficult

to weigh them or cut them through; no attempt to raise them, or to open the channel in any manner could be successful until the command of the shores on both sides should be obtained.

Other ranges of these machines had been sunk about three miles lower down the river; and some considerable works were in progress at Billingsport on the Jersey side, which were in such forwardness as to be provided with artillery. These works and machines were farther supported by several galleys mounting heavy cannon, together with two floating batteries, a number of armed vessels, and some fire ships.

The present relative situation of the armies gave a decisive importance to these works. Cutting off the communication of General Howe with his fleet, they prevented his receiving supplies by water, while the American vessels in the river above fort Mifflin, the name given to the fort on Mud Island, rendered it difficult to forage in Jersey, General Washington hoped to render his supplies on the side of Pennsylvania so precarious, as to compel him to evacuate Philadelphia.

The advantages of this situation were considerably diminished by the capture of the Delaware frigate.

The day after Lord Cornwallis entered Philadelphia, three batteries were commenced for the purpose of acting against any American ships which might appear before the town. While

September 27.

yet incomplete, they were attacked by two frigates, assisted by several galleys and gondolas.
The Delaware, being left by the tide while engaged with the battery, grounded and was captured; soon after which, the smaller frigate, and
the other vessels, retired under the guns of the
fort. This circumstance was the more interesting, as it gave the British General the command
of the ferry, and, consequently, free access to
Jersey, and enabled him to intercept the communication between the forts below, and Trenton, from which place the garrisons were to have
drawn their military stores.

Septem-
ber 28.

All the expected reinforcements, except the
state regiment and militia from Virginia, being
arrived, and the detached parties being called in,
the effective strength of the army amounted to
eight thousand continental troops, and three
thousand militia. With this force, General
Washington determined to approach the enemy,
and seize the first favourable moment to attack
him. In pursuance of this determination, the
army took a position on the Skippack road, about
twenty miles from Philadelphia, and sixteen
from Germantown,—a long village stretching
on both sides the great road leading northward
from Philadelphia, which forms one continued
street nearly two miles in length. The British
line of encampment crossed this village at right
angles near the centre, and Lord Cornwallis,
with four regiments of grenadiers, occupied

Septem-
ber 30.

Philadelphia. The immediate object of General Howe being the removal of the obstructions in the river, Colonel Stirling, with two regiments, had been detached to take possession of the fort at Billingsport, which he accomplished without opposition. This service being effected, and the works facing the water destroyed, Colonel Stirling was directed to escort a convoy of provisions from Chester to Philadelphia. Some apprehensions being entertained for the safety of this convoy, another regiment was detached from Germantown, with directions to join Colonel Stirling. *

This division of the British force appeared to Washington to furnish a fair opportunity to engage Sir William Howe with advantage. Determining to avail himself of it, he formed a plan for surprising the camp at Germantown, and attacking both wings, in front and rear, at the same instant.

The divisions of Sullivan and Wayne, flanked by Conway's brigade, were to march down the main road, and, entering the town by the way of Chesnut Hill, to attack the left wing; while General Armstrong, with the Pennsylvania militia, was to move down the Manatawny road† by Vanduring's mill, and turning the left flank to attack in the rear. The Commander-in-chief accompanied this column.

---

* Annual Register.—Stedman.
† Better known as the Ridge road.

The divisions of Greene and Stephen, flanked by M'Dougal's brigade, were to take a circuit by the Lime Kiln road, and, entering the town at the market house, to attack the right wing.

The militia of Maryland and Jersey, under Generals Smallwood and Forman, were to march down the old York road, and turning the right to fall upon its rear.

The division of Lord Stirling, and the brigades of Nash and Maxwell, were to form a corps de reserve.

Parties of cavalry were silently to scour the roads to prevent observation, and to keep up the communication between the heads of the several columns.

The necessary arrangements being made, the army moved from its ground at seven in the afternoon. Before sunrise the next morning, the advance of the column led by Sullivan, encountered and drove in a picket placed at Mount Airy, the house of Mr. Allen. † The main body followed close in the rear, and engaging the light infantry and the 40th regiment, posted at the head of the village, soon forced them to give way, leaving their baggage behind them. Though closely pursued, Lieutenant Colonel Musgrave threw himself with five companies of the 40th regiment into a large stone house belonging to Mr. Chew, which stood directly in the way of Wayne's division, and poured on the

† Since Robinson's.

Americans an incessant and galling fire of musketry from its doors and windows. After making some unsuccessful, and bloody attempts to carry this house by storm, and then battering it for a few minutes with field artillery, which was found too light to make any impression on its walls, a regiment was left to observe the party within it, while the troops who had been checked by Colonel Musgrave again moved forward, passing to the left of the house.

In rather more than half an hour after Sullivan had been engaged, the left wing, having formed the line, came also into action; and, attacking the light infantry posted in front of the British right wing, soon drove it from its ground. While rapidly pursuing the flying enemy, Woodford's brigade, ‡ which was on the right of this wing, was arrested by a heavy fire from Chew's house, directed against its right flank. The inefficiency of musketry against troops thus sheltered being instantly perceived, the brigade was drawn off to the left by its commanding officer, and the field-pieces attached to it were ordered up to play on the house, but were too light to be of service. Some time was consumed in this operation, and the advance of the brigade was, of course, retarded. This part of the line was consequently broken, and the two brigades composing the division of Stephen were not only

‡ The author was in this brigade, and describes this part of the action from his own observation.

separated from each other, but from the other division which was led by General Greene in person. That division, consisting of the brigades of Muhlenberg and Scott, pressing forward with eagerness, encountered and broke a part of the British right wing, entered the village, and made a considerable number of prisoners.

Thus far the prospect was flattering. The attack had been made with great spirit; several brigades had entered the town; and such an impression had been made on the British army as to justify the expectation that its wings might be separated from each other, and a complete victory be obtained. Had the American troops possessed the advantages given by experience; had every division of the army performed with precision the part allotted to it, there is yet reason to believe that the hopes inspired by this favourable commencement would not have been disappointed. But the face of the country, and the darkness of the morning produced by a fog of uncommon density, co-operating with the want of discipline in the army, and the derangements of the corps from the incidents at Chew's house, blasted their flattering appearances, and defeated the enterprise.

The grounds over which the British were pursued abounded with small and strong enclosures, which frequently broke the line of the advancing army. The two divisions of the right wing had been separated at Chew's house; and immediately after their passing it, the right of the left wing was stopped at the same place, so as to cause a division of that wing also. The darkness of the morning rendered it difficult to distinguish objects even at an inconsiderable distance; and it was impossible for the Commander-in-chief to learn the situation of the whole, or to correct the confusion which was commencing. The divisions and brigades separated at Chew's house could not be reunited; and, even among those parts which remained entire, a considerable degree of disorder was soon introduced by the impediments to their advance. Some regiments pursuing with more vivacity than others, they were separated from each other, their weight lessened, and their effect impaired. The darkness which obstructed the reunion of the broken parts of the American army, also prevented their discerning the real situation of the enemy, so as to improve the first impression; and, in some instances, some corps being in advance of others, produced uncertainty whether the troops, seen indistinctly, were friends or foes.

The attacks on the flanks and rear, which formed a part of the original plan, do not appear ever to have been made. The Pennsylvania militia came in view of the chasseurs who flanked the left of the British line, but did not engage them closely. The Maryland and Jersey militia just showed themselves on the right flank, about the time Greene was commencing a retreat.

These embarrassments gave the British time to recover from the consternation into which they had been thrown. General Knyphausen, who commanded their left, detached two brigades to meet the right of Sullivan which had penetrated far into the village, before his left, which had been detained at Chew's house, could rejoin him; and the action became warm in this quarter. The British right also recovered from its surprise, and advanced on that part of Greene's division which had entered the town.

The Americans repulsed.

After a sharp engagement these two brigades began to retreat, and those which were most in advance were surrounded and compelled to surrender. About the same time the right wing also began to retreat. It is understood that they had expended their ammunition.

Every effort to stop this retrograde movement proved ineffectual. The division of Wayne fell back on that of Stephen, and was for an instant mistaken for the enemy. General confusion prevailed, and the confidence felt in the beginning of the action was lost. With infinite chagrin General Washington was compelled to relinquish his hopes of victory, and turn his attention to the security of his army. The enemy not being sufficiently recovered to endanger his rear, the retreat was made without loss, under cover of the division of Stephen, which had scarcely been in the engagement.

In this battle, about two hundred Americans were killed, near three times that number wounded, and about four hundred were made prisoners. Among the killed was General Nash of North Carolina; and among the prisoners was Colonel Matthews of Virginia, whose regiment had penetrated into the centre of the town.

The loss of the British, as stated in the official return of General Howe, did not much exceed five hundred in killed and wounded, of whom less than one hundred were killed; among the latter were Brigadier General Agnew and Colonel Bird.

The American army retreated the same day, about twenty miles, to Perkyomy Creek, where a small reinforcement, consisting of fifteen hundred militia and a state regiment, was received from Virginia; after which it again advanced towards Philadelphia, and encamped once more on Skippack Creek.

The plan of the battle of Germantown must be admitted to have been judiciously formed; and, in its commencement, to have been happily conducted. But a strict adherence to it by those who were entrusted with the execution of its several parts, was indispensable to its success.

Major General Stephen, who commanded the right division of the left wing, was cashiered for misconduct on the retreat, and for intoxication.

Congress expressed, in decided terms, their approbation both of the plan of this enterprise, and of the courage with which it was executed; for which their thanks were given to the general and the army. *

The attention of both armies was most principally directed to the forts below Philadelphia.

The loss of the Delaware frigate, and of Billingsport, greatly discouraged the seamen by whom the galleys and floating batteries were manned. Believing the fate of America to be decided, an opinion strengthened by the intelligence received from their connexions in Philadelphia, they manifested the most alarming defection, and several officers as well as sailors deserted to the enemy. This desponding temper was checked by the battle of Germantown, and by throwing a garrison of continental troops into the fort at Red Bank, called fort Mercer, the defence of which had been entrusted to militia. This fort commanded the channel between the Jersey shore and Mud Island; and the American vessels were secure under its guns. The militia

---

* On hearing that General Howe had landed at the head of the Chesapeake, Sir Henry Clinton, for the purpose of averting those aids which Washington might draw from the north of the Delaware, entered Jersey at the head of three thousand men. On the approach of General M'Dougal with a body of continental troops from Peekskill, and on hearing that the militia were assembling under General Dickinson, he returned to New York and Staten Island with the cattle he had collected, having lost in the expedition only eight men killed and twice as many wounded.

M'Dougal continued his march towards the Delaware; and the utmost exertions were made both by Governor Livingston and General Dickinson to collect the militia for the purpose of aiding the army in Pennsylvania. The success of their exertions did not equal their wishes. The militia being of opinion that there was danger of a second invasion from New York, and that their services were more necessary at home than in Pennsylvania, assembled slowly and reluctantly.

of Jersey were relied on to reinforce its garrison, and also to form a corps of observation which might harass the rear of any detachment investing the place.

To increase the inconvenience of General Howe's situation by intercepting his supplies, six hundred militia, commanded by General Potter, crossed the Schuylkill, with orders to scour the country between that river and Chester; and the militia on the Delaware, above Philadelphia, were directed to watch the roads in that vicinity.

Measures taken by General Washington for cutting off supplies from Philadelphia.

The more effectually to stop those who were seduced by the hope of gold and silver to supply the enemy at this critical time, congress passed a resolution subjecting to martial law and to death, all who should furnish them with provisions, or certain other enumerated articles, who should be taken within thirty miles of any city, town or place, in Jersey, Pennsylvania, or Delaware, occupied by British troops.

Five or six hundred crossed the Delaware at Philadelphia, about the time Sir William Howe crossed the Schuylkill, and were employed in the removal of stores. On the approach of the British army, they were directed to avoid it by moving up the Frankford road; but the commanding officer, having separated himself from his corps, was taken by a party of British horse employed in scouring the country; on which the regiment dispersed, and returned by different roads to Jersey. With much labour General Dickinson assembled two other corps amounting to about nine hundred men, with whom he was about to cross the Delaware when intelligence was received of the arrival at New York of a reinforcement from Europe. He was detained in Jersey for the defence of the state, and the militia designed to serve in Pennsylvania were placed under General Forman. About six hundred of them reached the army a few days before the battle of Germantown, immediately after which they were permitted to return.

These· arrangements being made to cut off supplies from the country, General Washington reoccupied the ground from which he had marched to fight the battle of Germantown.

Meanwhile, General Howe was actively preparing to attack fort Mifflin from the Pennsylvania shore. He erected some batteries at the mouth of the Schuylkill, in order to command Webb's ferry, which were attacked by Commodore Hazlewood, and silenced; but, the following night, a detachment crossed over Webb's ferry into Province Island, and constructed a slight work opposite fort Mifflin, within two musket shots of the block-house, from which they were enabled to throw shot and shells into the barracks. When day-light discovered this work, three galleys and a floating battery were ordered to attack it, and the garrison surrendered: While the boats were bringing off the prisoners, a large column of British troops were seen marching into the fortress, upon which the attack on it was renewed, but without success; and two attempts made by Lieutenant Colonel Smith to storm it, failed. In a few nights, works were completed on the high ground of Province Island which enfiladed the principal battery of fort Mifflin, and rendered it necessary to throw up some cover on the platform to protect the men who worked the guns.

Attack upon
Fort
Mifflin.

The aids expected from the Jersey militia were not received. "Assure yourself," said

Lieutenant Colonel Smith, in a letter pressing earnestly for a reinforcement of continental troops, "that no dependence is to be put on the militia; whatever men your excellency determines on sending, no time is to be lost." The garrison of fort Mifflin was now reduced to one hundred and fifty-six effectives, and that of Red Bank did not much exceed two hundred.

In consequence of these representations, Colonel Angel, of Rhode Island, with his regiment, was ordered to Red Bank, and Lieutenant Colonel John Greene, of Virginia, with about two hundred men, to fort Mifflin.

Immediately after the battle of Brandywine, Admiral Howe sailed for the Delaware, where he expected to arrive in time to meet and co-operate with the army in and about Philadelphia. But the winds were so unfavourable, and the navigation of the bay of Delaware so difficult, that his van did not get into the river until the 4th of October. The ships of war and transports which followed, came up from the sixth to the eighth, and anchored from New Castle to Reedy Island.

The frigates, in advance of the fleet, had not yet succeeded in their endeavours to effect a passage through the lower double row of chevaux-de-frise. Though no longer protected by the fort at Billingsport, they were defended by the water force above, and the work was found more difficult than had been expected. It was

not until the middle of October that the impediments were so far removed as to afford a narrow
and intricate passage through them.   In the
mean time, the fire from the Pennsylvania shore
had not produced all the effect expected from
it; and it was perceived that greater exertions
would be necessary for the reduction of the works
than could safely be made in the present relative
situation of the armies.   Under this impression,
General Howe, soon after the return of the
American army to its former camp on the Skippack, withdrew his troops from Germantown
into Philadelphia, as preparatory to a combined
attack by land and water on forts Mercer and
Mifflin.

After effecting a passage through the works
sunk in the river at Billingsport, other difficulties
still remained to be encountered by the ships of
war.   Several rows of chevaux-de-frise had been
sunk about half a mile below Mud Island, which
were protected by the guns of the forts, as well
as by the moveable water force.   To silence these
works, therefore, was a necessary preliminary
to the removal of these obstructions in the
channel.

On the 21st of October, a detachment of Hessians, amounting to twelve hundred men, commanded by Colonel Count Donop, crossed the
Delaware at Philadelphia, with orders to storm
the fort at Red Bank.   The fortifications consisted of extensive outer works, within which

was an intrenchment eight or nine feet high, boarded and fraized. Late in the evening of the twenty-second, Count Donop appeared before the fort, and attacked it with great intrepidity. It was defended with equal resolution. The outer works being too extensive to be manned by the troops in the fort, were used only to gall the assailants while advancing. On their near approach, the garrison retired within the inner intrenchment, whence they poured upon the Hessians a heavy and destructive fire. Colonel Donop received a mortal wound; and Lieutenant Colonel Mengerode, the second in command, fell about the same time. Lieutenant Colonel Minsing, the oldest remaining officer, drew off his troops, and returned next day to Philadelphia. The loss of the assailants was estimated by the Americans at four hundred men. The garrison was reinforced from fort Mifflin, and aided by the galleys which flanked the Hessians in their advance and retreat. The American loss, in killed and wounded, amounted to only thirty-two men.

The ships having been ordered to co-operate with Count Donop, the Augusta, with four smaller vessels, passed the lower line of chevaux-de-frise, opposite to Billingsport, and lay above it, waiting until the assault should be made on the fort. The flood tide setting in about the time the attack commenced, they moved with it up the river. The obstructions sunk in the

Colonel
Donop
killed
and his
party
repulsed
with
considerable
loss.

Delaware had in some degree changed its channel, in consequence of which the Augusta and
the Merlin grounded, a considerable distance below the second line of chevaux-de-frise and a
strong wind from the north so checked the rising
of the tide, that these vessels could not be floated
by the flood. Their situation, however, was not
discerned that evening, as the frigates which
were able to approach the fort, and the batteries from the Pennsylvania shore, kept up an
incessant fire on the garrison, till night put an
end to the cannonade. Early next morning it
was recommenced, in the hope that, under its
cover, the Augusta and the Merlin might be got
off. The Americans, on discovering their situation, sent four fire ships against them, but without effect. Meanwhile, a warm cannonade took
place on both sides, in the course of which the
Augusta took fire, and it was found impracticable
to extinguish the flames. Most of the men were
taken out, the frigates withdrawn, and the Merlin set on fire; after which the Augusta blew
up, and a few of the crew were lost in her.

The
Augusta
frigate
blows up.

This repulse inspired congress with flattering
hopes for the permanent defence of the posts on
the Delaware. That body expressed its high
sense of the merits of Colonel Greene of Rhode
Island, who had commanded in fort Mercer; of
Lieutenant Colonel Smith of Maryland, who
had commanded in fort Mifflin; and of Commodore Hazlewood, who commanded the galleys;

and presented a sword to each of these officers, as a mark of estimation in which their services were held.

The situation of these forts was far from justifying this confidence of their being defensible. That on Mud Island had been unskilfully constructed, and required at least eight hundred men fully to man the lines. The island is about half a mile long. Fort Mifflin was placed at the lower end, having its principal fortifications in front for the purpose of repelling ships coming up the river. The defences in the rear consisted only of a ditch and palisade, protected by two block-houses, the upper story of one of which had been destroyed in the late cannonade. Above the fort were two batteries opposing those constructed by the British on Province and Carpenter's Islands, which were separated from Mud Island only by a narrow passage between four and five hundred yards wide.

The vessels of war, engaged in the defence of the Delaware, were partly in the service of the continent, and partly in that of the state of Pennsylvania, under a Commodore who received his commission from the state. A misunderstanding took place between him and Lieutenant Colonel Smith, and also between him and the officers of the continental navy; and it required all the authority of the Commander-in-chief to prevent these differences from essentially injuring the service.

The garrison of fort Mifflin consisted of only three hundred continental troops, who were worn down with fatigue, and constant watching, under the constant apprehension of being attacked from Province Island, from Philadelphia, and from the ships below.

Having failed in every attempt to draw the militia of Jersey to the Delaware, General Washington determined to strengthen the garrison by farther drafts from his army. Three hundred Pennsylvania militia were detached, to be divided between the two forts; and, a few

days afterwards, General Varnum was ordered, with his brigade, to take a position about Woodbury, near Red Bank, and to relieve and reinforce the garrisons of both forts as far as his strength would permit. The hope was entertained that the appearance of so respectable a continental force might encourage the militia to assemble in greater numbers.

Aware of the advantage to result from a victory over the British army while separated from the fleet, General Washington had been uniformly determined to risk much to gain one. He had, therefore, after the battle of Germantown, continued to watch assiduously for an opportunity to attack his enemy once more to advantage. The circumspect caution of General Howe afforded none. After the repulse at Red Bank, his measures were slow but certain; and were calculated to insure the possession of the forts

without exposing his troops to the hazard of an
assault.

In this state of things, intelligence was received of the successful termination of the northern campaign, in consequence of which great part of the troops who had been employed against Burgoyne, might be drawn to the aid of the army in Pennsylvania. But it was feared that, before these reinforcements could arrive, Sir William Howe would gain possession of the forts, and remove the obstructions to the navigation of the Delaware. This apprehension furnished a strong motive for vigorous attempts to relieve fort Mifflin. But the relative force of the armies, the difficulty of acting offensively against Philadelphia, and, above all, the reflection that a defeat might disable him from meeting his enemy in the field even after the arrival of the troops expected from the north, determined General Washington not to hazard a second attack under existing circumstances.

To expedite the reinforcements for which he waited, Colonel Hamilton was despatched to General Gates with directions to represent to him the condition of the armies in Pennsylvania; and to urge him, if he contemplated no other service of more importance, immediately to send the regiments of Massachusetts and New Hampshire to aid the army of the middle department. These orders were not peremptory, because it was possible that some other object (as the capture of New York) still more interesting than the expulsion of General Howe from Philadelphia, might be contemplated by Gates; and Washington meant not to interfere with the accomplishment of such object.

On reaching General Putnam, Colonel Hamilton found that a considerable part of the northern army had joined that officer, but that Gates had detained four brigades at Albany for an expedition intended to be made in the winter against Ticonderoga.

Having made such arrangements with Putnam as he supposed would secure the immediate march of a large body of continental troops from that station, Colonel Hamilton proceeded to Albany for the purpose of remonstrating to General Gates against retaining so large and valuable a part of the army unemployed at a time when the most imminent danger threatened the vitals of the country. Gates was by no means disposed to part with his troops. He could not believe that an expedition then preparing at New York, was designed to reinforce General Howe; and insisted that, should the troops then embarked at that place, instead of proceeding to the Delaware, make a sudden movement up the Hudson, it would be in their power, should Albany be left defenceless, to destroy the valuable arsenal which had been there erected, and the military stores captured with Burgoyne, which had been chiefly deposited in that town.

Having, after repeated remonstrances, obtained an order directing three brigades to the
Delaware, Hamilton hastened back to Putnam,
and found the troops which had been ordered
to join General Washington, still at Peekskill.
The detachment from New York had suggested
to Putnam the possibility of taking that place;
and he does not appear to have made very great
exertions to divest himself of a force he deemed
necessary for an object, the accomplishment of
which would give so much splendour to his military character. In addition to this circumstance,
an opinion had gained ground among the soldiers that their share of service for the campaign
had been performed, and that it was time for
them to go into winter quarters. Great discontents too prevailed concerning their pay, which
the government had permitted to be more than
six months in arrear; and in Poor's brigade, a
mutiny broke out, in the course of which a soldier who was run through the body by his captain, before he expired, shot the captain dead
who gave the wound. Colonel Hamilton came
in time to borrow money from the governor of
New York, to put the troops in motion; and
they proceeded by brigades to the Delaware.
But these several delays retarded their arrival
until the contest for the forts on that river was
terminated.

The preparations of Sir William Howe being
completed, a large battery on Province Island

of twenty-four and thirty-two pounders, and two howitzers of eight inches each, opened, early in the morning of the 10th of November, upon fort Mifflin, at the distance of five hundred yards, and kept up an incessant fire for several successive days. The block-houses were reduced to a heap of ruins; the palisades were beaten down; and most of the guns dismounted and otherwise disabled. The barracks were battered in every part, so that the troops could not remain in them. They were under the necessity of working and watching the whole night to repair the damages of the day, and to guard against a storm, of which they were in perpetual apprehension. If in the day, a few moments were allowed for repose, it was taken on the wet earth, which, in consequence of heavy rains, had become a soft mud. The garrison was relieved by General Varnum every forty-eight hours; but his brigade was so weak that half the men were constantly on duty.

Colonel Smith was decidedly of opinion, and General Varnum concurred with him, that the garrison could not repel an assault, and ought to be withdrawn; but General Washington still cherished the hope that the place might be maintained until he should be reinforced from the northern army. Believing that an assault would not be attempted until the works were battered down, he recommended that the whole night should be employed in making repairs. His orders were that the place should be defended to the last extremity; and never were orders more faithfully executed.

Several of the garrison were killed, and among them Captain Treat, a gallant officer, who commanded the artillery. Colonel Smith received a contusion on his hip and arm which compelled him to give up the command, and retire to Red Bank. Major Fleury, a French officer of distinguished merit, who served as engineer, reported to the Commander-in-chief that, although the block-houses were beaten down, all the guns in them, except two, disabled, and several breaches made in the walls, the place was still defensible; but the garrison was so unequal to the numbers required by the extent of the lines, and was so dispirited by watching, fatigue, and constant exposure to the cold rains which were almost incessant, that he dreaded the event of an attempt to carry the place by storm. Fresh troops were ordered to their relief from Varnum's brigade, and the command was taken, first by Colonel Russell, and afterwards by Major Thayer. The artillery, commanded by Captain Lee, continued to be well served. The besiegers were several times thrown into confusion, and a floating battery which opened on the morning of the 14th, was silenced in the course of the day.

The defence being unexpectedly obstinate, the assailants brought up their ships as far as the obstructions in the river permitted, and added their fire to that of the batteries, which was the more fatal as the cover for the troops had been greatly impaired. The brave garrison, however, still maintained their ground with unshaken firmness. In the midst of this stubborn conflict, the Vigilant and a sloop of war were brought up the inner channel, between Mud and Province Islands, which had, unobserved by the besieged, been deepened by the current in consequence of the obstructions in the main channel; and, taking a station within one hundred yards of the works, not only kept up a destructive cannonade, but threw hand grenades into them; while the musketeers from the round top of the Vigilant killed every man that appeared on the platform.

Major Thayer applied to the Commodore to remove these vessels, and he ordered six galleys on the service; but, after reconnoitring their situation, the galleys returned without attempting any thing. Their report was that these ships were so covered by the batteries on Province Island as to be unassailable.

Fort Mifflin evacuated and possession taken by the British.

It was now apparent to all that the fort could be no longer defended. The works were in ruins. The position of the Vigilant rendered any farther continuance on the island a prodigal and useless waste of human life; and on the 16th, November 16. about 11 at night, the garrison was withdrawn.*

---

* In stating the defence of Mud Island, the author has availed himself of the journal of Major Fleury.

A second attempt was made to drive the vessels from their stations with a determination, should it succeed, to repossess the island; but the galleys effected nothing; and a detachment from Province Island soon occupied the ground which had been abandoned.

The day after receiving intelligence of the evacuation of fort Mifflin, General Washington deputed Generals De Kalb, and Knox, to confer with General Varnum and the officers at fort Mercer on the practicability of continuing to defend the obstructions in the channel, to report thereon, and to state the force which would be necessary for that purpose. Their report was in favour of continuing the defence. A council of the navy officers had already been called by the Commodore in pursuance of a request of the Commander-in-chief made before the evacuation had taken place, who were unanimously of opinion that it would be impracticable for the fleet, after the loss of the island, to maintain its station, or to assist in preventing the chevaux-de-frise from being weighed by the ships of the enemy.

General Howe had now completed a line of defence from the Schuylkill to the Delaware; and a reinforcement from New York had arrived at Chester. These two circumstances enabled him to form an army in the Jerseys sufficient for the reduction of fort Mercer, without weakening himself so much in Philadelphia as to put his lines in hazard. Still deeming it of the utmost importance to open the navigation of the Delaware completely, he detached Lord Cornwallis about one in the morning of the 17th, with a strong body of troops to Chester. From that place, his lordship crossed over to Billingsport, where he was joined by the reinforcement from New York.

General Washington received immediate intelligence of the march of this detachment, which he communicated to General Varnum with orders that fort Mercer should be defended to the last extremity. With a view to military operations in that quarter, he ordered one division of the army to cross the river at Burlington, and despatched expresses to the northern troops who were marching on by brigades, directing them to move down the Delaware on its northern side until they should receive farther orders.

Major General Greene, an officer who had been distinguished early in the war by the Commander-in-chief for the solidity of his judgment and his military talents, was selected for this expedition. A hope was entertained that he would be able, not only to protect fort Mercer, but to obtain some decisive advantage over Lord Cornwallis; as the situation of the fort, which his lordship could not invest without placing himself between Timber and Manto Creeks, would expose the assailants to great peril from a respectable force in their rear. But, before

Greene could cross the Delaware, Lord Cornwallis approached with an army rendered more
powerful than had been expected by the junction of the reinforcement from New York; and
fort Mercer was evacuated.

A few of the smaller galleys escaped up the
river, and the others were burnt by their crews.

Washington still hoped to recover much of
what had been lost. A victory would restore the
Jersey shore, and this object was deemed so important, that General Greene's instructions indicated the expectation that he would be in a
condition to fight Lord Cornwallis.

That judicious officer feared the reproach of
avoiding an action less than the just censure of
sacrificing the real interests of his country by
engaging the enemy on disadvantageous terms.
The numbers of the British exceeded his, even
counting his militia as regulars; and he determined to wait for Glover's brigade, which was
marching from the north. Before its arrival,
Lord Cornwallis took post on Gloucester Point,
a point of land making deep into the Delaware,
which was entirely under cover of the guns of
the ships, from which place he was embarking
his baggage and the provisions he had collected
for Philadelphia. *

---

* While Lord Cornwallis lay on Gloucester Point, about
one hundred and fifty men of Morgan's rifle corps under
Lieutenant Colonel Butler, and an equal number of militia,
the whole under the Marquis de la Fayette, who still served
as a volunteer, attacked a picket consisting of about three
hundred men, and drove them with the loss of twenty or

Believing that Lord Cornwallis would immediately follow the magazines he had collected,
and that the purpose of Sir William Howe was,
with his united forces, to attack the American
army while divided, General Washington ordered Greene to recross the Delaware, and join
the army.

The enemy
succeeds in
opening a
free com-
munication
with his
fleet.

Thus after one continued struggle of more
than six weeks, in which the continental troops
displayed great military virtues, the army in
Philadelphia secured itself in the possession of
that city, by opening a free communication with
the fleet. †

While Lord Cornwallis was in Jersey, and
General Greene on the Delaware above him, the
reinforcements from the north being received,
an attack on Philadelphia was strongly pressed
by several officers high in rank; and was in some
measure urged by that torrent of public opinion,

---

thirty killed, and a greater number wounded, quite into
their camp; after which the Americans retired without
being pursued.

† While these transactions were passing on the Delaware,
General Dickinson projected another expedition against the
post on Staten Island. He collected about two thousand men,
and requested General Putnam to make a diversion on the
side of Kingsbridge, in order to prevent a reinforcement
from New York.

Knowing that success depended on secrecy, he had concealed his object even from his field-officers, until eight of
the night in which it was to be executed. Yet by three next
morning, information of his design was given to General
Skinner, who, being on his guard, saved himself and his
brigade, by taking refuge, on the first alarm, in some works
too strong to be carried by assault. A few prisoners were
made and a few men killed, after which General Dickinson
brought off his party with the loss of only three killed and
ten slightly wounded.

CHAP. IX

1777

Washington
urged to
attack
Philadelphia.

which, if not resisted by a very firm mind, over-
whelms the judgment, and by controlling measures not well comprehended, may frequently
produce, especially in military transactions, the
most disastrous effects.

It was stated to the Commander-in-chief, that
his army was now in greater force than he could
expect it to be at any future time; that being
joined by the troops who had conquered Burgoyne, his own reputation, the reputation of his
army, the opinion of congress, and of the nation,
required some decisive blow on his part. That
the rapid depreciation of the paper currency, by
which the resources for carrying on the war were
dried up, rendered indispensable some grand effort to bring it to a speedy termination.

The plan proposed was, that General Greene
should embark two thousand men at Dunks'
ferry, and descending the Delaware in the night,
land in the town just before day, attack the
enemy in the rear, and take possession of the
bridge over the Schuylkill. That a strong corps
should march down on the west side of that
river, occupy the heights enfilading the works
of the enemy, and open a brisk cannonade upon
them, while a detachment from it should march
down to the bridge, and attack in front at the
same instant, that the party descending the river
should commence its assault on the rear.

Not only the Commander-in-chief, but some
of his best officers, those who could not be im-

pelled by the clamours of the ill-informed to ruin the public interests, were opposed to this mad enterprise.

The two armies, they said, were now nearly equal in point of numbers, and the detachment under Lord Cornwallis could not be supposed to have so weakened Sir William Howe as to compensate for the advantages of his position. His right was covered by the Delaware, his left by the Schuylkill, his rear by the junction of those two rivers, as well as by the city of Philadelphia, and his front by a line of redoubts extending from river to river, and connected by an abattis, and by circular works. It would be indispensably necessary to carry all these redoubts; since to leave a part of them to play on the rear of the columns, while engaged in front with the enemy in Philadelphia, would be extremely hazardous.

Supposing the redoubts carried, and the British army driven into the town, yet all military men were agreed on the great peril of storming a town. The streets would be defended by an artillery greatly superior to that of the Americans, which would attack in front, while the brick houses would be lined with musketeers, whose first must thin the ranks of the assailants.

A part of the plan, on the successful execution of which the whole depended, was, that the British rear should be surprised by the corps descending the Delaware. This would require the concurrence of too many favourable circumstances to be calculated on with any confidence. As the position of General Greene was known, it could not be supposed that Sir William Howe would be inattentive to him. It was probable that not even his embarkation would be made unnoticed; but it was presuming a degree of negligence which ought not to be assumed, to suppose that he could descend the river to Philadelphia undiscovered. So soon as his movements should be observed, the whole plan would be comprehended, since it would never be conjectured that General Greene was to attack singly.

If the attack in front should fail, which was not even improbable, the total loss of the two thousand men in the rear must follow; and General Howe would maintain his superiority through the winter.

The situation of America did not require these desperate measures. The British general would be compelled to risk a battle on equal terms, or to manifest a conscious inferiority to the American army. The depreciation of paper money was the inevitable consequence of immense emissions without corresponding taxes. It was by removing the cause, not by sacrificing the army, that this evil was to be corrected.

Washington possessed too much discernment to be dazzled by the false brilliant presented by those who urged the necessity of storming Philadelphia, in order to throw lustre round his own fame, and that of his army; and too much firmness of temper, too much virtue and real patriotism, to be diverted from a purpose believed to be right, by the clamours of faction or the discontents of ignorance. Disregarding the importunities of mistaken friends, the malignant insinuations of enemies, and the expectations of the ill-informed; he persevered in his resolution to make no attempt on Philadelphia. He saved his army, and was able to keep the field in the face of his enemy; while the clamour of the moment wasted in air, and is forgotten.

The opinion that Sir William Howe meditated an attack on the American camp, was not ill founded. Scarcely had Lord Cornwallis returned to Philadelphia, and Greene to the American army, when unquestionable intelligence was received that the British general was preparing to march out in full strength, with the avowed object of forcing Washington from his position, and driving him beyond the mountains.

On the 4th of December, Captain M'Lane, a vigilant officer on the lines, discovered that an attempt to surprise the American camp at White Marsh was about to be made, and communicated the information to the Commander-in-chief. In the evening of the same day, General Howe marched out of Philadelphia with his whole force; and, about eleven at night, M'Lane, who had been detached with one hundred chosen men, attacked the British van at the Three Mile Run, on the Germantown road, and compelled their

front division to change its line of march. He
hovered on the front and flank of the advancing
army, galling them severely until three next
morning, when the British encamped on Chestnut Hill, in front of the American right, and
distant from it about three miles. A slight skirmish had also taken place between the Pennsylvania militia under General Irvine, and the advanced light parties of the enemy, in which the
general was wounded, and the militia, without
much other loss, were dispersed.

The range of hills on which the British were
posted, approached nearer to those occupied by
the Americans, as they stretched northward.

Having passed the day in reconnoitring the
right, Sir William Howe changed his ground in
the course of the night, and moving along the
hills to his right, took an advantageous position,
about a mile in front of the American left. The
next day he inclined still farther to his right,
and, in doing so, approached still nearer to the
left wing of the American army. Supposing a
general engagement to be approaching, Washington detached Gist with some Maryland militia, and Morgan with his rifle corps, to attack
the flanking and advanced parties of the enemy.
A sharp action ensued, in which Major Morris,
of Jersey, a brave officer in Morgan's regiment,
was mortally wounded, and twenty-seven of his
men were killed and wounded. A small loss was
also sustained in the militia. The parties first

CHAP. IX

1777

General
Howe
marches
out to
Chestnut
Hill.

attacked were driven in; but the enemy rein-forcing in numbers, and Washington, unwilling to move from the heights, and engage on the ground which was the scene of the skirmish, declining to reinforce Gist and Morgan, they, in turn, were compelled to retreat.

Sir William Howe continued to manœuvre towards the flank, and in front of the left wing of the American army. Expecting to be at-tacked in that quarter in full force, Washington made such changes in the disposition of his troops as the occasion required; and the day was con-sumed in these movements. In the course of it, the American chief rode through every brigade of his army, delivering, in person, his orders, re-specting the manner of receiving the enemy, ex-horting his troops to rely principally on the bayonet, and encouraging them by the steady firmness of his countenance, as well as by his words, to a vigorous performance of their duty.* The dispositions of the evening indicated an in-tention to attack him the ensuing morning; but in the afternoon of the eighth, the British sud-denly filed off from their right, which extended beyond the American left, and retreated to

Returns to
Philadelphia.

Philadelphia. The parties detached to harass their rear could not overtake it.

The loss of the British in this expedition, as stated in the official letter of General Howe, rather exceeded one hundred in killed, wounded,

---

* The author states this on his own observation.

and missing; and was sustained principally in the skirmish of the 7th, in which Major Morris fell.

On no former occasion had the two armies met, uncovered by works, with superior numbers on the side of the Americans. The effective force of the British was then stated at twelve thousand men. It has been since declared by an author † who then belonged to it, but who, though a candid writer, appears to have imbibed prejudices against Sir William Howe, to have amounted to fourteen thousand. The American army consisted of precisely twelve thousand one hundred and sixty-one continental troops, and three thousand two hundred and forty-one militia. This equality in point of numbers, rendered it a prudent precaution to maintain a superiority of position. As the two armies occupied heights fronting each other, neither could attack without giving to its adversary some advantage in the ground; and this was an advantage which neither seemed willing to relinquish.

The return of Sir William Howe to Philadelphia without bringing on an action, after marching out with the avowed intention of fighting, is the best testimony of the respect which he felt for the talents of his adversary, and the courage of the troops he was to encounter.

The cold was now becoming so intense that it was impossible for an army neither well

---

† Stedman.

clothed, nor sufficiently supplied with blankets, longer to keep the field in tents. It had become necessary to place the troops in winter quarters; but in the existing state of things the choice of winter quarters was a subject for serious reflection. It was impossible to place them in villages without uncovering the country, or exposing them to the hazard of being beaten in detachment.

To avoid these calamities, it was determined to take a strong position in the neighbourhood of Philadelphia, equally distant from the Delaware above and below that city; and there to construct huts, in the form of a regular encampment, which might cover the army during the winter. A strong piece of ground at Valley Forge, on the west side of the Schuylkill, between twenty and thirty miles from Philadelphia, was selected for that purpose; and some time before day on the morning of the 11th of December, the army marched to take possession of it. By an accidental concurrence of circumstances, Lord Cornwallis had been detached the same morning at the head of a strong corps, on a foraging party on the west side of the Schuylkill. He had fallen in with a brigade of Pennsylvania militia commanded by General Potter, which he soon dispersed; and, pursuing the fugitives, had gained the heights opposite Matron's ford, over which the Americans had thrown a bridge for the purpose of crossing the river, and had posted troops to command the defile called the Gulph, just as the front division of the American army reached the bank of the river. This movement had been made without any knowledge of the intention of General Washington to change his position, or any design of contesting the passage of the Schuylkill; but the troops had been posted in the manner already mentioned for the sole purpose of covering the foraging party.

Washington apprehended, from his first intelligence, that General Howe had taken the field in full force. He therefore recalled the troops already on the west side, and moved rather higher up the river, for the purpose of understanding the real situation, force, and designs of the enemy. The next day Lord Cornwallis returned to Philadelphia; and, in the course of the night, the American army crossed the river.

Here the Commander-in-chief communicated to his army, in general orders, the manner in which he intended to dispose of them during the winter. He expressed, in strong terms, his approbation of their conduct, presented them with an encouraging state of the future prospects of their country, exhorted them to bear with continuing fortitude the hardships inseparable from the position they were about to take, and endeavoured to convince their judgments that those hardships were not imposed on them by unfeel-

General Washington goes into winter quarters.

ing caprice, but were necessary for the good of their country.

The winter had set in with great severity, and the sufferings of the army were extreme. In a few days, however, these sufferings were considerably diminished by the erection of logged huts, filled up with mortar, which, after being dried, formed comfortable habitations, and gave content to men long unused to the conveniences of life. The order of a regular encampment was observed; and the only appearance of winter quarters, was the substitution of huts for tents.

CHAPTER X.

WHILE, with inferior numbers, General   ¹1777
Washington maintained a stubborn contest in
the middle states, events of great variety and
importance were passing in the north.

After Sir Guy Carleton had distributed his
army, for winter quarters, in the several villages
from the Isle Aux Noix and Montreal to Quebec,
General Burgoyne, who had served under him,
embarked for England, in order to communicate
a full statement of affairs in the northern department; and to assist in making arrangements
for the ensuing campaign. The American army,
having been formed for only one year, dissolved

of itself at the expiration of that term, and could scarcely furnish even the appearance of garrisons in their forts.

The defence of this frontier was assigned to the regiments directed to be raised in Massachusetts, New Hampshire, and the northwestern parts of New York; but the recruiting service advanced so slowly, and so much difficulty was found in clothing and arming those who were enlisted, that it became indispensable to call in the aid of the militia; and the plan of the campaign on the part of the British was involved in so much obscurity that General Washington deemed it adviseable to direct eight of the regiments of Massachusetts to rendezvous at Peekskill.

The service of General Schuyler in the northern department had been more solid than brilliant. Dissatisfied with his situation, and disgusted with the injustice * he supposed himself to experience, he had for some time meditated a resignation, and had been retained in the service only by the deep interest he felt in the struggle of his country for independence. So soon as his fears for Ticonderoga were removed by the partial opening of Lake Champlain, he waited

---

* When the command of the operating army was given to General Thomas in March 1776, the head quarters of General Schuyler had been fixed by congress at Albany, and that resolution remained in force. General Gates was now directed to repair to Ticonderoga and take command of the army; and Major General St. Clair was ordered to the same place to serve under him.

in person on congress for the purpose of adjusting his accounts, obtaining an inquiry into his
conduct, and supporting those necessary measures of defence in the north, which were suggested by his perfect knowledge of the country.
At his request, a committee, consisting of a
member from each state, was appointed to inquire into his conduct during the time he had
held a command in the army.   The arduous
services performed by this meritorious officer,
when investigated, were found so far to exceed
any estimate which had been made of them, that
congress deemed it essential to the public interest to prevail on him to retain his commission.
The resolution which fixed his head quarters at
Albany was repealed, and he was directed to
proceed forthwith to the northern department,
and to take the command of it.

On his arrival, he found the army of the north
not only too weak for the objects entrusted to
it, but badly supplied with arms, clothes, and
provisions.   From a spy who had been seized
near Onion River, he obtained information that
General Burgoyne was at Quebec, and was to
command the British forces in that department
so soon as they should march out of Canada.
That while Ticonderoga should be attacked by
the main army, Sir John Johnson, with a strong
body of British, Canadians, and Indians, was
to penetrate to the Mohawk by Oswego, and

CHAP. X

1777

An inquiry
into the
conduct of
General
Schuyler,
which
terminates
to his
honour.

May 22.

place himself between fort Stanwix and fort Edward.

General Schuyler was sensible of the danger which threatened him, and made every exertion to meet it. After completing his arrangements at Ticonderoga for sustaining a siege, he had proceeded to Albany, for the purpose of attending to his supplies, and of expediting the march of reinforcements, when he received intelligence from General St. Clair, who was entrusted with the defence of Ticonderoga, that Burgoyne had appeared before that place.

In the course of the preceding winter, a plan for penetrating to the Hudson, from Canada, by the way of the lakes, had been digested in the cabinet of London. General Burgoyne, who assisted in forming it, was entrusted with its execution, and was to lead a formidable army against Ticonderoga as soon as the season would permit. At the same time a smaller party under Colonel St. Leger, composed of Canadians, newly raised Americans, and a few Europeans, aided by a powerful body of Indians, was to march from Oswego, to enter the country by the way of the Mohawk, and to join the grand army on the Hudson.

Burgoyne reached Quebec as soon as it was practicable to sail up the St. Lawrence, and appeared in full force on the river Bouquet, on the western banks of lake Champlain, much earlier than the American general had supposed to be possible. At this place he met the Indians in a grand council, after which he gave them a war feast. Much of the cruelty afterwards perpetrated by the savages has been attributed to this unfortunate officer; but justice requires the admission that his speech was calculated rather to diminish than increase their habitual ferocity. He endeavoured to impress on them the distinction between enemies in the field, and the unarmed inhabitants, many of whom were friends; and, addressing himself to their avarice, promised rewards for prisoners, but none for scalps. It was perhaps fortunate for America, that, in some instances, peculiarly calculated to excite and interest the human feelings, these feeble restraints were disregarded.

After publishing a manifesto at Putnam River, designed to act on the hopes and fears of the people of the country through which he was to pass, he halted a few days at Crown Point, to make the necessary dispositions for investing Ticonderoga.

From Crown Point, the royal army advanced on both sides the lake, keeping up a communication between its divisions, by means of the fleet; and on the 1st of July encamped within four miles of the American works. A strong party was pushed forward to Three Mile Point; and the fleet anchored just beyond the range of the guns of the fort. The next day they took possession, without opposition, of the important post at Mount Hope, which commanded, in part, the lines on the northern side, and entirely cut off the communication with lake George.

The weakness of his garrison induced General St. Clair to give up this post without a struggle. Believing it to be impracticable to support it without hazarding a general action, he determined to concentrate his force about Ticonderoga and Mount Independence.

After taking possession of Mount Hope, the British lines were extended on the western side of Champlain, from the mountain quite to the lake, so as completely to inclose the garrison on that side. The German division under Major General Reidisel, which occupied the eastern shore of the lake, was encamped at Three Mile Point, and had pushed forward a detachment near the rivulet, which runs east of Mount Independence.

The besiegers laboured assiduously to bring up their artillery and complete their works. Sugar Hill, a rugged mountain standing at the confluence of the waters that unite at Ticonderoga, which overlooks the fortress and had been thought inaccessible, was examined; and the report being that the ascent, though extremely difficult, was practicable, the work was immediately commenced, and was pressed with so much vigour that the batteries might have opened next day. The garrison was not in a condition to check these operations.

The situation of St. Clair was now at its crisis. Only the ground between the Eastern run and the South River remained open; and this he was informed would be occupied the next day, so that the investment would be complete. The place must be immediately evacuated, or maintained at the hazard of losing the garrison when it should be no longer tenable.

Between these cruel alternations, General St. Clair did not hesitate to choose the first; but deeming it prudent to take the advice of a council of war, he convened the general officers, who unanimously advised the immediate evacuation of the fort.

Preparations for the retreat were instantly commenced. The invalids, the hospital, and such stores as could be moved in the course of the night, were put on board the batteaux, which proceeded under the guard of Colonel Long, up the South River to Skeensborough; and, before day on the morning of the 6th of July, the main body of the army directed its march to the same place.

In the hope of making considerable progress before his retreat should be discovered, General St. Clair had ordered the troops to observe the most profound silence, and, particularly, to set nothing on fire. These judicious orders were disobeyed; and, before the rear guard was in motion, the house which had been occupied by General De Fermoy was in flames. This served as a signal to the besiegers, who immediately entered the works. The main body of the retreating army was rapidly pursued by Generals Frazer and Reidisel, while General Burgoyne, in person, followed the detachment under Colonel Long.

The bridge, the boom, and those other works, the construction of which had employed the labour of ten months, were cut through by nine in the morning, so as to afford a passage for the Royal George and Inflexible frigates, as well as for the gun boats, which engaged the American galleys, about three in the afternoon, near the falls of Skeensborough.

In the mean time, three regiments had disembarked at some distance from the fort, with the intention of attacking it by land, and cutting off the retreat of the garrison, as well as that of the detachment in the boats and galleys. This manœuvre being discovered, the works and batteaux were set on fire, and the troops retired to fort Anne. On this occasion, the baggage of the army, and a great quantity of military stores, were either destroyed by the Americans, or taken by the British.

Knowing that he could save his army only by the rapidity of his march, General St. Clair reached Castletown, thirty miles from Ticonderoga, on the night succeeding the evacuation of the fort. The rear guard under Colonel Warner halted six miles short of that place. Having been augmented by those who from excessive fatigue had fallen out of the line of march, it amounted to rather more than one thousand men.

The next morning at five, they were overtaken and attacked by General Frazer with eight hundred and fifty men. The action was warm and well contested. In its commencement, two regiments of militia, which lay within two miles of Colonel Warner, were ordered to his assistance. Instead of obeying these orders, they consulted their own safety, and hastened to Castletown. Had these orders been executed, the corps which attacked Warner would probably have been cut to pieces. While the action was maintained with equal spirit on both sides, General Reidisel arrived with his division of Germans, and the Americans were routed.

July 7.

Colonel Warner attacked by General Frazer and obliged to retreat.

In this action, Colonel Francis, several other officers, and upwards of two hundred men were left dead on the field; and one colonel, seven captains, ten subalterns, and two hundred and ten privates were made prisoners. Near six hundred are supposed to have been wounded, many of whom must have perished in attempting to escape through the woods towards the inhabited country. The British state their own loss at thirty-five killed, among whom was one field officer, and one hundred and forty-four wounded, including two majors, and five inferior officers. It is scarcely credible, notwithstanding the difference in arms, that in a well contested action, the disparity in the killed could have been so considerable. It is the less probable, as the pursuit was not of long continuance.

To avoid that division of the British army which had proceeded up the North River, St. Clair changed his route; and directed his march to Rutland, to which place he ordered Warner also to retire. At Rutland he fell in with several soldiers who had been separated from their corps, and, two days afterwards, at Manchester, was joined by Warner with about ninety men. From this place he proceeded to fort Edward, where he met General Schuyler.

After taking possession of Skeensborough, Burgoyne had found it necessary to suspend the pursuit, and to give his army refreshment. The troops were in some disorder; distinct corps were intermingled, and his detachments were far apart from each other. He determined therefore to halt a few days at that place, in order to reassemble and arrange his army.

Colonel Long having been directed to defend fort Anne, the ninth regiment of British, under Lieutenant Colonel Hill, had been detached against that place. It being understood that the Americans were in some force, two other regiments, under Brigadier Powell, were ordered to support the first party. Before the arrival of this reinforcement, Colonel Long attacked the ninth regiment, and a sharp skirmish ensued, in which the British kept their ground, and the advantage was claimed by both parties. Hearing that a reinforcement was approaching, Long set fire to the works at fort Anne, and retired to fort Edward.

Colonel Long evacuates Fort Anne and retires to Fort Edward.

July 7.

At Stillwater, on his way to Ticonderoga, General Schuyler was informed of the evacuation of that place; and, on the same day, at Saratoga, of the loss of the stores at Skeensborough. He had heard nothing from General St. Clair; and was seriously apprehensive for that officer and his army, which, after the junction of Colonel Long, consisted of about fifteen hundred continental troops, and the same number of militia. They were dispirited by defeat, without tents, badly armed, and had lost great part of their stores and baggage. The country was generally much alarmed; and even the well affected discovered more inclination to take care of themselves than to join the army. In this gloomy state of things, no officer could have exerted more diligence and skill than were displayed by Schuyler. Having fixed his head quarters at fort Edward, he employed to the utmost advantage the short respite from action which Burgoyne unavoidably gave. The country between Skeensborough and fort Edward was almost entirely unsettled, was covered with thick woods, and of a surface extremely rough, and much intersected with creeks and morasses. Wood creek was navigable with batteaux as far as fort Anne; and military stores of every description might be transported up it. He obstructed its navigation by sinking numerous impediments in its course, broke up the bridges, and rendered the roads impassable. He was also indefatigable in driving the live stock out of the way, and in bringing from fort George to fort Edward, the ammunition and other military stores which had been deposited at that place. Still farther to delay the movements of the British, he posted Colonel Warner on their left flank, with instructions to raise the militia in that quarter. The hope was entertained, that the appearance of a respectable force, threatening the flank and rear of the invading army, would not only retard its advance, but would induce General Burgoyne to weaken it, in order to strengthen the garrison of Ticonderoga.

While thus endeavoring to obstruct the march of the enemy, Schuyler was not less attentive to the best means of strengthening his own army. Reinforcements of regular troops were earnestly solicited; the militia of New England and New York were required to take the field, and all his influence in the surrounding country was exerted to reanimate the people, and to prevent their defection from the American cause.

Proclamation
of Burgoyne
and counter-
proclamation
of Schuyler.

While at Skeensborough General Burgoyne issued a second proclamation* summoning the people of the adjacent country to send ten depu-

---

* Remem.

ties from each township to meet Colonel Skeene at Castletown, in order to deliberate on such measures as might still be adopted to save those who had not yet conformed to his first, and submitted to the royal authority. General Schuyler apprehending some effect from this paper, issued a counter proclamation, stating the insidious designs of the enemy. Warning the inhabitants, by the example of Jersey, of the danger to which their yielding to this seductive proposition would expose them, and giving them the most solemn assurances that all who should send deputies to this meeting, or in any manner aid the enemy, would be considered traitors, and should suffer the utmost rigour of the law.

The evacuation of Ticonderoga was a shock for which no part of the United States was prepared. Neither the strength of the invading army, nor of the garrison had been understood. When therefore intelligence was received that a place, on the fortifications of which much money and labour had been expended, which was considered as the key to the whole northwestern country, and supposed to contain a garrison nearly equal to the invading army, had been abandoned without a siege; that an immense train of artillery, and all the military stores, had either fallen into the hands of the enemy, or been destroyed; that the army, on its retreat, had been attacked, defeated, and dispersed; astonishment pervaded all ranks of men; and the conduct of the officers was universally condemned. Congress recalled all the generals of the department, and directed an inquiry into their conduct. Throughout New England especially, the most bitter aspersions were cast on them and General Schuyler, who, from some unknown cause, had never been viewed with favour in that part of the continent, was involved in the common charge of treachery, to which this accumulation of unlooked-for calamity was generally attributed by the mass of the people.

On the representations of General Washington, the recall of the officers was suspended, until he should be of opinion that the service would not suffer by the measure; and, on a full inquiry afterwards made into their conduct, they were acquitted of all blame.

In a letter of St. Clair to the Commander-in-chief, stating his motives for evacuating Ticonderoga, he represented the strength of his garrison, including nine hundred militia, who would consent to stay but a few days, at only three thousand effective rank and file, many of whom were without bayonets. The lines required ten thousand to man them properly. He also affirmed, that his supply of provisions was sufficient for only twenty days, and that the works on the Ticonderoga side were incomplete, with their flanks undefended. He justified his having failed to call in a larger reinforcement of militia, by the scarcity of provisions, the supply on hand not having been procured until General Schuyler had resumed the command in the department; and attributed his not having evacuated the place in time to preserve his army and stores, to the prevalent opinion that there was not a sufficient force in Canada to attempt so hardy an enterprise, and to his not being at liberty to adopt that measure but in the last necessity.

A court of inquiry justified his conduct, and he retained the confidence of the Commander-in-chief.

On learning the distressed state of the remnant of the army, General Washington made great exertions to repair its losses, and to reinforce it. The utmost industry was used to procure a supply of tents; artillery and ammunition were forwarded from Massachusetts; the remaining troops of that state were ordered to that department; and General Lincoln, who possessed, in a high degree, the confidence of the New England militia, was directed to raise and command them. General Arnold, so often distinguished for his gallantry in the field, was ordered to the northern army, in the hope that his presence and reputation might reanimate the troops; and Colonel Morgan, with his corps of riflemen, was detached on the same service. Through the present dark gloom, Washington discerned a ray of light, and already cherished the hope that much good might result from present evil. "The evacuation of Ticonderoga and

Mount Independence," said he in a letter of the 15th of July, to General Schuyler, "is an event of chagrin and surprise, not apprehended, nor within the compass of my reasoning. This stroke is severe indeed, and has distressed us much. But, notwithstanding, things at present wear a dark and gloomy aspect, I hope a spirited opposition will check the progress of General Burgoyne's arms, and that the confidence derived from success will hurry him into measures that will, in their consequences, be favourable to us. We should never despair. Our situation has before been unpromising, and has changed for the better. So, I trust, it will again. If new difficulties arise, we must only put forth new exertions, and proportion our efforts to the exigency of the times."

On receiving a letter from General Schuyler of the seventeenth, stating the divided situation of the British army, he seemed to anticipate the event which afterwards occurred, and to suggest the measure in which originated that torrent of misfortune with which Burgoyne was overwhelmed. "Though our affairs," he said in reply to this information, "have for some days past worn a dark and gloomy aspect, I yet look forward to a fortunate and happy change. I trust General Burgoyne's army will meet, sooner or later, an effectual check; and, as I suggested before, that the success he has met with will precipitate his ruin. From your accounts, he appears to be pursuing that line of conduct which, of all others, is most favourable to us. I mean acting in detachment. This conduct will certainly give room for enterprise on our part, and expose his parties to great hazard. Could we be so happy as to cut one of them off, though it should not exceed four, five, or six hundred men, it would inspirit the people, and do away much of their present anxiety. In such an event, they would lose sight of past misfortunes; and, urged at the same time by a regard for their own security, would fly to arms, and afford every aid in their power."

After allowing a short repose to his army, General Burgoyne proceeded with ardour to the remaining objects of the campaign. The toils and delays which must be encountered in reaching the Hudson were soon perceived. He found it necessary to open Wood creek, and to repair the roads and bridges which Schuyler had broken up. Such was the unavoidable delay of this difficult operation, that the army did not arrive on the Hudson, in the neighbourhood of fort Edward, till the fourteenth of July. At this place it was necessary again to halt, in order to bring artillery, provisions, batteaux, and other articles from fort George.

The time afforded by this delay had been employed by Schuyler to the utmost advantage. Some reinforcements of continental troops had arrived from Peekskill, and the militia had been

CHAP. X

1777

Burgoyne
approaches
Fort
Edward and
Schuyler
retires to
Saratoga.

From
thence to
Stillwater.

assembled; but his strength did not yet afford a reasonable prospect of success in a contest with the enemy opposed to him. On this account, as Burgoyne approached fort Edward, Schuyler retired over the Hudson to Saratoga, and soon afterwards to Stillwater, not far from the mouth of the Mohawk. At this place, General Lincoln, who had been detached to take command of the militia assembling at Manchester, was ordered to rejoin him, and he fortified his camp in the hope of being strong enough to defend it.

At Stillwater, information was obtained that Burgoyne had evacuated Castletown; so that the only communication with Ticonderoga, whence nearly all his supplies were drawn, was through Lake George; and that the garrison of that important place had been reduced to three hundred men. In consequence of this intelligence, the orders to General Lincoln were countermanded, and he was directed with the militia of Massachusetts, New Hampshire, and of the Grants, making, as was understood, a total of between two and three thousand men, to place himself in the rear of the British army, and cut off its communication with the lakes. Here too he was informed that Colonel St. Leger, with a large body of Indians, in addition to his regulars, had penetrated from Oswego, by the way of the Oneida lake and Wood creek, to the Mohawk, where he had laid siege to fort Schuyler, and had totally defeated General Herkimer, who had

raised the militia of Tryon county, in order to relieve the fort. The importance of protecting the
inhabitants from the savages, and of preventing
a junction between St. Leger and Burgoyne, and
the consequent loss of the country on the Mohawk, determined Schuyler, weak as he was, to
detach Major General Arnold with three continental regiments to raise the siege. The army
was so enfeebled by this measure, that its removal to a place of greater security became
necessary, and it was withdrawn to some islands
in the confluence of the Hudson and the Mohawk, where the camp was deemed more defensible. Burgoyne had now marched down the
east side of the Hudson, and his advanced parties had crossed the river, and occupied the
ground at Saratoga.

On the 3d of August, after a message vaunting
of his strength, and demanding a surrender,
which was answered by a declaration that the
fort would be defended to the last extremity, St.
Leger invested fort Schuyler. The garrison
amounted to six hundred men, all continental
troops, who were commanded by Colonel Gansevoort. The besieging army rather exceeded fifteen hundred, of whom from six to nine hundred
were Indians.

On the approach of the enemy, General Herkimer, who commanded the militia of Tryon
county, assembled them in considerable numbers, and gave information to the garrison, about

August 15.

St. Leger
invests
Fort
Schuyler.

eleven in the morning of the sixth, of his intention to force a passage that day through the besieging army. Gansevoort determined to favour the execution of this design by a vigorous sortie; and upwards of two hundred men, to be commanded by Lieutenant Colonel Willet, were drawn out for that purpose.

Unfortunately St. Leger received information the preceding day of Herkimer's approach, and, early in the morning, placed a strong party, composed of regulars and Indians, in ambuscade on the road along which he was to march. His first notice of it was given by a heavy discharge of small arms, which was followed by a furious attack from the Indians with their tomahawks. He defended himself with resolution; but was defeated with great slaughter. The general and several of the field officers were wounded; and many others, among whom were several persons of distinction, were killed or taken prisoners. The loss was estimated at four hundred men. The destruction was prevented from being still more complete, by the very timely sortie made by Lieutenant Colonel Willet, which checked the pursuit, and recalled those engaged in it to the defence of their own camp.

As soon as Gansevoort understood that Herkimer was advancing, the sortie which he had planned was made. Lieutenant Colonel Willet fell on the camp of the besiegers, and routed them at the first onset. After driving them, some into the woods, and others over the river, he returned to the fort without the loss of a man.

Burgoyne had received early intimation of the arrival of St. Leger before fort Schuyler; and was aware of the advantage to be derived from an immediate and rapid movement down the Hudson. But the obstacles to his progress multiplied daily, and each step produced new embarrassments. Not more than one-third of the horses expected from Canada had arrived; and Schuyler had been active in removing the draft cattle of the country. With unremitting exertion, he had been able to transport from fort George to the Hudson, a distance of eighteen miles, only twelve batteaux, and provisions for four days in advance. The defectiveness of his means to feed his army until it should reach the abundant country below him, presented an impediment to his farther progress, not readily to be surmounted. The difficulty of drawing supplies from fort George would increase every day with the increasing distance; and the communications, already endangered by a considerable body of militia assembling at White Creek, could be secured only by larger detachments from his army than he was in a condition to make. These were strong inducements to attempt some other mode of supply.

It was well known that large magazines of provisions for the use of the American army were collected at Bennington, which place was generally guarded by militia, whose numbers varied from day to day. The possession of these magazines would enable him to prosecute his ulterior plans without relying for supplies from Lake George; and he determined to seize them.

To try the affections of the country, to complete a corps of loyalists, and to mount Reidisel's dragoons, were subordinate objects of the expedition.* Lieutenant Colonel Baum with five hundred Europeans, and a body of American loyalists, was detached on this service.

Colonel Baum is detached to seize the magazines at Bennington.

To facilitate the enterprise, and be ready to take advantage of its success, Burgoyne moved down the east side of the Hudson, and threw a bridge of rafts over that river for the passage of his van, which took post at Saratoga. At the same time Lieutenant Colonel Brechman, with his corps, was advanced to Batten Hill, in order, if necessary, to support Colonel Baum.*

On approaching Bennington, Baum discovered that he should have to encounter a much more considerable force than had been suspected. The New Hampshire militia, commanded by General Starke, had reached that place on their way to camp; and, uniting with Colonel Warner, made in the whole about two thousand men.

Perceiving his danger, Baum halted about four miles from Bennington, and despatched an

* Letter of Burgoyne.

express for a reinforcement. In the mean time, he strengthened his position by intrenchments.

Lieutenant Colonel Brechman was immediately ordered to his assistance; but, such was the state of the roads that, though the distance was only twenty-four miles, and his march was pressed unremittingly from eight in the morning of the 15th, he did not reach the ground on which Baum had encamped, until four in the afternoon of the next day.†

In the mean time, General Starke determined to attack him in his intrenchments. So confident were the provincials belonging to this party, of the attachment of the country to the royal cause, that the American troops, while making their dispositions for the attack, were mistaken for armed friends coming to join them. On discovering his error, Baum prepared for the contest, and made a gallant defence. His works however were carried by storm, and great part of his detachment killed, or taken prisoners. A few escaped into the woods, and saved themselves by flight.

Is attacked in his intrenchments by General Starke, and entirely routed.

Brechman arrived during the pursuit, and obtained from the fugitives, the first intelligence of the disaster which had befallen them. He immediately attacked the parties of militia who were engaged in the pursuit, and gained some advantage over them. Fortunately for the Americans, Colonel Warner‡ came up at this critical juncture with his continental regiment,

Brechman advances to Baum's aid, is attacked by Colonel Warner, and defeated.

† Ibid.   ‡ Gordon.

and restored, and continued the action, until the main body of the militia re-assembled, and came to support him. Brechman in turn was compelled to retire; but he maintained the engagement until dark, when, abandoning his artillery and baggage, he saved his party under cover of the night.

One thousand stand of arms, and nine hundred swords were taken in this battle. General Burgoyne represented his loss in men at about four hundred; but thirty-two officers, and five hundred and sixty-four privates, including Canadians and loyalists, were made prisoners. The number of the dead was not ascertained, because the action with Brechman had been fought in the woods, and been continued for several miles.

The British general therefore must have included in his estimate of loss, only his European troops.

This important success was soon followed by another of equal influence on the fate of the campaign.

Fort Schuyler had been fortified with more skill, and was defended with more courage, than St. Leger had expected. His artillery made no impression on its walls; and his Indians, who were much better pleased with obtaining plunder and scalps, than besieging fortresses, became intractable, and manifested great disgust with the service. In this temper, they understood that Arnold was advancing with a large body of continental troops; and, soon afterwards were told that Burgoyne and his army had been totally defeated; a report probably founded on the affair at Bennington. Unwilling to share the misfortune of their friends, they manifested a determination not to await the arrival of Arnold. The efforts of St. Leger to detain them being ineffectual, many of them decamped immediately, and the rest threatened to follow.

The time for deliberation was past. The camp was broken up with indications of excessive alarm. The tents were left standing; and the artillery, with great part of the baggage, ammunition, and provisions, fell into the hands of the Americans. The retreating army was pursued by a detachment from the garrison; and it was stated by deserters, that the Indians plundered the remaining baggage of the officers, and massacred such soldiers as could not keep up with the line of march. St. Leger returned to Montreal, whence he proceeded to Ticonderoga, with the intention of joining General Burgoyne by that route.

St. Leger abandons the siege of Fort Schuyler, and retreats to Ticonderoga.

The decisive victory at Bennington, and the retreat of St. Leger from fort Schuyler, however important in themselves, were still more so in their consequences. An army, which had spread terror and dismay in every direction, which had, previously, experienced no reverse of fortune, was considered as already beaten; and the opinion became common, that the appearance of the great body of the people in arms, would secure the emancipation of their country. It was too an advantage of no inconsiderable importance resulting from this change of public opinion, that the disaffected became timid, and the wavering who, had the torrent of success continued, would have made a merit of contributing their aid to the victor, were no longer disposed to put themselves and their fortunes in hazard, to support an army whose fate was so uncertain.

The barbarities which had been perpetrated by the Indians belonging to the invading armies, excited still more resentment than terror. As the prospect of revenge began to open, their effect became the more apparent; and their influence on the royal cause was the more sensibly felt because they had been indiscriminate.

The murder
of Miss
M'Crea.

The murder of Miss M'Crea passed through all the papers of the continent: and the story, being retouched by the hand of more than one master, excited a peculiar degree of sensibility.* But there were other causes of still greater influence in producing the events which afterwards took place. The last reinforcements of continental troops arrived in camp about this time, and added both courage and strength to the army. The harvest, which had detained the northern militia upon their farms, was over; and General Schuyler, whose continued and eminent services had not exempted him from the imputa-

* See note No. IX. at the end of the volume.

tion of being a traitor, was succeeded by General Gates, who possessed a large share of the public confidence.

When Schuyler was directed by congress to resume the command of the northern department, Gates withdrew himself from it. When the resolution passed recalling the general officers who had served in that department, General Washington was requested to name a successor to Schuyler. On his expressing a wish to decline this nomination, and representing the inconvenience of removing all the general officers, Gates was again directed to repair thither and take the command, and their resolution to recall the brigadiers was suspended until the Commander-in-chief should be of opinion that it might be carried into effect with safety.

General Gates takes command of the Northern Army.

Schuyler retained the command until the arrival of Gates, which was on the 19th of August, and continued his exertions to restore the affairs of the department, though he felt acutely the disgrace of being recalled in this critical and interesting state of the campaign. "It is," said he, in a letter to the Commander-in-chief, "matter of extreme chagrin to me to be deprived of the command at a time when, soon if ever, we shall probably be enabled to face the enemy; when we are on the point of taking ground† where they must attack to a disadvantage, should our force be inadequate to facing them in the

---

† The islands in the mouth of the Mohawk.

field; when an opportunity will, in all probability, occur, in which I might evince that I am not what congress have too plainly insinuated by taking the command from me."

If error be attributable to the evacuation of Ticonderoga, no portion of it was committed by Schuyler. His removal from the command was probably severe and unjust as respected himself; but perhaps wise as repected America. The frontier towards the lakes was to be defended by the troops of New England; and, however unfounded their prejudices against him might be, it was prudent to consult them.

Notwithstanding the difficulties which multiplied around him, Burgoyne remained steady to his purpose. The disasters at Bennington and on the Mohawk produced no disposition to abandon the enterprise and save his army.

It had now become necessary to recur to the slow and toilsome mode of obtaining supplies from fort George. Having, with persevering labour, collected provision for thirty days in advance, he crossed the Hudson on the 13th and

14th of September, and encamped on the heights and plains of Saratoga, with a determination to decide the fate of the expedition in a general engagement.

General Gates, having been joined by all the continental troops destined for the northern department, and reinforced by large bodies of militia, had moved from his camp in the islands, and advanced to the neighbourhood of Stillwater.

The bridges between the two armies having been broken down, the roads being excessively bad, and the country covered with wood, the progress of the British army down the river was slow. On the night of the 17th, Burgoyne encamped within four miles of the American army, and the next day was employed in repairing the bridges between the two camps.* In the morning of the 19th he advanced in full force towards the American left. Morgan was immediately detached with his corps to observe the enemy, and to harass his front and flanks. He fell in with a picket in front of the right wing, which he attacked with vivacity, and drove in upon the main body. Pursuing with too much ardour, he was met in considerable force, and, after a severe encounter, was compelled, in turn, to retire in some disorder. Two regiments being advanced to his assistance, his corps was rallied, and the action became more general. The Americans were formed in a wood, with an open field in front, and invariably repulsed the British corps which attacked them; but when they pursued those corps to the main body, they were in turn driven back to their first ground. Reinforcements were continually brought up, and about four in the afternoon, upwards of three thousand

He attacks Gates at Stillwater.

September 19.

---

* Letter of Burgoyne.

American troops † were closely engaged with the whole right wing of the British army commanded by General Burgoyne in person. The conflict was extremely severe, and only terminated with the day. At dark, the Americans retired to their camp, and the British, who had found great difficulty in maintaining their ground, lay all night on their arms near the field of battle.

In this action the killed and wounded on the part of the Americans were between three and four hundred. Among the former were Colonels Coburn and Adams, and several other valuable officers. The British loss has been estimated at rather more than five hundred men.

Each army claimed the victory; and each believed itself to have beaten near the whole of the hostile army with only a part of its own force. The advantage, however, taking all circumstances into consideration, was decidedly with the Americans. In a conflict which nearly consumed the day, they found themselves at least equal to their antagonists. In every quarter they had acted on the offensive; and, after an encounter for several hours, had not lost an inch of ground. They had not been driven from the field, but had retired from it at the close of day, to the camp from which they had marched to battle. Their object, which was to check the

---

† The accounts of the day stated that the Americans were commanded by General Arnold, but General Wilkinson says that no general officer was in the field.

advancing enemy, had been obtained; while that
of the British general had failed. In the actual
state of things, to fight without being beaten
was, on their part, victory; while, on the part
of the British, to fight without a decisive victory, was defeat. The Indians, who found
themselves beaten in the woods by Morgan, and
restrained from scalping and plundering the unarmed by Burgoyne, who saw before them the
prospect of hard fighting without profit, grew
tired of the service, and deserted in great numbers. The Canadians and Provincials were not
much more faithful; and Burgoyne soon perceived that his hopes must rest almost entirely on
his European troops.

With reason, therefore, this action was celebrated throughout the United States as a victory, and considered as the precursor of the total
ruin of the invading army. The utmost exultation was displayed, and the militia were stimu-
dated to fly to arms, and complete the work
so happily begun.

General Lincoln, in conformity with directions which have been stated, had assembled a
considerable body of New England militia in
the rear of Burgoyne, from which he drew three
parties of about five hundred men each. One of
these was detached under the command of Colonel Brown, to the north end of Lake George,
principally to relieve a number of prisoners who
were confined there, but with orders to push his

success, should he be fortunate, as far as prudence would admit. Colonel Johnson, at the head of another party, marched towards Mount Independence, and Colonel Woodbury, with a third, was detached to Skeensborough to cover the retreat of both the others. With the residue, Lincoln proceeded to the camp of Gates.

Colonel Brown, after marching all night, arrived, at the break of day, on the north end of the lake, where he found a small post which he carried without opposition. The surprise was complete; and he took possession of Mount Defiance, Mount Hope, the landing place, and about two hundred batteaux. With the loss of only three killed and five wounded, he liberated one hundred American prisoners, and captured two hundred and ninety-three of the enemy. This success was joyfully proclaimed through the northern states. It was believed confidently that Ticonderoga and Mount Independence were recovered; and the militia were exhorted, by joining their brethren in the army, to insure that event if it had not already happened.

The attempt on those places however failed. The garrison repulsed the assailants; who, after a few days, abandoned the siege. On their return through Lake George in the vessels they had captured, the militia made an attack on Diamond Island, the depot of all the stores collected at the north end of the lake. Being again repulsed, they destroyed the vessels they had taken, and returned to their former station.*

The day after the battle of Stillwater, General Burgoyne took a position almost within cannon shot of the American camp, fortified his right, and extended his left to the river. Directly after taking this ground he received a letter from Sir Henry Clinton, informing him that he should attack fort Montgomery about the 20th of September. The messenger returned with information that Burgoyne was in extreme difficulty, and would endeavour to wait for aid until the 12th of October.†

Both armies retained their position until the 7th of October. Burgoyne, in the hope of being relieved by Sir Henry Clinton; and Gates, in the confidence of growing stronger every day.

Having received no farther intelligence from Sir Henry, and being reduced to the necessity of diminishing the ration issued to his soldiers, the British general determined to make one more trial of strength with his adversary. In execution of this determination, he drew out on his right fifteen hundred choice troops, whom he commanded in person, assisted by Generals Philips, Reidisel, and Frazer.

The right wing was formed within three-quarters of a mile of the left of the American camp; and a corps of rangers, Indians, and provincials, was pushed on through secret paths, to

---

* Remem. † Letter of Burgoyne.

show themselves in its rear, and excite alarm in that quarter.*

These movements were perceived by General Gates, who determined to attack their left, and, at the same time, to fall on their right flank. Poor's brigade, and some regiments from New Hampshire, were ordered to meet them in front; while Morgan with his rifle corps made a circuit unperceived, and seized a very advantageous height covered with wood on their right. As soon as it was supposed that Morgan had gained the ground he intended to occupy, the attack was made in front and on the left, in great force. At this critical moment Morgan poured in a deadly and incessant fire on the front and right flank.

While the British right wing was thus closely pressed in front, and on its flank, a distinct division of the American troops was ordered to intercept its retreat to camp, and to separate it from the residue of the army. Burgoyne perceived the danger of his situation, and ordered the light infantry under General Frazer, with part of the 24th regiment, to form a second line, in order to cover the light infantry of the right, and secure a retreat. While this movement was in progress, the left of the British right was forced from its ground, and the light infantry was ordered to its aid. In the attempt to execute this

* Remem.

order, they were attacked by the rifle corps, with great effect; and Frazer was mortally wounded. Overpowered by numbers, and pressed on all sides by a superior weight of fire, Burgoyne, with great difficulty, and with the loss of his field pieces, and great part of his artillery corps, regained his camp. The Americans followed close in his rear; and assaulted his works throughout their whole extent. Towards the close of day, the intrenchments were forced on their right; and General Arnold, with a few men, actually entered their works; but his horse being killed under him, and himself wounded, the troops were forced out of them; and it being nearly dark, they desisted from the assault. The left of Arnold's division was still more successful. Jackson's regiment of Massachusetts, then led by Lieutenant Colonel Brooks, turned the right of the encampment, and stormed the works occupied by the German reserve. Lieutenant Colonel Brechman who commanded in them was killed, and the works were carried. The orders given by Burgoyne to recover them were not executed; and Brooks maintained the ground he had gained.

Darkness put an end to the action; and the Americans lay all night with their arms in their hands, about half a mile from the British lines, ready to renew the assault with the return of day. The advantage they had gained was decisive. They had taken several pieces of artil-

lery, killed a great number of men, made upwards of two hundred prisoners, among whom
were several officers of distinction, and had penetrated the lines in a part which exposed the
whole to considerable danger.

Unwilling to risk the events of the next day
on the same ground, Burgoyne changed his position in the course of the night, and drew his
whole army into a strong camp on the river
heights, extending his right up the river. This
movement extricated him from the danger of
being attacked the ensuing morning by an enemy
already in possession of part of his works.

General Gates perceived the strength of this
position, and was not disposed to hazard an
assault. Aware of the critical situation of his
adversary, he detached a party higher up the
Hudson for the purpose of intercepting the British army on its retreat, while strong corps were
posted on the other side of the river to guard its
passage.

October 8.

Retreats to
Saratoga.

This movement compelled Burgoyne again to
change his position, and to retire to Saratoga.
About nine at night the retreat was commenced,
and was effected with the loss of his hospital,
containing about three hundred sick, and of several batteaux laden with provision and baggage.
On reaching the ground to be occupied, he found
a strong corps already intrenched on the opposite
side of the river, prepared to dispute its passage.

From Saratoga, Burgoyne detached a company of artificers, under a strong escort, to repair the roads and bridges towards fort Edward. Scarcely had this detachment moved, when the Americans appeared in force on the heights south of Saratoga creek, and made dispositions which excited the apprehension of a design to cross it and attack his camp. The Europeans escorting the artificers were recalled, and a provincial corps, employed in the same service, being attacked by a small party, ran away and left the workmen to shift for themselves.

No hope of repairing the roads remaining, it became impossible to move the baggage and artillery.

The British army was now almost completely environed by a superior force. No means remained of extricating itself from difficulties and dangers which were continually increasing, but fording a river, on the opposite bank of which a formidable body of troops was already posted; and then escaping to fort George, through roads impassable by artillery or wagons, while its rear was closely pressed by a victorious enemy.*

---

* Mr. Gordon, in his history of the war, states himself to have received from General Glover an anecdote, showing, that all these advantages were on the point of being exposed to imminent hazard. "On the morning of the eleventh, Gates called the general officers together, and informed them of his having received certain intelligence, which might be depended upon, that the main body of Burgoyne's army was marched off for fort Edward with what they could take; and that the rear guard only was left in the camp, who, after awhile, were to push off as fast as possible, leaving the heavy baggage behind. On this it was concluded to ad-

A council of general officers called to deliberate on their situation, took the bold resolution
to abandon every thing but their arms and such
provisions as the soldiers could carry; and, by a
forced march in the night up the river, to extricate themselves from the American army; and
crossing at fort Edward, or at a ford above it, to
press on to fort George.

Gates had foreseen this movement, and had
prepared for it. In addition to placing strong
guards at the fords of the Hudson, he had
formed an intrenched camp on the high grounds
between fort Edward and fort George. The
scouts sent to examine the route returned with
this information, and the plan was abandoned as
impracticable.

Nothing could be more hopeless than the condition of the British army, or more desperate
than that of their general, as described by him-

---

vance and attack the camp in half an hour. The officers
repaired immediately to their respective commands. General
Nixon's being the eldest brigade, crossed the Saratoga creek
first. Unknown to the Americans, Burgoyne had a line
formed behind a parcel of brush-wood, to support the park
of artillery where the attack was to be made. General
Glover was upon the point of following Nixon. Just as he
entered the water, he saw a British soldier making across,
whom he called and examined." This soldier was a deserter, and communicated the very important fact that the
whole British army were in their encampment. Nixon was
immediately stopped: and the intelligence conveyed to Gates,
who countermanded his orders for the assault, and called
back his troops, not without sustaining some loss from the
British artillery.

Gordon is confirmed by General Wilkinson, who was adjutant general in the American army. The narrative of the
general varies from that of Gordon only in minor circumstances.

self. In his letter to Lord George Germain, secretary of state for American affairs, he says, "A series of hard toil, incessant effort, stubborn action, until disabled in the collateral branches of the army by the total defection of the Indians; the desertion, or timidity of the Canadians and provincials, some individuals excepted; disappointed in the last hope of any co-operation from other armies; the regular troops reduced by losses from the best parts, to three thousand five hundred fighting men, not two thousand of which were British; only three days provisions, upon short allowance, in store; invested by an army of sixteen thousand men; and no appearance of retreat remaining; I called into council all the generals, field officers, and captains commanding corps, and by their unanimous concurrence and advice, I was induced to open a treaty with Major General Gates."

A treaty was opened with a general proposition, stating the willingness of the British general to spare the further effusion of blood, provided a negotiation could be effected on honourable terms.

This proposition was answered by a demand that the whole army should ground their arms in their encampment, and surrender themselves prisoners of war. This demand was instantly rejected, with a declaration that if General Gates designed to insist on it, the negotiation must immediately break off, and hostilities re-

CHAP. X

1777

Surrender
of the
army under
Burgoyne.

October 17.

commence. On receiving this decided answer, Gates receded from the rigorous terms at first proposed; and a convention was signed, in which it was agreed that the British army, after marching out of their encampment with all the honours of war, should lay down their arms, and not serve against the United States till exchanged. They were not to be detained in captivity, but to be permitted to embark for England.

The situation of the armies considered,* these terms were highly honourable to the British general, and favourable to his nation. They were probably more advantageous than would have been granted by General Gates, had he entertained no apprehension from Sir Henry Clinton, who was, at length, making the promised diversion on the North River, up which he had penetrated as far as Æsopus.

The drafts made from Peekskill for both armies had left that post in a situation to require the aid of militia for its security. The requisitions of General Putnam were complied with; but the attack upon them being delayed, the militia, who were anxious to seed their farms, became impatient; many deserted; and General Putnam was induced to discharge the residue.

---

* The American army consisted of nine thousand and ninety-three continental troops. The number of the militia fluctuated; but amounted, at the signature of the convention, to four thousand one hundred and twenty-nine. The sick exceeded two thousand five hundred men.

Governor Clinton immediately ordered out half the militia of New York, with assurances that they should be relieved in one month by the other half. This order was executed so slowly that the forts were carried before the militia were in the field.

Great pains had been taken, and much labour employed, to render this position, which is naturally strong, still more secure. The principal defences were forts Montgomery and Clinton. They had been constructed on the western bank of the Hudson, on very high ground, extremely difficult of access, and were separated from each other by a small creek which runs from the mountains into the river. These forts were too much elevated to be battered from the water, and the hills on which they stood were too steep to be ascended by troops landing at the foot of them. The mountains, which commence five or six miles below them, are so high and rugged, the defiles, through which the roads leading to them pass, so narrow, and so commanded by the heights on both sides, that the approaches to them are extremely difficult and dangerous.

To prevent ships from passing the forts, chevaux-de-frise had been sunk in the river, and a boom extended from bank to bank, which was covered with immense chains stretched at some distance in its front. These works were defended by the guns of the forts, and by a frigate and galleys stationed above them, capable of opposing with an equal fire in front any force which might attack them by water from below.

Fort Independence is four or five miles below forts Montgomery and Clinton, and on the opposite side of the river, on a high point of land; and fort Constitution is rather more than six miles above them, on an island near the eastern shore. Peekskill, the general head quarters of the officer commanding at the station, is just below fort Independence, and on the same side of the river. The garrisons had been reduced to about six hundred men; and the whole force under General Putnam did not much exceed two thousand. Yet this force, though far inferior to that which General Washington had ordered to be retained at the station, was, if properly applied, more than competent to the defence of the forts against any numbers which could be spared from New York. To insure success to the enterprise, it was necessary to draw the attention of Putnam from the real object, and to storm the works before the garrisons could be aided by his army. This Sir Henry Clinton accomplished.

Between three and four thousand men embarked at New York, and landed on the 5th of October at Verplank's Point, on the east side of the Hudson, a short distance below Peekskill, upon which General Putnam retired to the heights in his rear. On the evening of the same day, a part of these troops re-embarked, and the fleet moved up the river to Peekskill Neck, in order to mask King's ferry, which was below them. The next morning, at break of day, the troops destined for the enterprise, landed on the west side of Stony Point, and commenced their march through the mountains, into the rear of forts Clinton and Montgomery.* This disembarkation was observed; but the morning was so foggy that the numbers could not be distinguished; and a large fire, which was afterwards perceived at the landing place, suggested the idea that the sole object of the party on shore was the burning of some store houses. In the mean time, the manœuvres of the vessels, and the appearance of a small detachment left at Verplank's Point, persuaded General Putnam that the meditated attack was on fort Independence.

His whole attention was directed to this object; and the real designs of the enemy were not suspected, until a heavy firing from the other side of the river announced the assault on forts Clinton and Montgomery. Five hundred men were instantly detached to reinforce the garrisons of those places; but before this detachment could cross the river the forts were in possession of the British.

Having left a battalion at the pass of Thunderhill, to keep up a communication, Sir Henry Clinton had formed his army into two divisions; one of which consisting of nine hundred men,

Forts Montgomery and Clinton taken by the British.

---

* Letter of Sir Henry Clinton.

commanded by Lieutenant Colonel Campbell, made a circuit by the forest of Deane, in order to fall on the back of fort Montgomery; while the other, consisting of twelve hundred men, commanded by General Vaughan, and accompanied by Sir Henry Clinton in person, advanced slowly against fort Clinton.*

Both posts were assaulted about five in the afternoon. The works were defended with resolution, and were maintained until dark, when, the lines being too extensive to be completely manned, the assailants entered them in different places. The defence being no longer possible, some of the garrison were made prisoners, while their better knowledge of the country enabled others to escape. Governor Clinton passed the river in a boat, and General James Clinton, though wounded in the thigh by a bayonet, also made his escape. Lieutenant Colonels Livingston and Bruyn, and Majors Hamilton and Logan were among the prisoners. The loss sustained by the garrisons was about two hundred and fifty men. That of the assailants, was stated by Sir H. Clinton, at less than two hundred. Among the killed were Lieutenant Colonel Campbell, and two other field officers.

As the boom and chains drawn across the river could no longer be defended, the continental frigates and galleys lying above them were burnt, to prevent their falling into the hands

* Letter of Sir Henry Clinton.

of the enemy. Fort Independence and fort Constitution were evacuated the next day, and Putnam retreated to Fishkill. General Vaughan, after burning Continental village, where stores to a considerable amount had been deposited, proceeded, at the head of a strong detachment, up the river to Æsopus, which he also destroyed.†

Peekskill, together with Forts Independence and Constitution evacuated by the Americans.

October 8.

General Putnam, whose army had been augmented by reinforcements of militia to six thousand men, detached General Parsons with two thousand, to repossess himself of Peekskill, and of the passes in the highlands; while, with the residue, he watched the progress of the enemy up the river. The want of heavy artillery prevented his annoying their ships in the Hudson.

On the capitulation of Burgoyne, near five thousand men had been detached by Gates to his aid. Before their arrival, General Vaughan had returned to New York, whence a reinforcement to General Howe was then about to sail.

Great as was the injury sustained by the United States from this enterprise, Great Britain derived from it no solid advantage. It was undertaken at too late a period to save Burgoyne; and though the passes in the highlands were acquired, they could not be retained. The

† Intelligence of the success of Sir Henry Clinton on the North River was received by General Burgoyne, in the night after the convention at Saratoga had been agreed upon, but before the articles had been signed and executed. The British general had serious thoughts of breaking off the treaty.

British had reduced to ashes every village, and almost every house within their power; but this wanton and useless destruction served to irritate, without tending to subdue. A keenness was given to the resentment of the injured, which outlasted the contest between the two nations.

The army which surrendered at Saratoga exceeded five thousand men. On marching from Ticonderoga, it was estimated at nine thousand. In addition to this great military force, the British lost, and the Americans acquired, a fine train of artillery, seven thousand stand of excellent arms, clothing for seven thousand recruits, with tents, and other military stores, to a considerable amount.

The thanks of congress were voted to General Gates and his army; and a medal of gold, in commemoration of this great event, was ordered to be struck, and presented to him by the President, in the name of the United States. Colonel Wilkinson, his Adjutant General, whom he strongly recommended, was appointed Brigadier General by brevet.

In the opinion that the British would not immediately abandon the passes in the highlands, congress ordered Putnam to join General Washington with a reinforcement not exceeding two thousand five hundred men, and directed Gates to take command of the army on the Hudson, with unlimited powers to call for aids of

The Saratoga Battle Monument

Schuylerville, New York

"Nothing bespeaks more strongly the consummate tragedy of Benedict Arnold's career than the Battle Monument which rises on the banks of the Hudson to commemorate the victory of Saratoga. In the square shaft are four high Gothic arches, and in these are placed heroic statues of the generals who won the victory. Horatio Gates, unworthy though he was, stands there in bronze. The gallant Schuyler, the intrepid Morgan, honor the other two. But where is he whose valor turned back the advancing Saint-Leger? whose prompt decision saved the Continental position at Bemis Heights? whose military genius truly gained the day? A vacant niche—empty as England's rewards, void as his own life—speaks more eloquently than words, more strongly than condemnation, more pitifully than tears, of a mighty career blighted by treason and hurled into the bottomless pit of despair. This is America's way of honoring Arnold in his dishonor."

—From The Real America in Romance.

The Saratoga Battle Monument

Schuylerville, New York

"*Nothing bespeaks more strongly the consummate tragedy of Benedict Arnold's career than the Battle Monument which rises on the banks of the Hudson to commemorate the victory of Saratoga. In the square shaft are four high Gothic arches, and in these are placed heroic statues of the generals who won the victory. Horatio Gates, unworthy though he was, stands there in bronze. The gallant Schuyler, the intrepid Morgan, honor the other two. But where is he whose valor turned back the advancing Saint-Leger? whose prompt decision saved the Continental position at Bemis Heights? whose military genius truly gained the day? A vacant niche—empty as England's rewards, void as his own life—speaks more eloquently than words, more strongly than condemnation, more pitifully than tears, of a mighty career blighted by treason and hurled into the bottomless pit of despair. This is America's way of honoring Arnold in his dishonor.*"

—From The Real America in Romance.

militia from the New England States, as well as from New York and New Jersey.

A proposition to authorize the Commander-in-chief, after consulting with General Gates and Governor Clinton, to increase the detachment designed to strengthen his army, if he should then be of opinion that it might be done without endangering the objects to be accomplished by Gates, was seriously opposed. An attempt was made to amend this proposition so as to make the increase of the reinforcement to depend on the assent of Gates and Clinton; but this amendment was lost by a considerable majority, and the original resolution was carried. These proceedings were attended with no other consequences than to excite some degree of attention to the state of parties.

Soon after the capitulation of Burgoyne, Ticonderoga and Mount Independence were evacuated, and the garrison retired to Isle Aux Noix, and St. Johns.

Ticonderoga and Mount Independence evacuated by the enemy.

The effect produced by this event on the British cabinet and nation was great and immediate. It seemed to remove the delusive hopes of conquest with which they had been flattered, and suddenly to display the mass of resistance which must yet be encountered. Previous to the reception of this disastrous intelligence, the employment of savages in the war had been the subject of severe animadversion. Parliament was assembled on the 20th of November; and, as usual, addresses were proposed in answer to the speech from the throne, entirely approving the conduct of the administration. In the House of Lords, the Earl of Chatham moved to amend the address by introducing a clause recommending to his Majesty, an immediate cessation of hostilities, and the commencement of a treaty of conciliation, "to restore peace and liberty to America, strength and happiness to England, security and permanent prosperity to both countries." In the course of the very animated observations made by this extraordinary man in support of his motion, he said,* "But, my Lords, who is the man that, in addition to the disgraces and mischiefs of war, has dared to authorize and associate to our arms the tomahawk and scalping-knife of the savage? to call into civilized alliance the wild and inhuman inhabitant of the woods? to delegate to the merciless Indian the defence of disputed rights, and to wage the horrors of his barbarous war against our brethren? My Lords, these enormities cry aloud for redress and punishment. Unless thoroughly done away they will be a stain on the national character. It is not the least of our national misfortunes that the strength and character of our army are thus impaired. Familiarized to the horrid scenes of savage cruelty, it can no longer boast of the noble and generous principles which dignify a soldier. No longer sym-

* Life of Chatham.—Belsham.

pathize with the dignity of the royal banner, nor feel the pride, pomp, and circumstance of glorious war that makes ambition virtue. What makes ambition virtue? the sense of honour. But is this sense of honour consistent with the spirit of plunder, or the practice of murder? Can it flow from mercenary motives? or can it prompt to cruel deeds?" †

The conduct of administration, however, received the full approbation of large majorities; but the triumph these victories in Parliament afforded them was of short duration. The disastrous issue of an expedition from which the most sanguine expectations had been formed, was soon known, and the mortification it produced was extreme. A reluctant confession of the calamity was made by the minister, and a desire to restore peace on any terms consistent with the integrity of the empire found its way into the cabinet.

---

† See note No. X. at the end of the volume.

CHAPTER XI.

Defects in the Commissary department....Distress of the
army at Valley Forge....The army subsisted by im-
pressments....Combination in congress against General Washington....Correspondence between him and
General Gates....Distress of the army for clothes....
Washington's exertions to augment the army....
Congress sends a committee to camp....Attempt to
surprise Captain Lee....Congress determines on a
second expedition to Canada....Abandons it....Gen-
eral Conway resigns....The Baron Steuben appointed
Inspector General....Congress forbids the embarkation of Burgoyne's army....Plan of reconciliation
agreed to in Parliament....Communicated to congress
and rejected....Information of treaties between France
and the United States....Great Britain declares war
against France....The treaties with France ratified by
congress....Complaints of the treatment of prisoners
....A partial exchange agreed to.

1777   THE army under the immediate command of
General Washington was engaged through the
winter in endeavouring to stop the intercourse
between Philadelphia and the country. To
effect this object General Smallwood was detached with one division to Wilmington; Colonel Morgan was placed on the lines on the west
side of the Schuylkill; and General Armstrong,
with the Pennsylvania militia, was stationed
near the old camp at White Marsh. Major
Jameson, with two troops of cavalry, and
M'Lane's infantry, was directed to guard the

east, and Captain Lee with his troop, the west side of that river. General Count Pulaski, a Polish nobleman who commanded the horse, led the residue of the cavalry to Trenton, where he trained them for the ensuing campaign.

One of the first operations meditated by General Washington after crossing the Schuylkill was the destruction of a large quantity of hay which remained in the islands above the mouth of Derby Creek, within the power of the British. Early in the morning after his orders for this purpose had been given, Sir William Howe marched out in full force, and encamped between Derby and the middle party, so as completely to cover the islands; while a foraging party removed the hay. Washington, with the intention of disturbing this operation, gave orders for putting his army in motion, when the alarming fact was disclosed, that the commissary's stores were exhausted, and that the last ration had been delivered and consumed.

Accustomed as were the continental troops to privations of every sort, it would have been hazarding too much to move them, under these circumstances, against a powerful enemy. In a desert, or in a garrison where food is unattainable, courage, patriotism, and habits of discipline, enable the soldier to conquer wants which, in ordinary situations, would be deemed invincible. But to perish in a country abounding with provisions, requires something more than fortitude; nor can soldiers readily submit, while in such a country, to the deprivation of food. It is not therefore surprising that, among a few of the troops, some indications of a mutiny appeared. It is much more astonishing that the great body of the army bore a circumstance so irritating, and to them so unaccountable, without a murmur.

On receiving intelligence of the fact, General Washington ordered the country to be scoured, and provisions, for supplying the pressing wants of the moment, to be seized wherever found. In the mean time, light parties were detached to harass the enemy about Derby, where Sir William Howe, with his accustomed circumspection, kept his army so compact, and his soldiers so within the lines, that an opportunity to annoy him was seldom afforded even to the vigilance of Morgan and Lee. After completing his forage, he returned, with inconsiderable loss, to Philadelphia.

That the American army, while the value still retained by paper bills placed ample funds in the hands of government, should be destitute of food, in the midst of a state so abounding with provisions as Pennsylvania, is one of those extraordinary facts which can not fail to excite attention.

Early in the war, the office of commissary general had been confirmed on Colonel Trumbull,

of Connecticut, a gentleman fitted by his talents,
activity and zeal, for that important station.
Yet, from the difficulty of arranging so compli-
cated a department in its commencement, without the advantages of experience, complaints
were repeatedly made of the insufficiency of supplies.

The subject was taken up by congress; but the
remedy administered, as well from the time of
its application, as from the ingredients of which
it was composed, served only to increase the
disease. The system was not completed until
near midsummer; and then its arrangements
were such that Colonel Trumbull refused to accept the office assigned to him; and new men
were to be called into service at a time when
the strongest necessity required the exertions of
those who understood the plan of supplies for
the campaign in all its modifications. In addition to the commissary of purchases, and a commissary general of issues, each to be appointed
by congress, the new plan contemplated four
deputies in each department, also to be appointed by that body, who were not accountable
to, nor removeable by the head of the department, but might be suspended, and accused before congress who should examine the charge,
and either remove the accused from his office, or
reinstate him in it.

This *imperium in imperio*, erected in direct
opposition to the opinion of the Commander-in-

chief, drove Colonel Trumbull from the army. Congress, however, persisted in the system; and the effects of deranging so important a department as that which feeds the troops, in the midst of a campaign, were not long in unfolding themselves. In every military division of the continent, loud complaints were made of the deficiency of supplies. The success of Gates appears to have been more endangered by this cause, than by the movement of Sir Henry Clinton up the Hudson. The army of General Washington was often greatly embarrassed, and his movements not unfrequently suspended, by the want of provisions. The present total failure of all supply was preceded, for a few days, by the issuing of meat unfit to be eaten. Representations on this subject were made to the Commander-in-chief, who, on the morning that Sir William Howe moved out to Derby, and before intelligence of that movement had been received, communicated them to congress.

Distress
of the
American
army at
Valley Forge
for
provisions.

That body had authorized the Commander-in-chief to seize provisions for the use of his army within seventy miles of head quarters; and either to pay for them in money, or in certificates, for the redemption of which the faith of the United States was pledged. The odium of this measure was increased by the failure of the government to provide funds to take up these certificates when presented.

The army
subsisted in
a great
measure
by impress-
ments.

At the same time, the provisions carried into Philadelphia were paid for in specie at a good price. The inhabitants of that part of Pennsylvania were not zealous in support of the war, and the difference between prompt payment in gold or silver, and a certificate, the value of which was often diminished by depreciation before its payment, was too great not to influence their wishes and their conduct. Such was the dexterity they employed that, notwithstanding the rigour of the laws, and the vigilance of the troops stationed on the lines, they often succeeded in concealing their provisions from those who were authorized to impress for the army, and in conveying them privately into Philadelphia.

General Washington exercised the powers confided to him with caution, but he did exercise them; and by doing so, acquired considerable supplies. Congress appeared as much dissatisfied with the lenity of the Commander-in-chief, as the people were with his rigour, in consequence of which the subject was taken into consideration, his forbearance disapproved, and instructions given for the rigorous exertions in December 10. future of the powers with which he was invested. In reply to the letter communicating these resolves, the General stated the conduct he had observed, insisted that provisions had been taken very extensively, and repeated his opinion, that

such measures would be much more readily submitted to if executed by the civil authority.

In obedience, however, to the will of congress,
he issued a proclamation, requiring the farmers
within seventy miles of head quarters, to thrash
out one half of their grain by the first of February, and the residue by the first of March, under
the penalty of having the whole seized as straw.

The success of this experiment did not correspond with the wishes of congress. It was
attended with the pernicious consequences which
had been foreseen by the General, to avoid which
he had considered this system as a dernier ressort,
of which he was to avail himself only in extreme
cases. In answer to a letter on this subject from
the board of war, he said, "I shall use every exertion that may be expedient and practicable for
subsisting the army, and keeping it together; but
I must observe, that this never can be done by
coercive means. Supplies of provisions and
clothing must be had in another way, or it can
not exist. The small seizures that were made of
the former some time ago, in consequence of the
most pressing and urgent necessity—when the
alternative was to do that or dissolve—excited
the greatest alarm and uneasiness imaginable,
even among some of our best and warmest
friends. Such procedures may relieve for an instant, but eventually will prove of the most pernicious consequence. Besides spreading disaffection and jealousy among the people, they never

fail, even in the most veteran armies, to raise in the soldiery a disposition to licentiousness, plunder, and robbery, which it has ever been found exceeding difficult to suppress; and which has not only proved ruinous to the inhabitants, but, in many instances, to the armies themselves." In a subsequent letter to congress, he added, "I regret the occasion which compelled us to the measure the other day, and shall consider it as among the greatest of our misfortunes to be under the necessity of practising it again. I am now obliged to keep several parties from the army thrashing grain, that our supplies may not fail; but this will not do."

About this time, a strong combination was forming against the Commander-in-chief, into which several members of congress, and a very few officers of the army are believed to have entered.

Combination formed in Congress against General Washington.

The splendour with which the capture of a British army had surrounded the military reputation of General Gates, acquired some advocates for the opinion that the arms of America would be more fortunate, should that gentleman be elevated to the supreme command. He could not be supposed hostile himself to the prevalence of this opinion; and some parts of his conduct would seem to warrant a belief that, if it did not originate with him, he was not among the last to adopt it. After the victory of the seventh of October had opened to him the prospect

General Gates supposed to be concerned in it.

of subduing the arms of Burgoyne, he not only omitted to communicate his success to General Washington, but carried on a correspondence with General Conway, in which that officer expressed great contempt for the Commander-in-chief. When the purport of this correspondence was disclosed to General Washington, Gates demanded the name of the informer in a letter far from being conciliatory in its terms, which was accompanied with the very extraordinary circumstance of being passed through congress. *

Corre-
spondence
on this
subject
between
the two
generals.

The state of Pennsylvania too, chagrined at the loss of its capital, and forgetful of its own backwardness in strengthening the army, which had twice fought superior numbers in its defence, furnished many discontented individuals. They imputed it to General Washington as a fault that, with forces inferior to his enemy in numbers, and in every equipment, he had not effected the same result which had been produced in the north, by a continental army, in itself, much stronger than its adversary, and so reinforced by militia as to treble his numbers. On the report that General Washington was moving into winter quarters, the legislature of that state addressed a remonstrance to congress on the subject, manifesting, in very intelligible terms, their dissatisfaction with the Commander-in-chief. About the same time, a new board of war was created, of which General Gates was

* See note No. XI. at the end of the volume.

appointed the President; and General Mifflin, who was supposed to be of the party unfriendly to Washington, was one of its members. General Conway, who was probably the only brigadier in the army that had joined this faction, was appointed inspector general, and was promoted, above senior brigadiers, to the rank of major general. These were evidences that, if the hold which the Commander-in-chief had taken of the affections and confidence of the army and of the nation could be loosened, the party in congress disposed to change their general, was far from being contemptible in point of numbers. But to loosen this hold was impossible. The indignation with which the idea of such a change was received even by the victorious troops who had conquered under Gates, forms the most conclusive proof of its strength. Even the northern army clung to Washington as the saviour of his country.

These machinations to diminish the well-earned reputation of the Commander-in-chief, could not escape his notice. They made, however, no undue impression on his steady mind, nor did they change one of his measures. His sensibilities seem to have been those of patriotism, of apprehension for his country, rather than of wounded pride. His desire to remain at the head of the army seemed to flow from the conviction that his retaining that station would be useful to his country, rather than from the gratification his high rank might furnish to ambition. When he unbosomed himself to his private friends, the feelings and sentiments he expressed were worthy of Washington. To Mr. Laurens, the president of congress, and his private friend, who, in an unofficial letter, had communicated an anonymous accusation made to him as president, containing heavy charges against the Commander-in-chief, he said, "I can not sufficiently express the obligation I feel towards you for your friendship and politeness upon an occasion in which I am deeply interested. I was not unapprised that a malignant faction had been for some time forming to my prejudice, which, conscious as I am of having ever done all in my power to answer the important purposes of the trusts reposed in me, could not but give me some pain on a personal account; but my chief concern arises from an apprehension of the dangerous consequences which intestine dissensions may produce to the common cause.

"As I have no other view than to promote the public good, and am unambitious of honours not founded in the approbation of my country, I would not desire, in the least degree, to suppress a free spirit of inquiry into any part of my conduct that even faction itself may deem reprehensible. The anonymous paper handed you exhibits many serious charges, and it is my wish that it may be submitted to congress. This I am the more inclined to, as the suppression or concealment may possibly involve you in embarrassment hereafter, since it is uncertain how many, or who, may be privy to the contents.

"My enemies take an ungenerous advantage of me. They know the delicacy of my situation, and that motives of policy deprive me of the defence I might otherwise make against their insidious attacks. They know I can not combat their insinuations, however injurious, without disclosing secrets it is of the utmost moment to conceal. But why should I expect to be free from censure, the unfailing lot of an elevated station? Merit and talents which I can not pretend to rival, have ever been subject to it. My heart tells me it has been my unremitted aim to do the best which circumstances would permit. Yet I may have been very often mistaken in my judgment of the means, and may in many instances deserve the imputation of error." *

Fortunately for America, these combinations only excited resentment against those who were believed to be engaged in them.

Soon after being informed of the unfavourable disposition of some members of congress towards him, and receiving the memorial of the legislature of Pennsylvania against his going into winter quarters, the General also discovered the failure already mentioned in the commissary department. On this occasion, he addressed con-

December.

* See note No. XII. at the end of the volume.

gress in terms of energy and plainness which he had used on no former occasion. In his letter to that body he said, "Full as I was in my representation of the matters in the commissary's department yesterday, fresh and more powerful reasons oblige me to add that I am now convinced beyond a doubt that, unless some great and capital change suddenly takes place in that line, this army must inevitably be reduced to one or other of these three things—to starve, dissolve, or disperse in order to obtain subsistence. Rest assured, sir, that this is not an exaggerated picture, and that I have abundant reason to suppose what I say.

"Saturday afternoon, receiving information that the enemy, in force, had left the city, and were advancing towards Derby with apparent design to forage, and draw subsistence from that part of the country, I ordered the troops to be in readiness, that I might give every opposition in my power; when, to my great mortification, I was not only informed, but convinced, that the men were unable to stir on account of a want of provisions; and that a dangerous mutiny, begun the night before, and which with difficulty was suppressed by the spirited exertions of some officers, was still much to be apprehended from the want of this article.

"This brought forth the only commissary in the purchasing line in this camp, and with him

this melancholy and alarming truth, that he
had not a single hoof of any kind to slaughter,
and not more than twenty-five barrels of flour!
From hence, form an opinion of our situation,
when I add that he could not tell when to expect
any.

"All I could do under these circumstances,
was to send out a few light parties to watch and
harass the enemy, whilst other parties were instantly detached different ways to collect, if possible, as much provision as would satisfy the
present pressing wants of the soldiers; but will
this answer? No, sir. Three or four days of
bad weather would prove our destruction. What
then is to become of the army this winter? And
if we are now as often without provisions as
with them, what is to become of us in the spring,
when our force will be collected, with the aid
perhaps of militia, to take advantage of an early
campaign before the enemy can be reinforced?
These are considerations of great magnitude,
meriting the closest attention, and will, when
my own reputation is so intimately connected
with, and to be affected by the event, justify my
saying, that the present commissaries are by no
means equal to the execution of the office, or
that the disaffection of the people surpasses all
belief. The misfortune, however, does, in my
opinion, proceed from both causes; and, though
I have been tender heretofore of giving any opinion, or of lodging complaints, as the change in

that department took place contrary to my judgment, and the consequences thereof were predicted; yet, finding that the inactivity of the army, whether for want of provisions, clothes, or other essentials, is charged to my account, not only by the common vulgar, but by those in power; it is time to speak plain in exculpation of myself. With truth, then, I can declare that no man, in my opinion, ever had his measures more impeded than I have, by every department of the army. Since the month of July, we have had no assistance from the quartermaster general; and to want of assistance from this department, the commissary general charges great part of his deficiency. To this I am to add that, notwithstanding it is a standing order (often repeated) that the troops shall always have two days provisions by them, that they may be ready at any sudden call; yet, scarcely any opportunity has ever offered of taking advantage of the enemy, that has not been either totally obstructed, or greatly impeded, on this account; and this, the great and crying evil is not all. Soap, vinegar, and other articles allowed by congress, we see none of, nor have we seen them, I believe, since the battle of Brandywine. The

first, indeed, we have little occasion for; few men having more than one shirt, many, only the moiety of one, and some, none at all. In addition to which, as a proof of the little benefit from a clothier general, and at the same time, as a farther proof of the inability of an army under the circumstances of this to perform the common duties of soldiers, we have, by a field return this day made, besides a number of men confined to hospitals for want of shoes, and others in farmers' houses on the same account, no less than two thousand eight hundred and ninety-eight men, now in camp, unfit for duty, because they are bare-foot, and otherwise naked. By the same return, it appears that our whole strength in continental troops, including the eastern brigades, which have joined us since the surrender of General Burgoyne, exclusive of the Maryland troops sent to Wilmington, amounts to no more than eight thousand two hundred in camp fit for duty; notwithstanding which, and that since the fourth instant, our number fit for duty, from the hardships and exposures they have undergone, particularly from the want of blankets, have decreased near two thousand men, we find gentlemen, without knowing whether the army was really going into winter quarters or not, (for I am sure no resolution of mine would warrant the remonstrance), reprobating the measure as much as if they thought the soldiers were made of stocks or stones, and equally insensible of frost and snow; and moreover, as if they conceived it easily practicable for an inferior army, under the disadvantages I have described ours to be, which are by no means exaggerated, to confine a superior one, in all respects well appointed and provided for a winter's campaign, within the city of Philadelphia, and to cover from depredation and waste the states of Pennsylvania, Jersey, &c. But what makes this matter still more extraordinary in my eye is, that these very gentlemen, who were well apprised of the nakedness of the troops from ocular demonstration, who thought their own soldiers worse clad than others, and advised me, near a month ago, to postpone the execution of a plan I was about to adopt, in consequence of a resolve of Congress for seizing clothes, under strong assuraces that an ample supply would be collected in ten days, agreeably to a decree of the state; (not one article of which by the by is yet to come to hand,) should think a winter's campaign, and the covering of their states from the invasion of an enemy, so easy and practicable a business. I can assure those gentlemen, that it is a much easier and less distressing thing to draw remonstrances in a comfortable room, by a good fireside, than to occupy a cold bleak hill, and sleep under frost and snow, without clothes or blankets. However, although they seem to have little feeling for the naked and distressed soldiers, I feel superabundantly for them, and from my soul pity those miseries which it is not in my power either to relieve or to prevent."

The representations made in this letter were not exaggerated. The distresses of the army, however, so far as respected clothing, did not arise from the inattention of congress. Measures for the importation of clothes had been adopted early in the war, but had not produced the effect expected from them. Vigorous but ineffectual means had also been taken to obtain supplies from the interior. The unfortunate non-importation agreements which preceded the commencement of hosilities, had reduced the quantity of goods in the country below the ordinary amount, and the war had almost annihilated foreign commerce. The progress of manufactures did not equal the consumption; and such was the real scarcity, that exactions from individuals produced great distress, without relieving the wants of the army. A warm blanket was a luxury in which not many participated, either in the camp or in the country.

In the northern states, where the sea coast was too extensive, and the ports too numerous to be completely guarded, and where the people were more inclined to maritime enterprise, supplies both of arms and clothes were attainable in a more considerable degree than in those farther south; but the large sums of money expended in that part of the union for the support of the army, had lessened the value of the currency there more rapidly than elsewhere, and a consequent high nominal price was demanded for imported articles. Congress deemed the terms on which some large contracts had been made by the clothier general in Massachusetts, so exorbitant, as to forbid their execution; and at the same time, addressed a letter to the state government, requesting that the goods should be seized for the use of the army, at prices to be fixed by the legislature, in pursuance of a resolution of the 22d of November.

These recommendations from congress, so far as they exhorted the states to supply the wants of the soldiers, were strongly supported by the General. In his letters to the several governors, he represented the very existence of the army, and the continuance of the contest, as depending on their exertions in this respect.

General Washington's exertions to increase his force, and to place it on a respectable footing before the ensuing campaign.

To recruit the army for the ensuing campaign became again an object of vital importance; and the Commander-in-chief again pressed its necessity on congress, and on the states. To obtain a respectable number of men by voluntary enlistment had, obviously, become impossible. Coercion could be employed only by the state governments; and it required all the influence of General Washington to induce the adoption of a measure so odious in itself, but so indispensable to the acquirement of means to meet the crisis of the war, which, in his judgment, had not yet passed away. He enclosed to each state a return of its troops on continental establishment, thereby exhibiting to each its own deficiency. To those who had not resorted to coercive means, he stated the success with which they had been used by others; and he urged all, by every motive which could operate on the human mind, to employ those means early enough to enable him to anticipate the enemy in taking the field.

To the causes which had long threatened the destruction of the army, the depreciation of paper money was now to be added. It had become so considerable that the pay of an officer would not procure even those absolute necessaries which might protect his person from the extremes of heat and cold. The few who possessed small patrimonial estates found them melting away; and others were unable to appear as gentlemen. Such circumstances could not fail to excite disgust with the service, and a disposition to leave it. Among those who offered their commissions to the Commander-in-chief, were many who, possessing a larger portion of military pride, and therefore feeling with peculiar sensibility the degradation connected with poverty and rags, afforded the fairest hopes of becoming the ornaments of the army. This general indifference about holding a commission; this general opinion that an obligation was conferred, not received by continuing in the service, could not fail to be unfavourable, not only to that spirit of emulation which stimulates to bolder deeds than are required, but to a complete execution of orders, and to a rigid observance of duty.

An officer whose pride was in any degree wounded, whose caprice was not indulged, who

apprehended censure for a fault which his care-
lessness about remaining in the army had probably seduced him to commit, was ready to throw
up a commission which, instead of being valuable, was a burden almost too heavy to be borne.

With extreme anxiety the Commander-in-
chief watched the progress of a temper which,
though just commencing, would increase, he
feared, with the cause that produced it. He
was, therefore, early and earnest in pressing the
consideration of this important subject on the
attention of congress.

The weak and broken condition of the continental regiments, the strong remonstrances of
the General, the numerous complaints received
from every quarter, determined congress to depute a committee to reside in camp during the
winter, for the purpose of investigating the state
of the army, and reporting such reforms as the
public good might require.

January 10.

Congress
send a
committee
of their
own body
to the
army.

This committee repaired to head quarters in
the month of January. The Commander-in-
chief laid before them a general statement, taking a comprehensive view of the condition of
the army, and detailing the remedies necessary
for the correction of existing abuses, as well
as those regulations which he deemed essential
to its future prosperity.

This paper, exhibiting the actual state of the
army, discloses defects of real magnitude in the
existing arrangements. In perusing it, the reader

is struck with the numerous difficulties, in addition to those resulting from inferiority of numbers, with which the American general was under the necessity of contending. The memorial is too long to be inserted, but there are parts which ought not to be entirely overlooked. The neglect of the very serious representation it contained respecting a future permanent provision for the officers, threatened, at an after period, to be productive of such pernicious effects, that their insertion in this place will not, it is presumed, be unacceptable.

He recommended as the basis of every salutary reform, a comfortable provision for the officers, which should render their commissions valuable; to effect which the future, as well as the present, ought to be contemplated.

"A long and continual sacrifice of individual interest for the general good, ought not," he said, "to be expected or required. The nature of man must be changed, before institutions built on the presumptive truth of such a principle can succeed.

"This position," he added, "is supported by the conduct of the officers of the American army, as well as by that of all other men. At the commencement of the dispute, in the first effusions of zeal, when it was believed the service would be temporary, they entered into it without regard to pecuniary considerations. But finding its duration much longer than had been at

first expected, and that, instead of deriving advantage from the hardships and dangers to which
they are exposed, they were, on the contrary,
losers by their patriotism, and fell far short of
even a competency for their wants, they have
gradually abated in their ardour; and, with
many, an entire disinclination to the service, under present circumstances, has taken place. To
this, in an eminent degree, must be ascribed the
frequent resignations daily happening, and the
more frequent importunities for permission to
resign, from some officers of the greatest merit.

"To this also may be ascribed the apathy, inattention, and neglect of duty, which pervade all
ranks; and which will necessarily continue and
increase, while an officer, instead of gaining any
thing, is impoverished by his commission, and
conceives he is conferring, not receiving a favour,
in holding it. There can be no sufficient tie on
men possessing such sentiments. Nor can any
method be adopted to compel those to a punctual discharge of duty, whc are indifferent about
their continuance in the service, and are often
seeking a pretext to disengage themselves from
it. Punishment, in this case, would be unavailing. But when an officer's commission is made
valuable to him, and he fears to lose it, you may
exact obedience from him.

"It is not indeed consistent with reason or
justice that one set of men should make a sacrifice of property, domestic ease, and happiness;

encounter the rigours of the field, the perils and vicissitudes of war, without some adequate compensation, to obtain those blessings which every citizen will enjoy in common with them. It must also be a comfortless reflection to any man, that, after he may have contributed to secure the rights of his country, at the risk of his life, and the ruin of his fortune, there will be no provision made to prevent himself and his family, from sinking into indigence and wretchedness."

With these and other arguments, General Washington recommended, in addition to present compensation, a half pay and pensionary establishment for the army.

"I urge my sentiments," said he, "with the greater freedom, because I can not, and shall not, receive the smallest benefit from the establishment; and can have no other inducement for proposing it, than a full conviction of its utility and propriety."

The wants and distresses of the army, when actually seen by the committee of congress, made a much deeper impression than could have been received from any statement whatever. They endeavoured to communicate to congress the sentiments felt by themselves, and to correct the errors which had been committed. But a numerous body, if it deliberate at all, proceeds slowly in the conduct of executive business; and will seldom afford a prompt corrective to existing mischiefs, especially to those growing out of its own measures.

Much of the sufferings of the army was attributed to mismanagement in the quartermaster's department, which, notwithstanding the repeated remonstrances of the Commander-in-chief, had long remained without a head. This subject was taken up early by the committee, and proper representations made respecting it. But congress still remained under the influence of those opinions which had already produced such mischievous effects, and were still disposed to retain the subordinate officers of the department in a state of immediate dependence on their own

body. In this temper, they proposed a plan which, not being approved in camp, was never carried into execution.

While congress was deliberating on the reforms proposed, the distresses of the army approached their acme, and its dissolution was threatened. Early in February, the commissaries gave notice that the country, to a great distance, was actually exhausted; and that it would be impracticable to obtain supplies for the army longer than to the end of that month. Already the threatened scarcity began to be felt, and the rations issued were often bad in quality, and insufficient in quantity. General Washington found it necessary again to interpose his personal exertions to procure provisions from a distance.

In the apprehension that the resources of the commissary department would fail before the distant supplies he had taken measures to obtain could reach him, and that the enemy designed to make another incursion into the country around Philadelphia, for the purpose of gleaning what yet remained in possession of the inhabitants, he detached General Wayne, with orders to seize every article proper for the use of an army within fifteen miles of the Delaware, and to destroy the forage on the islands between Philadelphia and Chester.

To defeat the object of this foraging party, the inhabitants concealed their provisions and teams, and gave to the country every appearance of having been entirely pillaged. Before any sufficient aid could be obtained by these means, the bread, as well as the meat, was exhausted, and famine prevailed in camp.

In an emergency so pressing, the Commander-in-chief used every effort to feed his hungry army. Parties were sent out to glean the country; officers of influence were deputed to Jersey, Delaware and Maryland; and circular letters were addressed to the governors of states by the committee of congress in camp and by the Commander-in-chief, describing the wants of the army, and urging the greatest exertions for its immediate relief.

Fortunately for America, there were features in the character of Washington which, notwithstanding the discordant materials of which his army was composed, attached his officers and soldiers so strongly to his person, that no distress could weaken their affection, nor impair the respect and veneration in which they held him. To this sentiment is to be attributed, in a great measure, the preservation of a respectable military force, under circumstances but too well calculated for its dissolution.

Through this severe experiment on their fortitude, the native Americans persevered steadily in the performance of their duty; but the conduct of the Europeans, who constituted a large part of the army, was, to a considerable extent, less laudable; and at no period of the war was desertion so frequent as during this winter. Aided by the disaffected, deserters eluded the vigilance of the parties who watched the roads, and great numbers escaped into Philadelphia with their arms.

In a few days, the army was rescued from the famine with which it had been threatened, and considerable supplies of provisions were laid up in camp. It was perceived that the difficulties which had produced such melancholy effects, were created more by the want of due exertion in the commissary department, and by the efforts of the people to save their stock for a better market, than by any real deficiency of food in the country.

This severe demonstration seems to have convinced congress that their favourite system was radically vicious, and the subject was taken up with the serious intention of remodeling the commissary department on principles recommended by experience. But such were the delays inherent in the organization of that body, that the new system was not adopted until late in April.

At no period of the war had the situation of the American army been more perilous than at Valley Forge. Even when the troops were not entirely destitute of food, their stock of provisions was so scanty that a quantity sufficient for one week was seldom in store. Consequently, had General Howe moved out in force, the American army could not have remained in camp; and their want of clothes disabled them from keeping the field in the winter. The returns of the first of February exhibit the astonishing number of three thousand nine hundred and eighty-nine men in camp, unfit for duty for want of clothes. Scarcely one man of these had a pair of shoes. Even among those returned capable of doing duty, many were so badly clad, that exposure to the cold of the season must have destroyed them. Although the total of the army exceeded seventeen thousand men, the present effective rank and file amounted to only five thousand and twelve.

While the sufferings of the soldiers filled the hospitals, a dreadful mortality continued to prevail in those miserable receptacles of the sick. A violent putrid fever swept off much greater numbers than all the diseases of the camp.

If then during the deep snow which covered the earth for a great part of the winter, the British general had taken the field, his own army would indeed have suffered greatly, but the American loss is not to be calculated.

Happily, the real condition of Washington was not well understood by Sir William Howe; and the characteristic attention of that officer to the lives and comfort of his troops, saved the American army. Fortunately, he confined his operations to those small excursions that were calculated to enlarge the comforts of his own soldiers, who, notwithstanding the favourable dispositions of the neighbouring country, were much distressed for fuel, and often in great want of forage and fresh provisions. The vigilance of the parties on the lines, especially on the south side of the Schuylkill, intercepted a large portion of the supplies intended for the Philadelphia market; and corporal punishment was frequently inflicted on those who were detected in attempting this infraction of the laws. As Captain Lee was particularly active, a plan was formed, late in January, to surprise and capture him in his quarters. An extensive circuit was made by a large body of cavalry, who seized four

Attempt to
surprise
Captain Lee's
corps, and
the gallant
resistance
made
by him.

Washington's Headquarters at Valley Forge

Here on December 17, 1777, after the Battles of Brandywine and Germantown and the occupation of Philadelphia by the British, Washington established his headquarters for what may be paradoxically termed the darkest winter of the Revolutionary War. The American Commander-in-Chief chose this place partly for its defensibility and partly to protect Congress, then in session at York, Pennsylvania, from a sudden British attack. It was here that Washington and Baron Steuben planned the reorganization of the American army, and it was here, May 1, 1778, that news reached Washington of the consummation of the French alliance.

Washington's Headquarters at Valley Forge

Here on December 17, 1777, after the Battles of Brandywine and Germantown and the occupation of Philadelphia by the British, Washington established his headquarters for what may be paradoxically termed the darkest winter of the Revolutionary War. The American Commander-in-Chief chose this place partly for its defensibility and partly to protect Congress, then in session at York, Pennsylvania, from a sudden British attack. It was here that Washington and Baron Steuben planned the reorganization of the American army, and it was here, May 1, 1778, that news reached Washington of the consummation of the French alliance.

of his patrols without communicating an alarm.
About break of day the British horse appeared;
upon which Captain Lee placed his troopers that
were in the house, at the doors and windows, who
behaved so gallantly as to repulse the assailants
without losing a horse or man. Only Lieutenant
Lindsay and one private were wounded. The
whole number in the house did not exceed ten.*
That of the assailants was said to amount to two
hundred. They lost a sergeant and three men
with several horses, killed; and an officer and
three men wounded.

The result of this skirmish gave great pleasure
to the Commander-in-chief, who had formed a
high opinion of Lee's talents as a partisan. He
mentioned the affair in his orders with strong
marks of approbation; and, in a private letter to
the captain, testified the satisfaction he felt.
For his merit through the preceding campaign,
congress promoted him to the rank of major, and
gave him an independent partisan corps to consist of three troops of horse.

While the deficiency of the public resources,
arising from the alarming depreciation of the
bills of credit, manifested itself in all the military departments, a plan was matured in congress, and in the board of war, without consulting the Commander-in-chief, for a second irruption into Canada. It was proposed to place the

Congress
determine
upon a
second
expedition
against
Canada.

---

* Major Jameson was accidentally present, and engaged in
this skirmish.

Marquis de Lafayette at the head of this expedition, and to employ Generals Conway and Starke, as the second and third in command.

This young nobleman, possessing an excellent heart, and all the military enthusiasm of his country, had left France early in 1777, in opposition to the will of his sovereign, to engage in the service of the United States. His high rank, and supposed influence at the court of Versailles, secured him the unlimited respect of his countrymen in America; and, added to his frankness of manners and zeal in their cause, recommended him strongly to congress. While the claims of others of the same country to rank were too exorbitant to be gratified, he demanded no station in the army; would consent to receive no compensation, and offered to serve as a volunteer. He had stipulated with Mr. Deane for the rank of major general without emolument; and, on his arrival in America, that rank was conferred on him, but without any immediate command. In that capacity, he sought for danger, and was wounded at the battle of Brandywine. He attached himself with the ardour of youth to the Commander-in-chief, who smoothed the way to his receiving a command in the army equal to his rank.

The first intimation to General Washington that the expedition was contemplated, was given in a letter frrom the president of the board of war of the 24th of January, inclosing one of the same date to the Marquis, requiring the attendance of that nobleman on congress to receive his instructions. The Commander-in-chief was requested to furnish Colonel Hazen's regiment, chiefly composed of Canadians, for the expedition; and in the same letter, his advice and opinion were asked respecting it. The northern states were to furnish the necessary troops.

Without noticing the manner in which this business had been conducted, and the marked want of confidence it betrayed, General Washington ordered Hazen's regiment to march towards Albany; and the Marquis proceeded immediately to the seat of congress. At his request, he was to be considered as an officer detached from the army of Washington, to remain under his orders, and Major General the Baron de Kalb was added to the expedition; after which the Marquis repaired in person to Albany to take charge of the troops who were to assemble at that place in order to cross the lakes on the ice, and attack Montreal.

On arriving at Albany, he found no preparations made for the expedition. Nothing which had been promised being in readiness, he abandoned the enterprise as impracticable. Some time afterward, congress also determined to relinquish it; and General Washington was authorized to recall both the Marquis de Lafayette, and the Baron de Kalb.

Before its execution, it is abandoned

While the army lay at Valley Forge, the Baron Steuben arrived in camp. This gentleman was a Prussian officer, who came to the United States with ample recommendations. He was said to have served many years in the armies of the great Frederick; to have been one of the aids de camp of that consummate commander; and to have held the rank of lieutenant general. He was, unquestionably, versed in the system of field exercise which the king of Prussia had introduced, and was well qualified to teach it to raw troops. He claimed no rank, and offered to render his services as a volunteer. After holding a conference with congress, he proceeded to Valley Forge.

Although the office of inspector general had been bestowed on Conway, he had never entered on its duties; and his promotion to the rank of major general had given much umbrage to the brigadiers, who had been his seniors. That circumstance, in addition to the knowledge of his being in a faction hostile to the Commander-in-chief, rendered his situation in the army so uncomfortable, that he withdrew to York, in Pennsylvania, which was then the seat of congress. When the expedition to Canada was abandoned, he was not directed, with Lafayette and De Kalb, to rejoin the army. Entertaining no hope of being permitted to exercise the functions of his new office, he resigned his commission about the last of April, and, some time afterwards, re-

General Conway resigns. Duel between him and General Cadwallader.

turned to France. * On his resignation, the
Baron Steuben, who had, as a volunteer, performed the duties of inspector general, much to
the satisfaction of the Commander-in-chief, and
of the army, was, on the recommendation of
General Washington, appointed to that office
with the rank of major general, without exciting
the slightest murmur.

This gentleman was of real service to the
American troops. He established one uniform
system of field exercise; and, by his skill and
persevering industry, effected important improvements through all ranks of the army during its continuance at Valley Forge.

While it was encamped at that place, several
matters of great interest engaged the attention
of congress. Among them, was the stipulation
in the convention of Saratoga for the return of

CHAP. XI

1778

The Baron
Steuben
appointed
inspector
general.

---

* General Conway, after his resignation, frequently indulged in expressions of extreme hostility to the Commander-in-chief. These indiscretions were offensive to the
gentlemen of the army. In consequence of them, he was
engaged in an altercation with General Cadwallader, which
produced a duel, in which Conway received a wound, supposed for some time to be mortal. While his recovery was
despaired of, he addressed the following letter to General
Washington.

Philadelphia, July 23d, 1778.

Sir,—I find myself just able to hold the pen during a few
minutes, and take this opportunity of expressing my sincere
grief for having done, written, or said any thing disagreeable
to your excellency. My career will soon be over, therefore,
justice and truth prompt me to declare my last sentiments.
You are, in my eyes, the great and good man. May you
long enjoy the love, veneration, and esteem of these states,
whose liberties you have asserted by your virtues.

I am with the greatest respect, sir,

Your excellency's most obedient humble servant,

PHS. CONWAY.

the British army to England. Boston was named as the place of embarkation. At the time of the capitulation, the difficulty of making that port early in the winter was unknown to General Burgoyne. Consequently, as some time must elapse before a sufficient number of vessels for the transportation of his army could be collected, its embarkation might be delayed until the ensuing spring.

On receiving this unwelcome intelligence, he applied to General Washington to change the port of embarkation, and to substitute Newport, in Rhode Island, or some place on the Sound, for Boston. If any considerations not foreseen should make this proposal objectionable, he then solicited this indulgence for himself and his suite. This request was communicated to congress, in terms favourable to that part of the application which respected General Burgoyne and his suite; but the objections to any change in the convention which might expedite the transportation of the army, were too weighty to be disregarded; and the General pressed them earnestly on congress. This precaution was unnecessary. The facility with which the convention might be violated by the British, and the captured army be united to that under General Howe, seems to have suggested itself to the American government, as soon as the first rejoicings were over; and such was its then existing temper, that the faith and honour of British officers were believed to be no securities against their appearing again in the field. Under this impression, a resolution had passed early in November, directing General Heath to transmit to the board of war a descriptive list of all persons comprehended in the convention, "in order that, if any officer, soldier, or other person of the said army should hereafter be found in arms against these states in North America, during the present contest, he might be convicted of the offence, and suffer the punishment in such case inflicted by the law of nations."

No other notice was taken of the application made by General Burgoyne to congress through the Commander-in-chief, than to pass a resolution "that General Washington be directed to inform General Burgoyne that congress will not receive, nor consider, any proposition for indulgence, nor for altering the terms of the convention of Saratoga, unless immediately directed to their own body."

Contrary to expectation, a fleet of transports for the reception of the troops reached Rhode Island, on its way to Boston, in the month of December. But, before its arrival, the preconceived suspicions of congress had ripened into conviction several circumstances combined to produce this result. General Burgoyne, dissatisfied with the accommodations prepared for his officers in Boston, had, after a fruitless correspondence with General Heath, addressed a letter to General Gates, in which he complained of the inconvenient quarters assigned his officers, as a breach of the articles of the convention. This complaint was considered by congress as being made for the purpose of letting in the principle, that the breach of one article of a treaty discharges the injured party from its obligations.

This suspicion was strengthened by the indiscreet hesitation of General Burgoyne to permit the resolution requiring a descriptive list of his troops to be executed. His subsequent relinquishment of the objection did not remove the impression it had made.

It was also alleged, that the number of transports was not sufficient to convey the troops to Europe; nor was it believed possible that Sir William Howe could have laid in, so expeditiously, a sufficient stock of provisions for the voyage.

These objections to the embarkation of Burgoyne's troops were strengthened by some trivial infractions of the convention, which, it was contended, gave congress a strict right to detain them. It was stipulated that "the arms" should be delivered up; and it appeared that several cartouch boxes and other military accoutrements, supposed to be comprehended in the technical term *arms*, had been detained. This was deemed an infraction of the letter of the compact, which, on rigid principle, justified the measures after-wards adopted by congress.

The whole subject was referred to a committee who reported all the circumstances of the case, whereupon congress came to several resolutions, enumerating the facts already mentioned, the last of which was in these words: "Resolved, therefore, that the embarkation of Lieutenant General Burgoyne, and the troops under his command, be suspended, until a distinct and explicit ratification of the convention of Saratoga shall be properly notified by the court of Great Britain to congress."

Congress forbid the embarkation of the British troops taken at Saratoga

These resolutions, together with the report on which they were founded, were transmitted to the several states, and to General Washington. Two copies of them were sent to General Heath, with directions to deliver one of them to General Burgoyne, and with farther directions, "to order the vessels which may have arrived, or which shall arrive, for the transportation of the army under Lieutenant General Burgoyne, to quit, without delay, the port of Boston."

On receiving these resolutions, General Burgoyne addressed a letter to congress, containing papers, on which he founded a defence of his conduct, and insisted on the embarkation of his army, as stipulated in the convention; but the committee, to whom these papers were referred, reported their opinion, after the most attentive consideration of them, to be, "that nothing therein contained was sufficient to induce congress to recede from their resolves of the 8th of January last, respecting the convention of Saratoga." This application was accompanied by another letter from General Burgoyne, to be delivered if the army should still be detained, in

Burgoyne permitted to depart.

which, in consideration of the state of his health, he solicited permission to return to England. This request was readily granted.

The impression made on the British nation by the capitulation of Burgoyne, notwithstanding the persevering temper of the king, at length made its way into the cabinet, and produced resolutions in favour of pacific measures.

1778
February.

After the rejection of repeated motions made by the opposition members tending to the abandonment of the American war, Lord North gave notice, in the House of Commons, that he had digested a plan of reconciliation which he designed shortly to lay before the house.

Plan of reconciliation with America agreed to in Parliament.

In conformity with this notice, he moved for leave to bring in, "first, A bill for removing all doubts and apprehensions concerning taxation by the Parliament of Great Britain in any of the colonies and plantations of North America.

"Second. A bill to enable his Majestÿ to appoint commissioners with sufficient powers to treat, consult, and agree upon the means of quieting the disorders now subsisting in certain of the colonies of North America."

The first contained a declaration that Parliament will impose no tax or duty whatever payable within any of the colonies of North America, except only such duties as it may be expedient to impose for the purposes of commerce, the net produce of which should always be paid and applied to and for the use of the colonies in which the same shall be respectively levied, in like manner as other duties collected under the authority of their respective legislatures are ordinarily paid and applied.

The second authorized the appointment of commissioners by the crown, with power to treat either with the existing governments, or with individuals, in America; provided that no stipulations which might be entered into should have any effect until approved in Parliament, other than is afterward mentioned.

It is then enacted, that the commissioners may have power "to proclaim a cessation of hostilities in any of the colonies, to suspend the operation of the non-intercourse law; and farther, to suspend, during the continuance of the act, so much of all or any of the acts of Parliament which have passed since the 10th day of February, 1763, as relates to the colonies.

"To grant pardon to any number or description of persons, and to appoint a governor in any colony in which his majesty had heretofore exercised the power of making such appointments."

These bills passed both houses of Parliament with inconsiderable opposition.

Intelligence of the treaty between the United States and France having been received by the minister about the time of their being introduced, copies of them, before they had gone through the requisite forms, were hurried to America, to be laid before congress and the public, in the hope and expectation that they might counteract the effects which it was feared the treaty with France would produce.

General Washington received early information of their arrival, and entertained serious fears of their operation. He was apprehensive that the publication of a proposition for the restoration of peace on the terms originally required by America, would greatly increase the numbers of the disaffected; and immediately forwarded the bills to congress in a letter suggesting the policy of preventing their pernicious influence on the public mind by all possible means, and especially through the medium of the press.

This letter was referred to a committee, consisting of Messrs. Morris, Drayton, and Dana, by whom a report was made, investigating the bills with great acuteness as well as asperity. This report, and the resolutions upon it, were ordered to be published. Other resolutions were passed the succeeding day, recommending it to the states to pardon under such limitations as they might think proper to make, such of their misguided fellow-citizens as had levied war against the United States.

This resolution was accompanied by an order directing it to be printed in English and in German, and requesting General Washington to take such measures as he should deem most effectual for circulating the copies among the American recruits in the enemy's army. *

During these transactions, the frigate *La Sensible* arrived with the important intelligence that treaties of alliance and of commerce, had been formed between the United States of America and France. The treaties themselves were brought by Mr. Simeon Deane, the brother of the American Minister in Paris.

This event had long been anxiously expected, and the delay attending it had been such as to excite serious apprehension that it would never take place.

France was still extremely sore under the wounds inflicted during the war which terminated in 1763. It was impossible to reflect on a treaty which had wrested from her so fair a part

---

* This request afforded the Commander-in-chief a fair retort on Major General Tryon. That officer had addressed a letter to him enclosing the bills brought into Parliament, and containing, to use the language of General Washington himself, "the more extraordinary and impertinent request" that their contents should be communicated through him to the army. General Washington now acknowledged the receipt of this letter, and, in return, enclosed to Governor Tryon copies of the resolution just mentioned, with a request that he would be instrumental in making them known to the persons on whom they were to operate.

of North America, without feeling resentments which would seek the first occasion of gratification.

The growing discontents between Great Britain and her colonies were, consequently, viewed at a distance with secret satisfaction; but rather as a circumstance which might have some tendency to weaken and embarrass a rival, and which was to be encouraged from motives of general policy, than as one from which any definite advantage was to be derived. France appears, at that time, to have required, and wished for, repose. The great exertions of the preceding disastrous war had so deranged her finances, that the wish to preserve peace seems to have predominated in her cabinet. The young monarch, who had just ascended the throne, possessed a pacific unambitious temper, and the councils of the nation were governed by men alike indisposed to disturb the general tranquillity. The advice they gave the monarch was, to aid and encourage the colonies secretly, in order to prevent a reconciliation with the mother country, and to prepare privately for hostilities, by improving his finances, and strengthening his marine; but to avoid every thing which might give occasion for open war. The system which for a time regulated the cabinet of Versailles, conformed to this advice. While the utmost attention was paid to the Minister of Britain, and every measure to satisfy him was openly taken, intimation was privately given to those of the United States, that these measures were necessary for the present, but they might be assured of the good will of the French government.

During the public demonstration of dispositions favourable to England, means were taken to furnish aids of ammunition and arms, and to facilitate the negotiation of loans to the United States; and the owners of American privateers, though forbidden to sell their prizes, or to procure their condemnation, found means to dispose of them privately.

Meanwhile, another party was formed in the cabinet, to whose political system subsequent events gave the ascendency. Its avowed object was to seize the present moment to revenge past injuries, humble the haughty rival of France, and dismember her empire.

Matters remained in a fluctuating state until December, 1777. Privately encouraged, but discountenanced publicly, the prospects of the American Ministers varied according to the complexion of American affairs.

Intelligence of the convention of Saratoga reached France early in December, 1777. The American deputies took that opportunity to press the treaty which had been under consideration for the preceding twelve months; and to urge the importance, at this juncture, when Britain would, most probably, make proposals for an

CHAP. XI   accommodation, * of communicating to congress,
1778   precisely, what was to be expected from France
and Spain.

They were informed by M. Girard, one of the
secretaries of the king's council of state, that it
was determined to acknowledge the independence of the United States, and to make a treaty
with them. That his Most Christian Majesty
was resolved not only to acknowledge, but to
support their independence. That in doing this,
he might probably soon be engaged in a war;
yet he should not expect any compensation from
the United States on that account; nor was it
pretended that he acted wholly for their sakes;
since, besides his real good will to them, it was
manifestly the interest of France that the power
of England should be diminished by the separation of her colonies. The only condition he
should require would be that the United States,
in no peace to be made, should give up their
independence, and return to their obedience to
the British government.

On determining to take this decisive course,
the cabinet of Versailles had despatched a
courier to his Catholic majesty with information
of the line of conduct about to be pursued by
France. On his return, the negotiation was

---

* Congress, in their first instructions to their commissioners,
directed them to press the immediate declaration of France in
favour of the United States, by suggesting that a reunion
with Great Britain might be the consequence of delay.—
Secret Journals of Congress, v. ii. p. 30.

taken up in earnest, and a treaty of friendship and commerce was soon concluded. This was accompanied by a treaty of alliance eventual and defensive between the two nations, in which it was declared, that if war should break out between France and England during the existence of that with the United States, it should be made a common cause; and that neither of the contracting parties should conclude either truce or peace with Great Britain without the formal consent of the other, first obtained; and they mutually engaged "not to lay down their arms until the independence of the United States shall have been formally, or tacitly assured by the treaty, or treaties that shall terminate the war."

It was the wish of the ministers of the United States to engage France immediately in the war; and to make the alliance, not eventual, but positive. This proposition, however, was rejected.

In a few weeks after the conclusion of these negotiations, the Marquis de Noailles announced officially to the court of London, the treaty of friendship and commerce France had formed with the United States. The British government, considering this notification as a declaration of war, published a memorial for the purpose of justifying to all Europe the hostilities it had determined to commence.

Soon after their commencement, the Count de Vergennes received private intelligence that it was contemplated in the cabinet of London to offer to the United States an acknowledgment of their independence as the condition of a separate peace. He immediately communicated this intelligence to the American ministers, requesting them to lose no time in stating to congress that, though war was not declared in form, it had commenced in fact; and that he considered the obligations of the treaty of alliance as in full force; consequently that neither party was now at liberty to make a separate peace. Instructions of a similar import were given to the minister of France in the United States.

Information received of treaties of alliance and commerce being entered into between France and the United States.

The despatches containing these treaties were received by the president on Saturday the second of May, after congress had adjourned. That body was immediately convened, the despatches were opened, and their joyful contents communicated.

In the exultation of the moment, the treaty of alliance, as well as that of commerce and friendship was published; a circumstance which, not without reason, gave umbrage to the cabinet of Versailles; because that treaty, being only eventual, ought not to have been communicated to the public but by mutual consent.

From this event, which was the source of universal exultation to the friends of the revolution, the attention must be directed to one which was productive of very different sensations.

Among the various improvements which struggling humanity has gradually engrafted on the belligerent code, none have contributed more to diminish the calamities of war, than those which meliorate the condition of prisoners. No obligations will be more respected by the generous and the brave; nor are there any, the violation of which could wound the national character more deeply, or expose it to more lasting or better merited reproach.

In wars between nations nearly equal in power, and possessing rights acknowledged to be equal, a departure from modern usage in this respect is almost unknown; and the voice of the civilized world would be raised against the potentate who could adopt a system calculated to re-establish the rigours and misery of exploded barbarism. But in contests between different parts of the same empire, those practices which mitigate the horrors of war yield, too frequently, to the calculations of a blind and erring resentment. The party which supports the ancient state of things, often treats resistance as rebellion, and captives as traitors. The opposite party, supporting also by the sword principles believed to be right, will admit of no departure from established usage, to its prejudice; and may be expected, if possessing the power, to endeavour, by retaliating injuries, to compel the observance of a more just and humane system. But they participate in the fault imputable to their adversaries, by manifesting a disposition to punish those whom they deem traitors, with the same severity of which they so loudly and justly complain, when they are themselves its victims.

General Gage, as Commander-in-chief of the British army, in the harshness of spirit which had been excited while governor of Massachusetts, not only threw all his prisoners into a common jail, but rejected every proposition for an exchange of them. When the command devolved on Sir William Howe, this absurd system was abandoned, and an exchange * took place to a considerable extent. But the Americans had not made a sufficient number of prisoners to relieve all their citizens, and many of them still remained in confinement. Representations were continually received from these unfortunate men, describing in strong terms, the severity of their treatment. They complained of suffering almost the extremity of famine, that even the supply of provisions allowed them was unsound, and that they were crowded into prison-ships, where they became the victims of disease.

---

* In the execution of this agreement, the inconveniences arising from having committed the custody of prisoners to the several states, was severely felt. In addition to the delay inseparable from the necessity of inquiring for them, and collecting them from different places, they were often sent in without the knowledge of General Washington; and, in some instances, they passed unobserved, with permits from a state government, through his camp, into that of the enemy. These irregularities, and the remonstrances of the Commander-in-chief, at length, induced congress to appoint a commissary of prisoners.

When charged with conduct so unworthy of his character and station, Sir William Howe positively denied its truth.

It would be unjust to ascribe this excess of inhumanity to an officer who, though perhaps severe in his temper, did not mingle cruelties in his general system, which would excite universal indignation in other wars. It must be admitted that his supplies of provisions were neither good nor abundant; and that the American soldiers, in their own camp, were unhealthy. But the excessive mortality prevailing among the prisoners can be accounted for on no ordinary principles; and the candid, who were least inclined to criminate without cause, have ever been persuaded that, if his orders did not produce the distress which existed, his authority was not interposed with sufficient energy, to correct the abuses which prevailed.

The capture of General Lee furnished an additional ground of controversy on the subject of prisoners. As he had been an officer in the British service, whose resignation had not, perhaps, been received when he entered into that of America, a disposition was, at first, manifested to consider him as a deserter, and he was closely confined. On receiving information of this circumstance, congress directed General Howe to be assured that Lieutenant Colonel Campbell, and five Hessian field-officers, should be detained, and should experience precisely the fate of General Lee. These officers were taken into close custody, and informed that the resolution announced to General Howe should be strictly enforced.

The sentiments of the Commander-in-chief on the subject of retaliation, seem to have been less severe than those of congress. So great was his abhorrence of the cruelties such a practice must generate, that he was unwilling to adopt it in any case not of absolute and apparent necessity. Not believing that of General Lee to be such a case, he remonstrated strongly against these resolutions. But congress remained inflexible; and the officers designated as the objects of retaliation, were kept in rigorous confinement until General Lee was declared to be a prisoner of war. *

The resolutions of congress respecting the prisoners taken at the Cedars, were also the source of much embarrassment and chagrin to the Commander-in-chief. Alleging that the capitulation had been violated on the part of the enemy, and that the savages had been permitted to murder some of the prisoners, and to plunder others, they withheld their sanction from the agreement entered into by General Arnold with Captain Forster, and refused to allow other prisoners to be returned in exchange for those liberated under that agreement, until the murderers should be given up, and compensa-

* See note No. XIII. at the end of the volume.

tion made for the baggage said to have been plundered. As the fact alleged was not clearly established, Sir William Howe continued to press General Washington on this subject. Reminding him of the importance of a punctilious observance of faith, plighted in engagements like that made by General Arnold, he persisted to hold the Commander-in-chief personally bound for an honourable compliance with military stipulations entered into by an officer under his authority.

General Washington, feeling the keenness of the reproach, pressed congress to change their resolution on this subject; but his remonstrances were, for a long time, unavailing.

After the sufferings of the prisoners in New York had been extreme, and great numbers had perished in confinement, the survivors were liberated for the purpose of being exchanged; but so miserable was their condition, that many of them died on their way home. For the dead as well as the living, General Howe claimed a return of prisoners, while General Washington contended that reasonable deductions should be made for those who were actually dead, of diseases under which they laboured when permitted to leave the British prisons.

Until this claim should be admitted, General Howe rejected any partial exchange. General Washington was immoveable in his determination to repel it; and thus all hope of being relieved in the ordinary mode appeared to be taken from those whom the fortune of war had placed in the power of the enemy.

In the mean time, the sufferings of the American prisoners increased with the increasing severity of the season. Information continued to be received, that they suffered almost the extremity of famine. Repeated remonstrances, made on this subject to the British general, were answered by a denial of the fact. He continued to aver that the same food, both in quantity and quality, was issued to the prisoners, as to British troops when in transports, or elsewhere, not on actual duty; and that every tenderness was extended to them, which was compatible with the situation of his army. He yielded to the request made by General Washington to permit a commissary to visit the jails, and demanded passports for an agent to administer to the wants of British prisoners.

Complaints
made by
General
Washington
of the
treatment
of American
prisoners in
possession
of the
enemy.

When Mr. Boudinot, the American commissary of prisoners, who was appointed by General Washington to visit the jails in Philadelphia, met Mr. Ferguson, the British commissary, he was informed that General Howe thought it unnecessary for him to come into the city, as he would himself inspect the situation and treatment of the prisoners. There is reason to believe that their causes of complaint, so far as respected provisions, did not exist afterwards in the same degree as formerly; and that the strong measures subsequently taken by congress, were founded on facts of an earlier date.

But clothes and blankets were also necessary, and the difficulty of furnishing them was considerable. General Howe would not permit the purchase of those articles in Philadelphia; and they were not attainable elsewhere.

To compel him to abandon this distressing restriction, and to permit the use of paper money within the British lines, congress resolved, that no prisoner should be exchanged until all the expenditures made in paper for the supplies they received from the United States, should be repaid in specie, at the rate of four shillings and sixpence for each dollar. They afterwards determined, that from the 1st day of February, no British commissary should be permitted to purchase any provisions for the use of prisoners west of New Jersey, but that all supplies for persons of that description should be furnished from British stores.

Proceedings of congress on this subject.

Sir William Howe remonstrated against the last resolution with great strength and justice, as a decree which doomed a considerable number of prisoners, far removed into the country, to a slow and painful death by famine; since it was impracticable to supply them immediately from Philadelphia. The severity of this order was in some degree mitigated by a resolution that each British commissary of prisoners should receive provisions from the American commissary of purchases, to be paid for in specie, according to the resolution of the 19th of December, 1777.

About the same time, an order was hastily given by the board of war, which produced no inconsiderable degree of embarrassment; and exposed the Commander-in-chief to strictures not less severe than those he had applied to the British general.

General Washington had consented that a quartermaster, with a small escort, should come out of Philadelphia, with clothes and other comforts for the prisoners who were in possession of the United States. He had expressly stipulated for their security, and had given them a passport.

While they were travelling through the country, information was given to the board of war that General Howe had refused to permit provisions to be sent in to the American prisoners in Philadelphia by water. This information was not correct. General Howe had only requested that flags should not be sent up or down the river without previous permission obtained from himself. On this information, however, the board ordered Lieutenant Colonel Smith im-

January 26.

mediately to seize the officers, though protected by the passport of General Washington, their horses, carriages, and the provisions destined for the relief of the British prisoners; and to secure them until farther orders, either from the board or from the Commander-in-chief.

General Washington, on hearing this circumstance, despatched one of his aids with orders for the immediate release of the persons and property which had been confined; but the officers refused to proceed on their journey, and returned to Philadelphia. *

This untoward event was much regretted by the Commander-in-chief. In a letter received some time afterwards, General Howe, after expressing his willingness that the American prisoners should be visited by deputy commissaries, who should inspect their situation, and supply their wants required, as the condition on which this indulgence should be granted, "that a similar permit should be allowed to persons appointed by him, which should be accompanied with the assurance of General Washington, that his authority will have sufficient weight to prevent any interruption to their progress, and any insult to their persons." This demand was ascribed to the treatment to which officers under the protection of his passport had already been exposed.

General Washington lamented the impediment to the exchange of prisoners, which had hitherto appeared to be insuperable; and made repeated, but ineffectual efforts to remove it.

* They alleged that their horses had been disabled, and the clothing embezzled.

General Howe had uniformly refused to proceed with any cartel, unless his right to claim for all the diseased and infirm, whom he had liberated, should be previously admitted.

At length, after all hope of inducing him to recede from that high ground had been abandoned, he suddenly relinquished it of his own accord, and acceded completely to the proposition of General Washington for the meeting of commissioners, in order to settle equitably the number to which he should be entitled for those he had discharged in the preceding winter. This point being adjusted, commissaries were mutually appointed, who were to meet on the 10th of March, in Germantown, to arrange the details of a general cartel.

The Commander-in-chief had entertained no doubt of his authority to enter into this agreement.

On the fourth of March, however, he had the mortification to perceive in a newspaper, a resolution of congress calling on the several states for the amounts of supplies furnished the prisoners, that they might be adjusted according to the rule of the 10th of December, before the exchange should take place.

On seeing this embarrassing resolution, General Washington addressed a letter to Sir William Howe, informing him that particular circumstances had rendered it inconvenient for the American commissioners to attend at the time appointed, and requesting that their meeting should be deferred from the 10th to the 21st of March. The interval was successfully employed in obtaining a repeal of the resolution.

It would seem probable that the dispositions of congress on the subject of an exchange, did not correspond with those of General Washington. From the fundamental principle of the military establishment of the United States at its commencement, an exchange of prisoners would necessarily strengthen the British, much more than the American army. The war having been carried on by troops raised for short times, aided by militia, the American prisoners, when exchanged, returned to their homes as citizens, while those of the enemy again took the field.

General Washington, who was governed by a policy more just, and more permanently beneficial, addressed himself seriously to congress, urging, as well the injury done the public faith, and his own personal honour, by this infraction of a solemn engagement, as the cruelty and impolicy of a system which must cut off for ever all hopes of an exchange, and render imprisonment as lasting as the war. He represented in strong terms the effect such a measure must have on the troops on whom they should thereafter be compelled chiefly to rely, and its impression on the friends of those already in captivity. These remonstrances produced the desired effect, and the resolutions were repealed. The commissioners met according to the second appointment; but, on examining their powers, it appeared that those given by General Washington were expressed to be in virtue of the authority vested in him; while those given by Sir William Howe contained no such declaration.

This omission produced an objection on the part of the United States; but General Howe refused to change the language, alleging that he designed the treaty to be of a personal nature, founded on the mutual confidence and honour of the contracting generals; and had no intention either to bind his government, or to extend the cartel beyond the limits and duration of his own command.

This explanation being unsatisfactory to the American commissioners, and General Howe persisting in his refusal to make the required alteration in his powers, the negotiation was broken off, and this fair prospect of terminating the distresses of numerous unfortunate persons passed away, without effecting the good it had promised.

Some time after the failure of this negotiation for a general cartel, Sir William Howe proposed that all prisoners actually exchangeable should be sent in to the nearest posts, and returns made of officer for officer of equal rank, and soldier for soldier, as far as numbers would admit; and that if a surplus of officers should remain, they should be exchanged for an equivalent in privates.

On the representations of General Washington, congress acceded to this proposition, so far as related to the exchange of officer for officer, and soldier for soldier; but rejected the part which admitted an equivalent in privates for a surplus of officers, because the officers captured with Burgoyne were exchangeable within the powers of General Howe. Under this agreement, an exchange took place to a considerable extent; but as the Americans had lost more prisoners than they had taken, unless the army of Burgoyne should be brought into computation, many of their troops were still detained in captivity.

NOTES.

NOTE—No. I. *See Page* 5

It will not be unacceptable to the reader to peruse this first report of a young gentleman who afterwards performed so distinguished a part in the revolution of his country, it is therefore inserted at large.

I was commissioned and appointed by the Hon. Robert Dinwiddie, Esq. Governor &c. of Virginia, to visit and deliver a letter to the commandant of the French forces on the Ohio, and set out on the intended journey on the same day: the next, I arrived at Fredericksburg, and engaged Mr. Jacob Vanbraam to be my French interpreter, and proceeded with him to Alexandria, where we provided necessaries. From thence we went to Winchester, and got baggage, horses, &c. and from thence we pursued the new road to Wills' Creek, where we arrived the 14th November.

Here I engaged Mr. Gist to pilot us out, and also hired four others as servitors, Barnaby Currin, and John M'Quire, Indian traders, Henry Steward, and William Jenkins; and in company with those persons left the inhabitants the next day.

The excessive rains and vast quantity of snow which had fallen, prevented our reaching Mr. Frazier's, an Indian trader, at the mouth of Turtle creek, on Monongahela river, until Thursday the 22d. We were informed here, that expresses had been sent a few days before to the traders down the river, to acquaint them with the French general's death, and the return of the major part of the French army into winter quarters.

The waters were quite impassable without swimming our horses, which obliged us to get the loan of a canoe from Frazier, and to send Barnaby Currin and Henry Steward down the Monongahela, with our baggage, to meet us at the forks of Ohio, about ten miles; there, to cross the Alleghany.

As I got down before the canoe, I spent some time in viewing the rivers, and the land in the fork, which I think extremely well situated for a fort, as it has the absolute command of both rivers. The land at the point is twenty, or twenty-five feet above the common surface of the water; and a considerable bottom of flat, well timbered land all around it very convenient for building. The rivers are each a quarter of a mile or more across, and run here very nearly at right angles; Alleghany, bearing northeast; and Monongahela, southeast. The former of these two is a very rapid and swift running water, the other deep and still, without any perceptible fall.

About two miles from this, on the southeast side of the river, at the place where the Ohio company intended to erect a fort, lives Shingiss, king of the Delawares. We called upon him, to invite him to council at the Loggstown.

As I had taken a good deal of notice yesterday of the situation at the fork, my curiosity led me to examine this more particularly, and I think it greatly inferior, either for defence or advantages; especially the latter. For a fort at the fork would be equally well situated on the Ohio, and have the entire command of the Monongahela, which runs up our settlement, and is extremely well designed for water carriage, as it is of a deep, still nature. Besides, a fort at the fork might be built at much less expense than at the other places.

Nature has well contrived this lower place for water defence; but the hill whereon it must stand being about a quarter of a mile in length, and then descending gradually on the land side, will render it difficult and very expensive to make a sufficient fortification there. The whole flat upon the hill must be taken in, the side next the descent made extremely high, or else the hill itself cut away: otherwise, the enemy may raise batteries within that distance without being exposed to a single shot from the fort.

Shingiss attended us to the Loggstown, where we arrived between sun-setting and dark, the twenty-fifth day after I left Williamsburg. We travelled over some extremely good and bad land to get to this place.

As soon as I came into town, I went to Monakatoocha (as the half king was out at his hunting cabin on Little Beaver creek, about fifteen miles off) and informed him by John Davidson, my Indian interpreter, that I was sent a messenger to the French general; and was ordered to call upon the sachems of the Six Nations to acquaint them with it. I gave him a string of wampum and a twist of tobacco, and desired him to send for the half king, which he promised to do by a runner in the morning, and for other sachems. I invited him and the other great men present, to my tent, where they stayed about an hour and returned.

According to the best observations I could make, Mr. Giff's new settlement (which we passed by) bears about west northwest seventy miles from Wills' creek; Shanapins, or the forks, north by west, or north northwest about fifty miles from that; and from thence to the Loggstown, the course is nearly west about eighteen or twenty miles: so that the whole distance, as we went and computed it, is, at least, one hundred and thirty-five or one hundred and forty miles from our back inhabitants.

25th. Came to town, four of ten Frenchmen, who had deserted from a company at the Kuskuskas, which lies at the mouth of this river. I got the following account from them. They were sent from New Orleans with a hundred men, and eight canoe loads of provisions, to this place, where they expected to have met the same number of men, from the forts on this side of lake Erie, to convoy them and the stores up, who were not arrived when they ran off.

I inquired into the situation of the French on the Mississippi, their numbers, and what forts they had built. They informed me, that there were four small forts between New Orleans and the Black Islands, garrisoned with about thirty or forty men, and a few small pieces in each. That at New Orleans, which is near the mouth of the Mississippi, there are thirty-five companies of forty men each, with a pretty strong fort mounting eight carriage guns; and at the Black Islands there are several companies and a fort with six guns. The Black Islands are about a hundred and thirty leagues above the mouth of the Ohio, which is about three hundred and fifty above New Orleans. They also acquainted me, that there was a small pallisadoed fort on the Ohio, at the mouth of the Obaish, about sixty leagues from the Mississippi. The Obaish heads near the west end of lake Erie, and affords the communication between the French on the Mississippi and those on the lakes. These deserters came up from the lower Shannoah town with one Brown, an Indian trader, and were going to Philadelphia.

About three o'clock this evening the half king came to town. I went up and invited him with Davidson, privately, to my tent; and desired him to relate some of the particulars of his journey to the French commandant, and of his reception there; also, to give me an account of the ways and distance. He told me, that the nearest and levelest way was now impassable, by reason of many large miry savannas; that we must be obliged to go by Venango, and should not get to the near fort in less than five or six nights sleep, good travelling. When he went to the fort, he said he was received in a very stern manner by the late commander, who asked him very abruptly, what he had come about, and to declare his business: which he said he did in the following speech:

"Fathers, I am come to tell you your own speeches; what your own mouths have declared. Fathers, you, in former days, set a silver basin before us, wherein there was the leg of a beaver, and desired all the nations to come and eat of it, to eat in peace and plenty, and not to be churlish to one another: and that if any such person should be found to be a disturber, I here lay down by the edge of the dish a rod, which you must scourge them with; and if your father should get foolish, in my old days, I desire you may use it upon me as well as others.

"Now, fathers, it is you who are the disturbers in this land, by coming and building your towns; and taking it away unknown to us, and by force.

"Fathers, we kindled a fire a long time ago, at a place called Montreal, where we desired you to stay, and not to come and intrude upon our land. I now desire you may despatch to that place; for be it known to you, fathers, that this is our land and not yours.

"Fathers, I desire you may hear me in civilness; if not, we must handle that rod which was laid down for the use of the obstreperous. If you had come in a peaceable manner, like our brothers the English, we would not have been against your trading with us, as they do; but to come, fathers, and build houses upon our land, and to take it by force, is what we can not submit to.

"Fathers, both you and the English are white, we live in a country between; therefore, the land belongs to neither one nor the other. But the great Being above allowed it to be a place of residence for us; so, fathers, I desire you to withdraw, as I have done our brothers the English; for I will keep you at arm's length. I lay this down as a trial for both, to see which will have the greatest regard to it, and that side we will stand by, and make equal sharers with us. Our brothers, the English, have heard this, and I come now to tell it to you; for I am not afraid to discharge you off this land."

This he said was the substance of what he spoke to the general, who made this reply.

"Now, my child, I have heard your speech: you spoke first, but it is my time to speak now. Where is my wampum that you took away, with the marks of towns in it? This wampum I do not know, which you have discharged me off the land with: but you need not put yourself to the trouble of speaking, for I will not hear you. I am not afraid of flies or mus-quitoes, for Indians are such as those: I tell you down that river I will go, and build upon it, according to my command. If the river was blocked up, I have forces sufficient to burst it open, and tread under my feet all that stand in opposition, together with their alliances; for my force is as the sand upon the sea shore: therefore here is your wampum; I sling it at you. Child, you talk foolish; you say this land belongs to you, but there is not the black of my nail yours. I saw that land sooner than you did, before the Shannoahs and you were at war; Lead was the man who went down and took possession of that river. It is my land, and I will have it, let who will stand up for, or say against it. I will buy and sell with the English (mockingly). If people will be ruled by me, they may expect kindness, but not else."

The half king told me he had inquired of the general after two Englishmen, who were made prisoners, and received this answer:

'Child, you think it a very great hardship that I made prisoners of those two people at Venango. Don't you concern yourself with it: we took and carried them to Canada, to get intelligence of what the English were doing in Virginia."

He informed me that they had built two forts, one on lake Erie, and another on French creek, near a small lake, about fifteen miles asunder, and a large wagon road between. They are both built after the same model, but different in size: that on the lake the largest. He gave me a plan of them of his own drawing.

The Indians inquired very particularly after their brothers in Carolina gaol.

They also asked what sort of a boy it was who was taken from the south branch; for they were told by some Indians, that a party of French Indians had carried a white boy by Kuskuska town, towards the lakes.

26th. We met in council at the long house about nine o'clock, when I spoke to them as follows:

"Brothers, I have called you together in council, by order of your brother the governor of Virginia, to acquaint you, that

I am sent with all possible despatch, to visit and deliver a letter to the French commandant, of very great importance to your brothers the English; and I dare say to you, their friends and allies.

"I was desired, brothers, by your brother the governor to call upon you, the sachems of the nations, to inform you of it, and to ask your advice and assistance to proceed the nearest and best road to the French. You see, brothers, I have gotten thus far on my journey.

"His honour likewise desired me to apply to you for some of your young men to conduct and provide provisions for us on our way; and be a safeguard against those French Indians who have taken up the hatchet against us. I have spoken thus particularly to you, brothers, because his honour our governor treats you as good friends and allies, and holds you in great esteem. To confirm what I have said, I give you this string of wampum."

After they had considered for some time on the above discourse, the half king got up and spoke.

"Now, my brother, in regard to what my brother the governor had desired of me, I return you this answer.

"I rely upon you as a brother ought to do, as you say we are brothers, and one people. We shall put heart in hand and speak to our fathers, the French, concerning the speech they made to me; and you may depend that we will endeavour to be your guard.

"Brother, as you have asked my advice, I hope you will be ruled by it, and stay until I can provide a company to go with you. The French speech belt is not here; I have it to go for to my hunting cabin. Likewise, the people whom I have ordered in are not yet come, and can not until the third night from this; until which time, brother, I must beg you to stay.

"I intend to send the guard of Mingos, Shannoahs, and Delawares, that our brothers may see the love and loyalty we bear them."

As I had orders to make all possible despatch, and waiting here was very contrary to my inclination, I thanked him in the most suitable manner I could; and told him that my business required the greatest expedition, and would not admit of that delay. He was not well pleased that I should offer to go before the time he had appointed, and told me, that he could not consent to our going without a guard, for fear some accident should befall us, and draw a reflection upon him. Besides, said he, this is a matter of no small moment, and must not be entered into without due consideration; for I intend to deliver up the French speech belt, and make the Shannoahs and Delawares do the same. And accordingly he gave orders to king Shingiss, who was present, to attend on Wednesday night with the wampum; and two men of their nation to be in readiness to set out with us next morning. As I found it was impossible to get off without affronting them in the most egregious manner, I consented to stay.

I gave them back a string of wampum which I met with at Mr. Frazier's, and which they sent with a speech to his honour the governor, to inform him, that three nations of French Indians, viz. Chippoways, Ottoways, and Orundaks, had taken up the hatchet against the English; and desired them to repeat it over again. But this they postponed doing until they met in full council with the Shannoah and Delaware chiefs.

27th. Runners were despatched very early for the Shannoah chiefs. The half king set out himself to fetch the French speech belt from his hunting cabin.

28th. He returned this evening, and came with Monaka-toocha, and two other sachems to my tent; and begged (as they had complied with his honour the governor's request, in providing men, &c.) to know on what business we were going to the French? This was a question I had all along expected, and had provided as satisfactory answers to as I could; which allayed their curiosity a little.

Monakatoocha informed me, that an Indian from Venango brought news, a few days ago, that the French had called all the Mingos, Delawares, &c. together at that place; and told them that they intended to have been down the river this fall, but the waters were growing cold, and the winter advancing, which obliged them to go into quarters; but that they might assuredly expect them in the spring, with a far greater number; and desired that they might be quite passive, and not intermeddle unless they had a mind to draw all their force upon them: for that they expected to fight the English three years (as they supposed there would be some attempts made to stop them) in which time they should conquer. But that if they should prove equally strong, they and the English would join to cut them all off, and divide the land between them: that though they had lost their general, and some few of their soldiers, yet there were men enough to reinforce them, and make them masters of the Ohio.

This speech, he said, was delivered to them by one Captain Joncaire, their interpreter in chief, living at Venango, and a man of note in the army.

29th. The half king and Monakatoocha, came very early and begged me to stay one day more: for notwithstanding they had used all the diligence in their power, the Shannoah chiefs had not brought the wampum they ordered, but would certainly be in to night; if not, they would delay me no longer, but would send it after us as soon as they arrived. When I found them so pressing in their request, and knew that returning of wampum was the abolishing of agreements; and giving this up was shaking off all dependence upon the French, I consented to stay, as I believed an offence offered at this crisis, might be attended with greater ill consequence, than another day's delay. They also informed me, that Shingiss could not get in his men; and was prevented from coming himself by his wife's sickness; (I believe, by fear of the French) but that the wampum of that nation was lodged with Kustalogo, one of their chiefs, at Venango.

In the evening, late, they came again, and acquainted me that the Shannoahs were not yet arrived, but that it should not retard the prosecution of our journey. He delivered in my hearing the speech that was to be made to the French by Jeskakake, one of their old chiefs, which was giving up the belt the late commandant had asked for, and repeating nearly the same speech he himself had done before.

He also delivered a string of wampum to this chief, which was sent by king Shingiss, to be given to Kustalogo, with orders to repair to the French, and deliver up the wampum.

He likewise gave a very large string of black and white wampum, which was to be sent up immediately to the Six Nations, if the French refused to quit the land at this warning; which was the third and last time, and was the right of this Jeskakake to deliver.

30th. Last night, the great men assembled at their council house, to consult further about this journey, and who were to go: the result of which was, that only three of their chiefs, with one of their best hunters, should be our convoy. The reason they gave for not sending more, after what had been proposed at council the 26th, was, that a greater number might give the French suspicions of some bad design, and cause them to be treated rudely: but I rather think they could not get their hunters in.

We set out about nine o'clock with the half king, Jeskakake, White Thunder, and the Hunter; and travelled on the road to Venango, where we arrived the fourth of December, without any thing remarkable happening but a continued series of bad weather.

This is an old Indian town, situated at the mouth of French creek, on Ohio; and lies near north about sixty miles from the Loggstown, but more than seventy the way we were obliged to go.

We found the French colours hoisted at a house from which they had driven Mr. John Frazier, an English subject. I immediately repaired to it, to know where the commander resided. There were three officers, one of whom, Captain Joncaire, informed me that he had the command of the Ohio; but that there was a general officer at the near fort, where he advised me to apply for an answer. He invited us to sup with them, and treated us with the greatest complaisance.

The wine, as they dosed themselves pretty plentifully with it, soon banished the restraint which at first appeared in their conversation, and gave a license to their tongues to reveal their sentiments more freely.

They told me, that it was their absolute design to take possession of the Ohio, and by G**d they would do it: for that, although they were sensible the English could raise two men for their one, yet they knew their motions were too slow and dilatory to prevent any undertaking of theirs. They pretend to have an undoubted right to the river from a discovery made by one La Salle, sixty years ago: and the rise of this expedition is, to prevent our settling on the river or waters of it, as they heard of some families moving out in order thereto. From the best intelligence I could get, there have been fifteen hundred men on this side Ontario lake. But upon the death of the general, all were recalled to about six or seven hundred, who were left to garrison four forts, one hundred and fifty or thereabout in each. The first of them is on French creek, near a small lake, about sixty miles from Venango, near north northwest: the next lies on lake Erie, where the greater part of their stores are kept, about fifteen miles from the other: from this it is one hundred and twenty miles to the carrying place, at the falls of Lake Erie, where there is a small fort, at which they lodge their goods in bringing them from Montreal, the place from whence all their stores are brought. The next fort lies about twenty miles from this, on Ontario lake. Between this fort and Montreal, there are three others, the first of which is nearly opposite to the English fort Oswego. From the fort on lake Erie to Montreal is about six hundred miles, which, they say, requires no more (if good weather,) than four weeks voyage, if they go in barks or large vessels, so that they may cross the lake: but if they come in canoes, it will require five or six weeks, for they are obliged to keep under the shore.

5th. Rained excessively all day, which prevented our travelling. Captain Joncaire sent for the half king, as he had but just heard that he came with me. He affected to be much concerned that I did not make free to bring them in before. I excused it in the best manner of which I was capable, and told him, I did not think their company agreeable, as I had heard him say a good deal in dispraise of Indians in general: but another motive prevented me from bringing them into his company: I knew that he was an interpreter, and a person of very great influence among the Indians, and had lately used all possible means to draw them over to his interest; therefore, I was desirous of giving him no opportunity that could be avoided.

When they came in, there was great pleasure expressed at seeing them. He wondered how they could be so near without coming to visit him, made several trifling presents, and applied liquor so fast, that they were soon rendered incapable of the business they came about, notwithstanding the caution which was given.

6th. The half king came to my tent, quite sober, and insisted very much that I should stay and hear what he had to say to the French. I fain would have prevented him from speaking any thing until he came to the commandant, but could not prevail. He told me, that at this place a council fire was kindled, where all their business with these people was to be transacted, and that the management of the Indian affairs was left solely to Monsieur Joncaire. As I was desirous of knowing the issue of this, I agreed to stay; but sent our horses a little way up French creek, to raft over and encamp; which I knew would make it near night.

About ten o'clock, they met in council. The king spoke much the same as he had before done to the general; and offered the French speech belt which had before been demanded, with the marks of four towns on it, which Monsieur Joncaire refused to receive, but desired him to carry it to the fort to the commander.

7th. Monsieur La Force, Commissary of the French stores, and three other soldiers, came over to accompany us up. We found it extremely difficult to get the Indians off to-day, as every stratagem had been used to prevent their going up with me. I had last night left John Davidson (the Indian interpreter) whom I brought with me from town, and strictly charged him not to be out of their company, as I could not get them over to my tent; for they had some business with Kustologa, chiefly to know why he did not deliver up the French speech belt which he had in keeping: but I was obliged to send Mr. Gist over to-day to fetch them, which he did with great persuasion.

At twelve o'clock, we set out for the fort, and were prevented from arriving there until the eleventh by excessive rains, snows, and bad travelling through many mires and swamps; these we were obliged to pass to avoid crossing the creek, which was impossible, either by fording or rafting, the water was so high and rapid.

We passed over much good land since we left Venango, and through several extensive and very rich meadows, one of which, I believe, was nearly four miles in length, and considerably wide in some places.

12th. I prepared early to wait upon the commander, and was received, and conducted to him by the second officer in command. I acquainted him with my business, and offered my commission and letter: both of which he desired me to keep until the arrival of Monsieur Reparti, captain at the next fort, who was sent for and expected every hour.

This commander is a knight of the military order of St. Louis, and named Legardeur de St. Pierre. He is an elderly gentleman, and has much the air of a soldier. He was sent over to take the command, immediately upon the death of the late general, and arrived here about seven days before me.

At two o'clock, the gentleman who was sent for arrived, when I offered the letter, &c. again, which they received, and adjourned into a private apartment for the captain to translate, who understood a little English. After he had done it, the commander desired I would walk in and bring my interpreter to peruse and correct it; which I did.

13th. The chief officers retired to hold a council of war, which gave me an opportunity of taking the dimensions of the fort, and making what observations I could.

It is situated on the south, or west fork of French creek, near the water; and is almost surrounded by the creek, and a small branch of it which forms a kind of island. Four houses compose the sides. The bastions are made of piles driven into the ground, standing more than twelve feet above it, and sharp at top; with port holes cut for cannon, and loop holes for the small arms to fire through. There are eight six pound pieces mounted in each bastion, and one piece of four pound before the gate. In the bastions are a guard house, chapel, doctor's lodging, and the commander's private store: round which are laid platforms for the cannon and men to stand on. There are several barracks without the fort, for the soldiers' dwelling, covered, some with bark, and some with boards, made chiefly of logs. There are also several other houses, such as stables, smith's shop, &c.

I could get no certain account of the number of men here; but according to the best judgment I could form, there are an hundred, exclusive of officers, of which there are many. I also gave orders to the people who were with me, to take an exact account of the canoes which were hauled up to convey their forces down in the spring. This they did, and told fifty of birch bark, and an hundred and seventy of pine; besides many others which were blocked out, in readiness for being made.

14th. As the snow increased very fast, and our horses daily became weaker, I sent them off unloaded, under the care of Barnaby Currin and two others, to make all convenient despatch to Venango, and there to wait our arrival, if there was a prospect of the river's freezing: if not, then to continue down to Shanapin's town, at the forks of Ohio, and there to wait until we came to cross the Alleghany; intending myself to go down by water, as I had the offer of a canoe or two.

As I found many plots concerted to retard the Indians' business, and prevent their returning with me, I endeavoured all that lay in my power to frustrate their schemes, and hurried them on to execute their intended design. They accordingly pressed for admittance this evening, which at length was granted them, privately, to the commander and one or two other officers. The half king told me that he offered the wampum to the commander, who evaded taking it, and made many fair promises of love and friendship; said he wanted to live in peace and trade amicably with them, as a proof of which, he would send some goods immediately down to the Loggstown for them. But I rather think the design of that is to bring away all our straggling traders they meet with, as I privately understood they intended to carry an officer, &c. with them. And what rather confirms this opinion, I was inquiring of the commander by what authority he had made prisoners of several of our English subjects. He told me that the country belonged to them; that no Englishman had a right to trade upon those waters; and that he had orders to make every person prisoner who attempted it on the Ohio, or the waters of it.

I inquired of Captain Reparti about the boy that was carried by this place, as it was done while the command devolved on him, between the death of the late general, and the arrival of the present. He acknowledged that a boy had been carried past: and that the Indians had two or three white men's scalps, (I was told by some of the Indians at Venango, eight) but pretended to have forgotten the name of the place where the boy came from, and all the particular facts, though he had questioned him for some hours, as they were carrying past. I likewise inquired what they had done with John Trotter and James M'Clocklan, two Pennsylvania traders, whom they had taken with all their goods. They told me that they had been sent to Canada, but were now returned home.

This evening, I received an answer to his honour the governor's letter, from the commandant.

15th. The commandant ordered a plentiful store of liquor, provision, &c. to be put on board our canoes, and appeared to be extremely complaisant, though he was exerting every artifice which he could invent to set our Indians at variance with us, to prevent their going until after our departure: presents, rewards, and every thing which could be suggested by him or his officers. I can not say that ever in my life I suffered so much anxiety as I did in this affair. I saw that every stratagem, which the most fruitful brain could invent, was practised to win the half king to their interest; and that leaving him there was giving them the opportunity they aimed at. I went to the half king and pressed him in the strongest terms to go; he told me that the commandant would not discharge him until the morning. I then went to the commandant, and desired him to do their business, and complained of ill treatment; for keeping them, as they were part of my company, was detaining me. This he promised not to do, but to forward my journey as much as he could. He protested he did not keep them, but was ignorant of the cause of their stay; though I soon found it out. He had promised them a present of guns, &c. if they would wait until the morning. As I was very much pressed by the Indians to wait this day for them, I consented, on a promise that nothing should hinder them in the morning.

16th. The French were not slack in their inventions to keep the Indians this day also. But as they were obliged, according to promise, to give the present, they then endeavoured to try the power of liquor, which I doubt not would have prevailed at any other time than this: but I urged and insisted with the king so closely upon his word, that he refrained, and set off with us as he had engaged.

We had a tedious and very fatiguing passage down the creek. Several times we had like to have been staved against rocks; and many times were obliged all hands to get out and remain in the water half an hour or more, getting over the shoals. At one place, the ice had lodged, and made it impassable by water; we were, therefore, obliged to carry our canoe across the neck of land, a quarter of a mile over. We did not reach Venango until the 22d, where we met with our horses.

This creek is extremely crooked. I dare say the distance between the fort and Venango, can not be less than one hundred and thirty miles to follow the meanders.

23d. When I got things ready to set off, I sent for the half king, to know whether he intended to go with us, or by water. He told me that White Thunder had hurt himself much, and was sick, and unable to walk; therefore he was obliged to carry him down in a canoe. As I found he intended to stay here a day or two, and knew that Monsieur Joncaire would employ every scheme to set him against the English, as he had before done, I told him, I hoped he would guard against his flattery, and let no fine speeches influence him in their favour. He desired I might not be concerned, for he knew the French too well, for any thing to engage him in their favour; and that though he could not go down with us, he yet would endeavour to meet at the forks with Joseph Campbell, to deliver a speech for me to carry to his honour the governor. He told me he would order the Young Hunter to attend us, and get provisions, &c. if wanted.

Our horses were now so weak and feeble, and the baggage so heavy, (as we were obliged to provide all the necessaries which the journey would require) that we doubted much their performing it. Therefore, myself and others, except the drivers, who were obliged to ride, gave up our horses for packs, to assist along with the baggage. I put myself in an Indian walking dress, and continued with them three days, until I found there was no probability of their getting home in any reasonable time. The horses became less able to travel every day; the cold increased very fast; and the roads were becoming much worse by a deep snow, continually freezing: therefore, as I was uneasy to get back, to make report of my proceedings to his honour the governor, I determined to prosecute my journey, the nearest way through the woods, on foot.

Accordingly, I left Mr. Vanbraam in charge of our baggage, with money and directions to provide necessaries from place to place for themselves and horses, and to make the most convenient despatch in travelling.

I took my necessary papers, pulled off my clothes, and tied myself up in a watch coat. Then, with gun in hand, and pack on my back, in which were my papers and provisions, I set out with Mr. Gist, fitted in the same manner, on Wednesday the 26th. The day following, just after we had passed a place called Murdering town, (where we intended to quit the path and steer across the country for Shanapin's town) we fell in with a party of French Indians, who had laid in wait for us. One of them fired at Mr. Gist or me, not fifteen steps off, but fortunately missed. We took this fellow into custody, and kept him until about nine o'clock at night, then let him go, and walked all the remaining part of the night without making any stop, that we might get the start, so far, as to be out of the reach of their pursuit the next day, since we were well assured they would follow our track as soon as it was light. The next day we continued travelling until quite dark, and got to the river about two miles above Shanapin's. We expected to have found the river frozen, but it was not, only about fifty yards from each shore. The ice, I suppose, had broken up above, for it was driving in vast quantities.

There was no way for getting over but on a raft, which we set about, with but one poor hatchet, and finished just after sun setting. This was a whole day's work: we next got it launched, then went on board of it, and set off; but before we were half way over, we were jammed in the ice, in such a manner, that we expected every moment our raft to sink, and ourselves to perish. I put out my setting pole to try to stop the raft, that the ice might pass by, when the rapidity of the stream threw it with so much violence against the pole, that it jerked me out into ten feet water; but I fortunately saved myself by catching hold of one of the raft logs. Notwithstanding all our efforts, we could not get to either shore, but were obliged, as we were near an island, to quit our raft and make to it.

The cold was so extremely severe, that Mr. Gist had all his fingers, and some of his toes frozen, and the water was shut up so hard, that we found no difficulty in getting off the island on the ice in the morning, and went to Mr. Frazier's. We met here with twenty warriors, who were going to the southward to war; but coming to a place on the head of the great Kanawa, where they found seven people killed and scalped, (all but one woman with very light hair) they turned about and ran back, for fear the inhabitants should rise and take them as the authors of the murder. They report that the bodies were lying about the house, and some of them much torn and eaten by the hogs. By the marks which were left, they say they were French Indians of the Ottoway nation, &c. who did it.

As we intended to take horses here, and it required some time to find them, I went up about three miles to the mouth of Yohogany, to visit queen Alliquippa, who had expressed great concern that we passed her in going to the fort. I made her a present of a watch coat and a bottle of rum, which latter was thought much the best present of the two.

Tuesday, the first of January, we left Mr. Frazier's house, and arrived at Mr. Gist's, at Monongahela, the second, where I bought a horse, saddle, &c. The sixth, we met seventeen horses loaded with materials and stores for a fort at the forks of Ohio, and the day after, some families going out to settle. This day, we arrived at Wills' creek, after as fatiguing a journey as it is possible to conceive, rendered so by excessive bad weather. From the first day of December to the fifteenth, there was but one day on which it did not rain or snow incessantly; and throughout the whole journey, we met with nothing but one continued series of cold, wet weather, which occasioned very uncomfortable lodgings, especially after we had quitted our tent, which was some screen from the inclemency of it.

On the 11th, I got to Belvoir, where I stopped one day to take necessary rest; and then set out and arrived in Williamsburg the 16th, when I waited upon his honour the governor, with the letter I had brought from the French commandant, and to give an account of the success of my proceedings. This

I beg leave to do by offering the foregoing narrative, as it contains the most remarkable occurrences which happened in my journey.

I hope what has been said will be sufficient to make your honour satisfied with my conduct; for that was my aim in undertaking the journey, and chief study throughout the prosecution of it.

———

NOTE—No. II. *See Page* 10.

The author is indebted, for the letter alluded to, to the Editor of the Lancaster Journal.

SIR,—I am really sorry that I have it not in my power to answer your request, in a more satisfactory manner. If you had favoured me with the journal a few days sooner, I would have examined it carefully, and endeavoured to point out such errors as might conduce to your use, my advantage, and the public satisfaction; but now it is out of my power.

I had no time to make any remarks upon that piece which is called my journal. The enclosed are observations on the French notes. They are of no use to me separated, nor will they, I believe, be of any to you; yet I send them unconnected and incoherent as they were taken, for I have no opportunity to correct them.

In regard to the journal, I can only observe in general, that I kept no regular one during that expedition: rough minutes of occurrences I certainly took, and find them as certainly and strangely metamorphosed—some parts left out which I remember were entered, and many things added that never were thought of; the names of men and things egregiously miscalled; and the whole of what I saw Englished, is very incorrect and nonsensical:—yet, I will not pretend to say that the little body who brought it to me, has not made a literal translation, and a good one.

Short as my time is, I can not help remarking on Villiers' account of the battle of, and transactions at the Meadows, as it is very extraordinary, and not less erroneous than inconsistent. He says the French received the first fire. It is well known that we received it at six hundred paces distance. He also says, our fears obliged us to retreat in the most disorderly manner after the capitulation. How is this consistent with his other account? He acknowledges that we sustained the attack, warmly, from ten in the morning until dark, and that he called first to parley, which strongly indicates that we were not totally absorbed in fear. If the gentleman in his account had adhered to the truth, he must have confessed, that we looked upon his offer to parley as an artifice to get into and examine our trenches, and refused on this account, until they desired an officer might be sent to them, and gave their parole for his safe return. He might also, if he had been as great a lover of the truth as he was of vain glory, have said, that we absolutely refused their first and second proposals, and would consent to capitulate on no other terms than such as we obtained. That we were wilfully, or ignorantly deceived by our interpreter in regard to the word *assassination,* I do aver, and will to my dying moment; so will every officer that was present. The interpreter was a Dutchman, little acquainted with the English tongue, therefore might not advert to the tone and meaning of the word in English; but, whatever his motives were for so doing, certain it is, he called it the *death,* or the *loss* of the Sieur Jumonville. So we received and so we understood it, until to our great surprise and mortification, we found it otherwise in a literal translation. That we left our baggage and horses at the Meadows is certain; that there was not even a possibility to bring them away is equally certain, as we had every horse belonging to the camp killed or taken away during the action; so that it was impracticable to bring any thing off that our shoulders were not able to bear, and to wait there was impossible, for we had scarce three days provisions, and were seventy miles from a supply; yet, to say we came off precipitately is absolutely false; notwithstanding they did, contrary to articles, suffer their Indians to pillage our baggage, and commit all kinds of irregularity, we were with them until ten o'clock the next day; we destroyed our powder and other stores, nay, even our private baggage, to prevent its falling into their hands, as we could not bring it off. When we had got about a mile from the place of action, we missed two or three of the wounded, and sent a party back to bring them up—this is the party he speaks of. We brought them all safe off, and encamped within three miles of the Meadows. These are circumstances, I think, that make it evidently clear, that we were not very apprehensive of danger. The colours he speaks of to be left, was a large flag of immense size and weight; our regimental colours were brought off and are now in my possession. Their gasconades, and boasted clemency, must appear in the most ludicrous light to every considerate person who reads Villiers' journal;—such preparations for an attack, such vigour and intrepidity as he pretends to have conducted his march with, such revenge, as by his own account, appeared in his attack, considered, it will hardly be thought that compassion was his motive for calling a parley. But to sum up the whole, Mr. Villiers pays himself no great compliment, in saying, we were struck with a panic when matters were adjusted. We surely could not be afraid without cause, and if we had cause after capitulation, it was a reflection upon himself.

I do not doubt, but your good nature will excuse the badness of my paper, and the incoherence of my writing—think you see me in a public house in a crowd, surrounded with noise, and you hit my case. You do me particular honour in offering your friendship: I wish I may be so happy as always to merit it, and deserve your correspondence, which I should be glad to cultivate.

NOTE—No. III. *See Page* 51.

SIR,—We your most obedient and affectionate officers, beg leave to express our great concern, at the disagreeable news we have received of your determination to resign the command of that corps, in which we have under you long served.

The happiness we have enjoyed, and the honour we have acquired together, with the mutual regard that has always subsisted between you and your officers, have implanted so sensible an affection in the minds of us all, that we can not be silent on this critical occasion.

In our earliest infancy you took us under your tuition, trained us up in the practice of that discipline, which alone can constitute good troops, from the punctual observance of which you never suffered the least deviation.

Your steady adherence to impartial justice, your quick discernment, and invariable regard to merit, wisely intended to inculcate those genuine sentiments of true honour and passion for glory, from which the greatest military achievements have been derived, first heightened our natural emulation and our desire to excel. How much we improved by those regulations and your own example, with what alacrity we have hitherto discharged our duty, with what cheerfulness we have encountered the severest toils, especially while under your particular directions, we submit to yourself, and flatter ourselves that we have in a great measure answered your expectations.

Judge, then, how sensibly we must be affected with the loss of such an excellent commander, such a sincere friend, and so affable a companion. How rare is it to find those amiable qualifications blended together in one man! How great the loss of such a man! Adieu to that superiority, which the enemy have granted us over other troops, and which even the regulars and provincials have done us the honour publicly to acknowledge! Adieu to that strict discipline and order, which you have always maintained! Adieu to that happy union and harmony, which have been our principal cement!

It gives us additional sorrow, when we reflect, to find our unhappy country will receive a loss no less irreparable than our own. Where will it meet a man so experienced in military affairs—one so renowned for patriotism, conduct, and courage? Who has so great a knowledge of the enemy we have to deal with?—who so well acquainted with their situation and strength?—who so much respected by the soldiery? —who, in short, so able to support the military character of Virginia?

Your approved love to your king and country, and your uncommon perseverance in promoting the honour and true interest of the service, convince us that the most cogent reasons only could induce you to quit it; yet we, with the greatest deference, presume to intreat you to suspend those thoughts for another year, and to lead us on to assist in the glorious work of extirpating our enemies, towards which, so considerable advances have been already made. In you, we place the most implicit confidence. Your presence only will cause a steady firmness and vigour to actuate in every breast, despising the greatest dangers, and thinking light of toils and hardships, while led on by the man we know and love.

But if we must be so unhappy as to part, if the exigencies of your affairs force you to abandon us, we beg it as our last request, that you will recommend some person most capable to command, whose military knowledge, whose honour, whose conduct, and whose disinterested principles, we may depend on.

Frankness, sincerity, and a certain openness of soul, are the true characteristics of an officer, and we flatter ourselves that you do not think us capable of saying any thing contrary to the purest dictates of our minds. Fully persuaded of this, we beg leave to assure you, that, as you have hitherto been the actuating soul of our whole corps, we shall at all times pay the most invariable regard to your will and pleasure, and will always be happy to demonstrate by our actions with how much respect and esteem we are, &c.

NOTE—No. IV. *See Page* 54.

The delegates of the United Colonies of New Hampshire, Massachusetts Bay, Rhode Island, Connecticut, New York, New Jersey, Pennsylvania, the counties of Newcastle, Kent and Sussex on Delaware, Maryland, Virginia, North Carolina and South Carolina:

To George Washington, esquire.

We, reposing special trust and confidence in your patriotism, valour, conduct, and fidelity, do, by these presents constitute and appoint you to be general and commander-in-chief of the army of the United Colonies, and of all the forces now raised, or to be raised by them, and of all others who shall voluntarily offer their service, and join the said army for the defence of American liberty, and for repelling every hostile invasion thereof: and you are hereby invested with full power and authority to act as you shall think for the good and welfare of the service.

And we do hereby strictly charge and require all officers and soldiers under your command, to be obedient to your orders, and diligent in the exercise of their several duties.

And we also enjoin and require you to be careful in executing the great trust reposed in you, by causing strict discipline and order to be observed in the army, and that the soldiers be duly exercised and provided with all convenient necessaries.

And you are to regulate your conduct in every respect by the rules and discipline of war, (as herewith given you) and punctually to observe and follow such orders and directions from time to time as you shall receive from this or a future congress of these United Colonies, or committee of congress.

This commission to continue in force, until revoked by us, or a future congress.

———

NOTE—No. V. *See Page* 78.

This letter is so truly characteristic of the writer, and treats in a manner so peculiar to himself, the measures of congress on this subject, that, although it may not be immediately connected with the Life of General Washington, the reader will not be displeased with its insertion

Stamford, January 22, 1779.

SIR,—As General Washington has informed the congress of his motives for detaching me, it is needless to trouble you upon the subject. I am therefore only to inform you that I have collected a body of about twelve hundred men from the colony of Connecticut, whose zeal and ardour demonstrated on this occasion can not be sufficiently praised. With this body I am marching directly to New York to execute the different purposes for which I am detached. I am sensible, sir, that nothing can carry the air of greater presumption than a servant intruding his opinion unasked upon his master, but at the same time there are certain seasons when the real danger of the master may not only excuse, but render laudable, the servant's officiousness. I therefore flatter myself that the congress will receive with indulgence and lenity the opinion I shall offer. The scheme of simply disarming the tories seems to me totally ineffectual; it will only embitter their minds and add virus to their venom. They can, and will, always be supplied with fresh arms by the enemy. That of seizing the most dangerous will, I apprehend, from the vagueness of the instruction, be attended with some bad consequences, and can answer no good one. It opens so wide a door for partiality and prejudice to the different congresses and committees on the continent, that much discord and animosity will probably ensue; it being next to impossible to distinguish who are, and who are not the most dangerous. The plan of explaining to these deluded people the justice and merits of the American cause is certainly generous and humane, but I am afraid, will be fruitless. They are so riveted in their opinions, that I am persuaded should an angel descend from heaven with his golden trumpet, and ring in their ears that their conduct was criminal, he would be disregarded. I had lately myself an instance of their infatuation which, if it is not impertinent, I will relate. At Newport I took the liberty, without any authority but the conviction of necessity, to administer a very strong oath to some of the leading tories, for which liberty I humbly ask pardon of the congress. One article of this oath was to take arms in defence of their country, if called upon by the voice of the congress. To this Colonel Wanton and others flatly refused their assent; to take arms against their sovereign, they said, was too monstrous an impiety. I asked them if they had lived at the time of the revolution whether they would have been revolutionists—their answers were at first evasive, circuitous, and unintelligible, but, by fixing them down precisely to the question, I at length drew from them a positive confession that no violence, no provocation on the part of the court, could prevail upon them to act with the continent. Such, I am afraid, is the creed and principles of the whole party great and small.—Sense, reason, argument, and eloquence, have been expended in vain; and in vain you may still argue and reason to the end of time. Even the common feelings and resentments of humanity have not aroused them, but rather with a malignant pleasure they have beheld the destruction of their fellow-citizens and relations. But I am running into declamation, perhaps impertinent and presuming, when I ought to confine myself to the scheme I submit to your consideration. It is, sir, in the first place, to disarm all the manifestly disaffected, as well of the lower as the higher class, not on the principle of putting them in a state of impotence (for this I observed before will not be the case) but to supply our troops with arms of which they stand in too great need. Secondly, to appraise their estates and oblige them to deposite at least the value of one half of their respective property in the hands of the continental congress as a security for their good behaviour. And lastly, to administer the strongest oath that can be devised to act offensively and defensively in support of the common rights. I confess that men so eaten up with bigotry, as the bulk of them appear to be, will not consider themselves as bound by this oath; particularly as it is in some measure forced, they will argue that it is by no means obligatory; but if I mistake not, it will be a sort of criterion by which you will be able to distinguish the desperate fanatics from those who are reclaimable. The former must of course be secured and carried to some interior parts of the continent where they can not be dangerous. This mode of proceeding I conceive (if any can) will be effectual—but whether it meets with the approbation or disapprobation of the congress, I most humbly conjure them not to attribute the proposal to arrogance, or self-conceit, or pragmatical officiousness, but, at worst, to an intemperate zeal for the public service.

Notwithstanding the apparent slimness of the authority, as I am myself convinced that it is substantial, I think it my duty to communicate a circumstance to congress. I have with me here, sir, a deserter from Captain Wallace's ship before Newport. It is necessary to inform you that this Captain Wallace has the reputation of being the most imprudent and rash of all mortals—particularly when he is heated with wine, which, as reported, is a daily incident: that in these moments he blabs his most secret instructions even to the common men. This deserter, then, informs us that the captain a few days ago assembled the sailors and marines on the quarter-deck, and assured them, by way of encouragement, that they were to proceed very soon to New York, where they were to be joined by his majesty's most loyal subjects of White Plains, Poughkeepsie, and Long Island, and at the same time bestowed abundantly his curses on the admiral and general for their dilatoriness and scandalous conduct in not availing themselves sooner of the invitation they had received from the worthy gentlemen. The congress will make what comments they please on this information, which I must repeat I thought it my duty to communicate. Upon the whole, sir, you may be assured that it is the intention of the ministerialists to take possession, and immediately, of New York. The intercepted letters, the unguarded expressions of their officers, in their interviews with ours on the lines, but above all the manifest advantages resulting to their cause from this measure, put their intention beyond dispute. With submission therefore to the wisdom of the congress, it behooves them, I should think, not to lose a moment in securing this important post, which, if in the hands of the enemy, must cut the continent in twain, and render it almost impossible for the northern and southern colonies to support each other. This crisis, when every thing is at stake, is not a time to be over complacent to the timidity of the inhabitants of any particular spot. I have now under my command a respectable force adequate to the purpose of securing the place, and purging all its environs of traitors, on which subject I shall expect with impatience the determination of the congress. Their orders I hope to receive before or immediately on my arrival.

This instant, the enclosed, express from the provincial congress of New York, was delivered into my hands, but as these gentlemen probably are not fully apprised of the danger hanging over their heads, as I have received intelligence from the camp that the fleet is sailed, and that it is necessary to urge my march, I shall proceed with one division of the forces under my command to that city. A moment's delay may be fatal. The force I shall carry with me is not strong enough to act offensively, but just sufficient to secure the city against any immediate designs of the enemy. If this is to give umbrage, if the governor and captain of the man of war are pleased to construe this step as an act of positive hostility, if they are to prescribe what number of your troops are and what number are not to enter the city, all I can say is that New York must be considered as the minister's place, and not the continent. I must now, sir, big pardon for the length of this letter, and more so, for the presumption in offering so freely my thoughts to the congress, from whom it is my duty simply to receive my orders, and as a servant and soldier strictly to obey; which none can do with greater ardour and affection than,

Sir,
Your most obedient humble servant,
CHARLES LEE.

To the honourable John Hancock, esquire, president of the continental congress.

NOTE—No. VI. *See Page* 153.

THE NAMES OF THE MEMBERS WHO SUBSCRIBED THE DECLARATION OF INDEPENDENCE WERE AS FOLLOWS, VIZ:

New Hampshire.

Josiah Bartlett,   Matthew Thornton.
William Whipple,

Massachusetts Bay.

Samuel Adams,   Robert Treat Paine,
John Adams,   Elbridge Gerry.

Rhode Island, &c.

Stephen Hopkins,   William Ellery.

Connecticut.

Roger Sherman,	William Williams,
Samuel Huntington,	Oliver Wolcott.

New York.

William Floyd,	Francis Lewis,
Philip Livingston,	Lewis Morris.

New Jersey.

Richard Stockton,	John Hart,
John Witherspoon,	Abram Clark.
Francis Hopkinson,	

Pennsylvania

Robert Morris,	James Smith,
Benjamin Rush,	George Taylor,
Benjamin Franklin,	James Wilson,
John Morton,	George Ross.
George Clymer,	

Delaware.

Cesar Rodney,	George Reed.

Maryland.

Samuel Chase,	Thomas Stone,
William Paca,	Charles Carroll, *of Carrollton.*

Virginia.

George Wythe,	Thomas Nelson, jun.
Richard Henry Lee,	Francis Lightfoot Lee,
Thomas Jefferson,	Carter Braxton.
Benjamin Harrison,	

North Carolina.

William Hooper,	John Penn.
Joseph Hughes,	

South Carolina.

Edward Rutledge,	Thomas Lynch, jun.
Thomas Heyward, jun.	Arthur Middleton.

Georgia.

Button Gwinn,	Lyman Hall.
George Walton,	

The people of the United States have taken such universal interest in the composition of this celebrated instrument as to excuse a more minute attention to it than has been bestowed on the other cotemporaneous state papers.

Mr. Jefferson has preserved a copy of the original draft as reported by the committee, with the amendments made to it in congress, which has been published in his correspondence. The following is extracted from that work.

Mr. Jefferson's draft as reported by the committee.	*As amended by congress.*
A declaration by the representatives of the United States of America in *general* congress assembled.	A declaration by the representatives of the United States of America in congress assembled.
When in the course of human events it becomes necessary for one people to dissolve the political bonds which have connected them with another, and to assume among the powers of the earth the separate and equal station to which the laws of nature and of nature's God entitle them, a decent respect for the opinions of mankind requires that they should declare the causes which impel them to the separation.	Not altered.
We hold these truths to be self-evident, that all men are created equal; that they are endowed by their creator with *inherent and* inalienable rights; that among these are life, liberty, and the pursuit of happiness; that to secure these rights, governments are instituted among men, deriving their just powers from the consent of the governed; that whenever any form of government becomes destructive of these ends, it is the right of the people to alter or to abolish it, and to institute new government, laying its foundation on such principles, and organising its powers in	We hold these truths to be self-evident, that all men are created equal; that they are endowed by their creator with *certain* inalienable rights; that among these are life, liberty, and the pursuit of happiness; that to secure these rights, governments are instituted among men, deriving their just powers from the consent of the governed; that whenever any form of government becomes destructive of these ends, it is the right of the people to alter or to abolish it, and to institute new government, laying its foundation on such principles, and organising its

such form, as to them shall seem most likely to effect their safety and happiness. Prudence indeed will dictate that governments long established should not be changed for light and transient causes; and accordingly all experience hath shown that mankind are more disposed to suffer while evils are sufferable, than to right themselves by abolishing the forms to which they are accustomed. But when a long train of abuses and usurpations *begun at a distinguished period and* pursuing invariably the same object, evinces a design to reduce them under absolute despotism, it is their right, it is their duty to throw off such government, and to provide new guards for their future security. Such has been the patient sufferings of these colonies; and such is now the necessity which constrains them to *expunge* their former systems of government. The history of the present king of Great Britain is a history of *unremitting* injuries and usurpations *among which appears no solitary fact to contradict the uniform tenor of the rest, but all have* in direct object the establishment of an absolute tyranny over these states. To prove this let facts be submitted to a candid world, *for the truth of which we pledge*

powers in such form, as to them shall seem most likely to effect their safety and happiness. Prudence indeed will dictate that governments long established should not be changed for light and transient causes; and accordingly all experience hath shown that mankind are more disposed to suffer while evils are sufferable, than to right themselves by abolishing the forms to which they are accustomed. But when a long train of abuses and usurpations pursuing invariably the same object, evinces a design to reduce them under absolute despotism, it is their right, it is their duty to throw off such government, and to provide new guards for their future security. Such has been the patient sufferance of these colonies, and such is now the necessity which constrains them to *alter* their former systems of government. The history of the present king of Great Britain is a history of *repeated* injuries and usurpations, *all having* in direct object the establishment of an absolute tyranny over these states. To prove this let facts be submitted to a candid world.

a faith yet unsullied by false-hood.

He has refused his assent to laws the most wholesome and necessary for the public good.

Not altered.

He has forbidden his governors to pass laws of immediate and pressing importance, unless suspended in their operation till his assent should be obtained; and when so suspended he has utterly neglected to attend to them.

Not altered.

He has refused to pass other laws for the accommodation of large districts of people, unless those people would relinquish the right of representation in the legislature, a right inestimable to them, and formidable to tyrants only.

Not altered.

He has called together legislative bodies at places unusual, uncomfortable, and distant from the depository of their public records, for the sole purpose of fatiguing them into compliance with his measures.

Not altered.

He has dissolved representative houses repeatedly *and continually,* for opposing with manly firmness his invasions on the rights of the people.

He has dissolved representative houses repeatedly for opposing with manly firmness his invasions on the rights of the people.

He has refused for a long time after such dissolutions to cause others to be elected, whereby the legislative powers, incapable of annihilation, have returned to the people at large for their exercise,

Not altered.

the state remaining, in the mean time, exposed to the dangers of invasion from without **and** convulsions within.

He has endeavoured to prevent the population of these states; for that purpose obstructing the laws for the naturalization of foreigners, refusing to pass others to encourage their migrations hither, and raising the conditions of new appropriations of lands.

Not altered.

He has *suffered* the administration of justice *totally to cease in some of these states,* refusing his assent to laws for establishing judiciary powers.

He has *obstructed* the administration of justice *by* refusing his assent to laws for establishing judiciary powers.

He has made *our* judges dependent on his will alone for the tenure of their offices, and the amount and payment of their salaries.

He has made judges dependent on his will alone for the tenure of their offices, and the amount and payment of their salaries.

He has erected a multitude of new offices, *by a self-assumed power,* and sent hither swarms of new officers to harass our people and eat out their substance.

He has erected a multitude of new offices, and sent hither swarms of new officers to harass our people and eat out their substance.

He has kept among us in times of peace standing armies *and ships of war* without the consent of our legislatures.

He has kept among us in times of peace standing armies without the consent of our legislatures.

He has affected to render the military independence of and superior to the civil power.

Not altered.

He has combined with others to subject us to a jurisdiction foreign to our consti-

He has combined with others to subject us to a jurisdiction foreign to our constitututions and unacknowledged by our laws, giving his assent to their acts of pretended legislation for quartering large bodies of armed troops among us; for protecting by a mock trial from punishment for any murders which they should commit on the inhabitants of these states; for cutting off our trade with all parts of the world; for imposing taxes on us without our consent; for depriving us of the benefits of trial by jury; for transporting us beyond seas to be tried for pretended offences; for abolishing the free system of English laws in a neighbouring province, establishing therein an arbitrary government, and enlarging its boundaries, so as to render it at once an example and fit instrument for introducing the same absolute rule into these *states;* for taking away our charters, abolishing our most valuable laws, and altering fundamentally the forms of our governments; for suspending our own legislatures, and declaring themselves invested with power to legislate for us in all cases whatsoever.

He has abdicated government here, *withdrawing his governors and declaring us out of his allegiance and protection.*

He has plundered our seas, ravaged our coasts, burnt our

tions and unacknowledged by our laws, giving his assent to their acts of pretended legislation for quartering large bodies of armed troops among us; for protecting by a mock trial from punishment for any murders which they should commit on the inhabitants of these states; for cutting off our trade with all parts of the world; for imposing taxes on us without our consent; for depriving us *in many cases* of the benefits of trial by jury; for transporting us beyond seas to be tried for pretended offences; for abolishing the free system of English laws in a neighbouring province, establishing therein an arbitrary government, and enlarging its boundaries, so as to render it at once an example and fit instrument for introducing the same absolute rule into these *colonies;* for taking away our charters, abolishing our most valuable laws, and altering fundamentally the forms of our governments; for suspending our own legislatures, and declaring themselves invested with power to legislate for us in all cases whatsoever.

He has abdicated government here *by declaring us out of his protection and waging war against us.*

Not altered.

towns and destroyed the lives of our people.

He is at this time transporting large armies of foreign mercenaries to complete the works of death, desolation and tyranny already begun with circumstances of cruelty and perfidy unworthy the head of a civilized nation.

He is at this time transporting large armies of foreign mercenaries to complete the works of death, destruction and tyranny already begun with circumstances of cruelty and perfidy *scarcely paralleled in the most barbarous ages and totally* unworthy the head of a civilized nation.

He has constrained our fellow-citizens taken captive on the high seas to bear arms against their country, to become the executioners of their friends and brethren, or to fall themselves by their hands.

Not altered.

He has endeavoured to bring on the inhabitants of the frontiers the merciless Indian savages whose known rule of warfare is an undistinguished destruction of all ages, sexes and conditions *of existence.*

He has *excited domestic insurrections among us and has* endeavoured to bring on the inhabitants of the frontiers the merciless Indian savages whose known rule of warfare is an undistinguished destruction of all ages, sexes, and conditions.

He has excited treasonable insurrections of our fellow-citizens, with the allurements of forfeiture and confiscation of our property.

Struck out.

He has waged cruel war against human nature itself, violating its most sacred rights of life and liberty in the persons of a distant people who never offended him, captivating and carrying them into slavery in another hemisphere, or to incur miserable death in their transportation thither. This piratical warfare, the opprobrium of INFIDEL powers, is the warfare of the CHRISTIAN king of Great Britain. Determined to keep open a market where MEN should be bought and sold, he has prostituted his negative for suppressing every legislative attempt to prohibit or to restrain this execrable commerce. And that this assemblage of horrors might want no fact of distinguished die, he is now exciting those very people to rise in arms among us, and to purchase that liberty of which he has deprived them, by murdering the people on whom he also obtruded them; thus paying off former crimes committed against the LIBERTIES of one people with crimes which he urges them to commit against the LIVES of another.

Struck out.

In every stage of these oppressions we have petitioned for redress in the most humble terms; our repeated petitions have been answered only by repeated injuries.

Not altered.

A prince whose character is thus marked by every act which may define a tyrant is unfit to be the ruler of a people *who mean to be free. Future ages will scarcely believe that the hardiness of one man adventured, within the short compass of twelve years only, to lay a foundation so*

A prince whose character is thus marked by every act which may define a tyrant is unfit to be the ruler of a *free* people.

broad and so undisguised for tyranny over a people fostered and fixed in principles of freedom.

Nor have we been wanting in attention to our British brethren. We have warned them from time to time of attempts by their legislature to extend *a* jurisdiction over *these our states.* We have reminded them of the circumstances of our emigration and settlement here; *no one of which could warrant so strange a pretension; these were effected at the expense of our own blood and treasure, unassisted by the wealth or the strength of Great Britain; that in constituting indeed our several forms of government, we had adopted one common king; thereby laying a foundation for perpetual league and amity with them; but that submission to their parliament was no part of our constitution, nor ever in idea if history may be credited; and* we appealed to their native justice and magnanimity, *as well as to* the ties of our common kindred, to disavow these usurpations which *were likely to* interrupt our connexion and correspondence. They too have been deaf to the voice of justice and of consanguinity, *and when occasions have been given them by the regular course of their laws, of removing from their*

Nor have we been wanting in attention to our British brethren. We have warned them from time to time of attempts by their legislature to extend *an unwarrantable* jurisdiction over *us.* We have reminded them of the circumstances of our emigration and settlement here; we *have* appealed to their native justice and magnanimity, *and we have conjured them by* the ties of our common kindred to disavow these usurpations which *would inevitably* interrupt our connexion and correspondence. They too have been deaf to the voice of justice and of consanguinity. *We must therefore* acquiesce in the necessity which denounces our separation, *and hold them* as we hold the rest of mankind, enemies in war, in peace friends.

councils the disturbers of our harmony, they have by their free election re-established them in power. At this very time too, they are permitting their chief magistrate to send over not only soldiers of our common blood, but Scotch and foreign mercenaries to invade and destroy us. These facts have given the last stab to agonizing affection, and manly spirit bids us to renounce for ever these unfeeling brethren. We must endeavour to forget our former love for them, and hold them as we hold the rest of mankind, enemies in war, in peace friends. We might have been a free and a great people together; but a communication of grandeur and of freedom, it seems, is below their dignity. Be it so, since they will have it. The road to happiness and to glory is open to us too. We will tread it apart from them, and acquiesce in the necessity which denounces our *eternal* separation.

We, therefore, the representatives of the United States of America in general congress assembled, do, in the name and by the authority of the good people of these states, *reject and renounce all allegiance and subjection to the kings of Great Britain, and all others who may hereafter claim by, through or*

We, therefore, the representatives of the United States of America in general congress assembled, *appealing to the supreme judge of the world for the rectitude of our intentions,* do in the name, and by the good people of these *colonies, solemnly publish and declare that these united colonies are and of*

under them; we utterly dis- right ought to be free and in-
solve all political connexion dependent states; that they
which may heretofore have are absolved from all alle-
subsisted between us and the giance to the British crown,
people or parliament of Great and that all political con-
Britain; and finally we do as- nexion between them and the
sert and declare these colonies state of Great Britain is, and
to be free and independent ought to be, totally dissolved;
states, and that as free and and that as free and inde-
independent states, they have pendent states they have full
full power to levy war, con- power to levy war, conclude
clude peace, contract alliances, peace, contract alliances, es-
establish commerce, and to do tablish commerce, and to do
all other acts and things all other acts and things
which independent states may which independent states may
of right do. of right do.

And for the support of this And for the support of this
declaration, we mutually declaration, *with a firm reli-*
pledge to each other our lives, *ance on the protection of di-*
our fortunes, and our sacred *vine providence,* we mutually
honour. pledge to each other our lives,
our fortunes, and our sacred
honour.

The words expunged from the original draft are distinguished by italics, as are the words that were introduced by
congress.

NOTE—No. VII. *See Page* 229.

"My reasons for this measure," said the Commander-in-
chief in his letter to General Lee, ordering him to cross the
Hudson, "and which I think must have weight with you,
are, that the enemy are evidently changing the seat of war
to this side of the North river; that this country, therefore,
will expect the continental army to give what support they
can; and, if disappointed in this, will cease to depend upon,
or support a force by which no protection is given to them.
It is, therefore, of the utmost importance that at least an
appearance of force should be made, to keep this state in
connexion with the others. If that should not continue, it
is much to be feared that its influence on Pennsylvania would
be very considerable; and the public interests would be more

and more endangered. Unless, therefore, some new event should occur, or some more cogent reason present itself, I would have you move over by the easiest and best passage. I am sensible your numbers will not be large, and that the movement may not perhaps be agreeable to your troops. As to the first, report will exaggerate them, and there will be preserved the appearance of an army, which will, at least, have the effect of encouraging the desponding here; and, as to the other, you will doubtless represent to them, that in duty and gratitude, their service is due wherever the enemy may make the greatest impression, or seem to intend to do so."

NOTE—No. VIII. *See Page* 268.

In a postscript, it is stated, that an accurate return could not be obtained, but that from the best estimate he could form, the whole force in Jersey fit for duty was under three thousand; all of whom, except nine hundred and eighty-one, were militia, who stood engaged only until the last of that month. The continental troops under inoculation, including their attendants, amounted to about one thousand.

In a letter of the sixth of March to Governor Trumbull, calling on the state of Connecticut for two thousand militia to be marched to Peekskill, after complaining of the militia he had called from the southern states, who came and went as their own caprice might direct, he says, "I am persuaded, from the readiness with which you have ever complied with all my demands, that you will exert yourself in forwarding the aforementioned number of men, upon my bare request. But I hope you will be convinced of the necessity of the demand, when I tell you, in confidence, that after the 15th of this month, when the time of General Lincoln's militia expires, I shall be left with the remains of five Virginia regiments, not amounting to more than as many hundred men, and parts of two or three other continental battalions, all very weak. The remainder of the army will be composed of small parties of militia from this state and Pennsylvania, on whom little dependence can be put, as they come and go when they please. I have issued peremptory orders to every colonel in the regular service, to send in what men he has recruited, even if they amount to but one hundred to a regiment: if they would do this, it would make a considerable force upon the whole. The enemy must be ignorant of our numbers and situation, or they would never suffer us to remain unmolested; and I almost tax myself with imprudence in committing the secret to paper; not that I distrust you, of whose inviolable attachment I have had so many proofs; but for fear the letter should by any accident fall into other hands than those for which it is intended."

NOTE—No. IX. *See Page* 382.

Justice to the unfortunate demands that an extract from the correspondence between Generals Burgoyne and Gates on this subject should be inserted.

The British general had complained of the harsh treatment experienced by the provincial prisoners taken at Bennington, and requested that a surgeon from his army should be permitted to visit the wounded; and that he might be allowed to furnish them with necessaries and attendants. "Duty and principle," he added, "make me a public enemy to the Americans, who have taken up arms; but I seek to be a generous one; nor have I the shadow of resentment against any individual, who does not induce it by acts derogatory to those maxims, upon which all men of honour think alike." In answer to this letter, General Gates, who had just taken command of the American army, said, "that the savages of America should, in their warfare, mangle and scalp the unhappy prisoners who fall into their hands is neither new nor extraordinary, but that the famous Lieutenant General Burgoyne, in whom the fine gentleman is united with the soldier and the scholar, should hire the savages of America to scalp Europeans, and the descendants of Europeans; nay more, that he should pay a price for each scalp so barbarously taken, is more than will be believed in Europe, until authenticated facts shall, in every gazette, confirm the truth of the horrid tale.

"Miss M'Crea, a young lady, lovely to the sight, of virtuous character, and amiable disposition, engaged to an officer of your army, was, with other women and children, taken out of a house near fort Edward, carried into the woods, and there scalped and mangled in a most shocking manner. Two parents with their six children, were all treated with the same inhumanity, while quietly resting in their once happy and peaceful dwelling. The miserable fate of Miss M'Crea was particularly aggravated, by being dressed to receive her promised husband; but met her murderer employed by you. Upwards of one hundred men, women and children, have perished by the hands of the ruffians to whom, it is asserted, you have paid the price of blood."

To this part of his letter, General Burgoyne replied, "I have hesitated, sir, upon answering the other paragraphs of your letter. I disdain to justify myself against the rhapsodies of fiction and calumny, which from the first of this contest, it has been an unvaried American policy to propagate, but which no longer imposes on the world. I am induced to deviate from this general rule, in the present instance, lest my silence should be construed an acknowledgment of the truth of your allegations, and a pretence be thence taken for exercising future barbarities by the American troops.

"By this motive, and upon this only, I condescend to inform you, that I would not be conscious of the acts you presume to impute to me, for the whole continent of America, though the wealth of worlds was in its bowels, and a paradise upon its surface.

"It has happened, that all my transactions with the Indian nations, last year and this, have been clearly heard, distinctly understood, accurately minuted, by very numerous, and in many parts, very unprejudiced persons. So immediately opposite to the truth is your assertion that I have paid a price for scalps, that one of the first regulations established by me at the great council in May, and repeated and enforced, and invariably adhered to since, was, that the Indians should receive compensation for prisoners, because it would prevent cruelty; and that not only such compensation should be withheld, but a strict account demanded for scalps. These pledges of conquest, for such you well know they will ever esteem them, were solemnly and peremptorily prohibited to be taken from the wounded, and even the dying, and the persons of aged men, women, children, and prisoners, were pronounced sacred, even in an assault.

"In regard to Miss M'Crea, her fall wanted not the tragic display you have laboured to give it, to make it as sincerely abhorred and lamented by me, as it can be by the tenderest of her friends. The fact was no premeditated barbarity. On the contrary, two chiefs who had brought her off for the purpose of security, not of violence to her person, disputed which should be her guard, and in a fit of savage passion in one, from whose hands she was snatched, the unhappy woman became the victim. Upon the first intelligence of this event, I obliged the Indians to deliver the murderer into my hands, and though to have punished him by our laws, or principles of justice, would have been perhaps unprecedented, he certainly should have suffered an ignominious death, had I not been convinced from my circumstances and observation, beyond the possibility of a doubt, that a pardon under the terms which I presented, and they accepted, would be more efficacious than an execution, to prevent similar mischiefs.

"The above instance excepted, your intelligence respecting the cruelty of the Indians is false.

"You seem to threaten me with European publications, which affect me as little as any other threats you could make; but in regard to American publications, whether your charge against me, which I acquit you of believing, was penned *from* a gazette, or *for* a gazette, I desire and demand of you, as a man of honour, that should it appear in print at all this answer may follow it."

NOTE—No. X. *See Page* 405.

Lord Suffolk, secretary of state, contended for the employment of Indians, in the war. "Besides its policy and necessity," his lordship said, "that the measure was also allowable on principle, for that it was perfectly justifiable to use all the means that God and nature had put into our hands."

This moving the indignation of Lord Chatham, he suddenly rose, and gave full vent to his feelings in one of the most extraordinary bursts of eloquence that the pen of history has recorded: "I am astonished," exclaimed his lordship, "shocked to hear such principles confessed; to hear them avowed in this house or even this country. My lords, I did not intend to have encroached again on your attention, but I can not repress my indignation. I feel myself impelled to speak. My lords, we are called upon as members of this house, as men, as christians, to protest against such horrible barbarity. That God and nature had put into our hands! what ideas of God and nature that noble lord may entertain I know not, but I know that such detestable principles are equally abhorrent to religion and humanity. What, to attribute the sacred sanction of God and nature to the massacres

of the Indian scalping knife! to the cannibal savage, tortur-
ing, murdering, devouring, drinking the blood of his mangled
victims! such notions shock every precept of morality, every
feeling of humanity, every sentiment of honour. These
abominable principles and this more abominable avowal of
them, demand the most decisive indignation. I call upon
that right reverend and this most learned bench to vindicate
the religion of their God, to support the justice of their country. I call upon the bishops to interpose the unsullied sanctity
of their lawn, upon the judges to interpose the purity of their
ermine, to save us from this pollution. I call upon the honour
of your lordships, to reverence the dignity of your ancestors,
and to maintain your own. I call upon the spirit and humanity of my country, to vindicate the national character.
I invoke the genius of the constitution. From the tapestry
that adorns these walls, the immortal ancestor of this noble
lord, frowns with indignation at the disgrace of his country.
In vain did he defend the liberty, and establish the religion
of Britain against the tyranny of Rome, if these worse than
popish cruelties and inquisitorial practices are endured among
us. To send forth the merciless cannibal thirsting for blood!
—against whom?—Your protestant brethren—to lay waste
their country, to desolate their dwellings, and extirpate their
race and name, by the aid and instrumentality of these horrible hell-hounds of war! Spain can no longer boast pre-
eminence of barbarity. She armed herself with blood-hounds
to extirpate the wretched natives of Mexico, but we more
ruthless, loose these dogs of war against our countrymen in
America, endeared to us by every tie that should sanctify
humanity. My lords, I solemnly call upon your lordships,
and upon every order of men in the state, to stamp upon
this infamous procedure the indelible stigma of the public
abhorrence. More particularly I call upon the holy prelates
of our religion to do away this iniquity; let them perform a
lustration to purify their country from this deep and deadly
sin. My lords, I am old and weak, and at present unable to
say more, but my feelings and indignation were too strong
to have said less. I could not have slept this night in my
bed, nor reposed my head upon my pillow, without giving
this vent to my eternal abhorrence of such enormous and
preposterous principles."

NOTE—No. XI. *See Page* 414.

The following are the letters which passed between the two generals on this subject:

Albany, December 18, 1777.

SIR,—I shall not attempt to describe what, as a private gentleman, I can not help feeling, on representing to my mind the disagreeable situation which confidential letters, when exposed to public inspection, may place an unsuspecting correspondent in; but, as a public officer, I conjure your excellency, to give me all the assistance you can, in tracing out the author of the infidelity, which put extracts from General Conway's letters to me into your hands. Those letters have been stealingly copied; but, which of them, when, or by whom, is to me, as yet, an unfathomable secret.

There is not one officer in my suite, or amongst those who have a free access to me, upon whom I could, with the least justification to myself, fix the suspicion; and yet, my uneasiness may deprive me of the usefulness of the worthiest men. It is, I believe, in your excellency's power to do me, and the United States, a very important service, by detecting a wretch who may betray me, and capitally injure the very operations under your immediate direction. For this reason, sir, I beg your excellency will favour me with the proofs you can procure to that effect. But, the crime being, eventually so important, that the least loss of time may be attended with the worst consequences; and, it being unknown to me whether the letter came to you from a member of congress, or from an officer, I shall have the honour of transmitting a copy of this to the president, that congress may, in concert with your excellency, obtain, as soon as possible, a discovery which so deeply affects the safety of the states. Crimes of that magnitude ought not to remain unpunished.

I have the honour to be,

Sir,

With the greatest respect,
Your excellency's most humble
and most obedient servant,

HORATIO GATES.

His excellency General Washington.

———

Valley Forge, January 4, 1778.

SIR,—Your letter of the 18th ultimo, came to my hands a few days ago, and to my great surprise informed me, that a copy of it had been sent to congress, for what reason, I find myself unable to account; but, as some end doubtless was intended to be answered by it, I am laid under the disagreeable necessity of returning my answer through the same channel, lest any member of that honourable body should harbour an unfavourable suspicion of my having practised some indiscreet means to come at the contents of the confidential letters between you and General Conway.

I am to inform you then, that **********, on his way to congress in the month of October last, fell in with Lord Stirling at Reading: and, not in confidence that I ever understood, informed his aid-de-camp, Major M'Williams, that General Conway had written thus to you, "heaven has been determined to save your country, or a weak general and bad counsellors * would have ruined it." Lord Stirling, from motives of friendship, transmitted the account with this remark. "The enclosed was communicated by ********** to Major M'Williams; such wicked duplicity of conduct I shall always think it my duty to detect."

In consequence of this information, and without having any thing more in view, than merely to show that gentleman that I was not unapprised of his intriguing disposition, I wrote him a letter in these words.

"Sir, a letter which I received last night contained the following paragraph.

"In a letter from General Conway to General Gates, he says, heaven has been determined to save your country, or a weak general and bad counsellors would have ruined it. I am, sir, &c."

Neither the letter, nor the information which occasioned it, was ever, directly, or indirectly, communicated by me to a single officer in this army (out of my own family) excepting the Marquis de Lafayette, who having been spoken to on the subject, by General Conway, applied for, and saw, under injunctions of secrecy, the letter which contained this information; so desirous was I of concealing every matter that could, in its consequences, give the smallest interruption to the tranquillity of this army, or afford a gleam of hope to the enemy by dissensions therein.

Thus, sir, with an openness and candour, which I hope will ever characterize and mark my conduct, have I complied with your request. The only concern I feel upon the occasion,

* One of whom, by the by, he was.

finding how matters stand, is, that in doing this, I have necessarily been obliged to name a gentleman, who, I am persuaded, (although I never exchanged a word with him upon the subject) thought he was rather doing an act of justice, than committing an act of infidelity; and sure I am, that, until Lord Stirling's letter came to my hands, I never knew that General Conway, (whom I viewed in the light of a stranger to you) was a correspondent of yours, much less did I suspect that I was the subject of your confidential letters. Pardon me then for adding, that, so far from conceiving that the safety of the states can be affected, or in the smallest degree injured, by a discovery of this kind, or that I should be called upon in such solemn terms to point out the author, that I considered the information as coming from yourself, and given with a friendly view to forewarn, and consequently forearm me, against a secret enemy, or in other words, a dangerous incendiary, in which character sooner or later, this country will know General Conway. But, in this, as well as other matters of late, I have found myself mistaken. I am, sir,

Your most obedient servant,
GEO: WASHINGTON.

To Major General Gates.

NOTE—No. XII. *See Page 417.*

During the existence of this faction, an attempt appears to have been made to alienate the affections of the leading political personages in the states from the commander-in-chief. The following letters exhibit a very unsuccessful effort of this sort, which was made on Governor Henry, of Virginia, by a gentleman not supposed to be a member of congress from that state.

Williamsburgh, February 20, 1778.

DEAR SIR,—You will no doubt be surprised at seeing the enclosed letter, in which the encomiums bestowed on me are as undeserved, as the censures aimed at you are unjust. I am sorry there should be one man who counts himself my friend, who is not yours.

Perhaps I give you needless trouble in handing you this paper. The writer of it may be too insignificant to deserve any notice. If I knew this to be the case, I should not have intruded on your time, which is so precious. But there may possibly be some scheme or party forming to your prejudice. The enclosed leads to such a suspicion. Believe me, sir, I have too high a sense of the obligations America has to you, to abet or countenance so unworthy a proceeding. The most exalted merit hath ever been found to attract envy. But I please myself with the hope, that the same fortitude and greatness of mind which have hitherto braved all the difficulties and dangers inseparable from your station, will rise superior to every attempt of the envious partisan.

I really can not tell who is the writer of this letter, which not a little perplexes me. The hand writing is altogether strange to me.

To give you the trouble of this, gives me pain. It would suit my inclination better, to give you some assistance in the great business of the war. But I will not conceal any thing from you, by which you may be affected, for I really think your personal welfare and the happiness of America are intimately connected. I beg you will be assured of that high regard and esteem with which I ever am,

Dear sir,

Your affectionate friend and very humble servant,

P. HENRY.

His excellency General Washington.

(Letter enclosed in the preceding.)

Yorktown, January 12, 1778.

DEAR SIR,—The common danger of our country first brought you and me together. I recollect with pleasure the influence of your conversation and eloquence upon the opinions of this country in the beginning of the present controversy. You first taught us to shake off our idolatrous attachment to royalty, and to oppose its encroachments upon our liberties with our very lives. By these means you saved us from ruin. The independence of America is the offspring of that liberal spirit of thinking, and acting, which followed the destruction of the sceptres of kings and the mighty power of Great Britain.

But, sir, we have only passed the Red Sea. A dreary wilderness is still before us, and unless a Moses or a Joshua are raised up in our behalf, we must perish before we reach the promised land. We have nothing to fear from our enemies on the way. General Howe, it is true, has taken Philadelphia; but he has only changed his prison. His dominions are bounded on all sides by his outsentries. America can only be undone by herself. She looks up to her councils and arms for protection; but alas! what are they? her representation in congress dwindled to only twenty-one members—her Adams—her Wilson—her Henry, are no more among them. Her councils weak—and partial remedies applied constantly for universal diseases. Her army—what is it? a major general belonging to it called it a few days ago in my hearing a *mob*. Discipline unknown or *wholly* neglected. The quartermaster and commissary's departments filled with idleness, ignorance and peculation—our hospitals crowded with six thousand sick, but half provided with necessaries or accommodations, and more dying in them in one month, than perished in the field during the whole of the last campaign.

The money depreciating without any effectual measures being taken to raise it—the country distracted with the Don Quixote attempts to regulate the prices of provisions, an *artificial* famine created by it, and a *real* one dreaded from it. The spirit of the people failing through a more intimate acquaintance with the causes of our misfortunes—many submitting daily to General Howe, and more wishing to do it, only to avoid the calamities which threaten our country. But is our case desperate? by no means. We have wisdom, virtue, and strength *eno'* to save us if they could be called into action. The northern army has shown us what Americans are capable of doing with A GENERAL at their head. The spirit of the southern army is no ways inferior to the spirit of the northern. A Gates—a Lee, or a Conway would, in a few weeks, render them an irresistible body of men. The last of the above officers has accepted of the new office of inspector general of our army, in order to reform abuses —but the remedy is only a palliative one. In one of his letters to a friend he says, "a great and good God hath decreed America to be free—or the ********** and weak counsellors would have ruined her long ago"—you may rest assured of *each* of the facts related in this letter. The author of it is one of your Philadelphia friends. A hint of his name, if found out by the hand writing, must not be mentioned to your most intimate friend. Even the letter *must* be thrown in the fire. But some of its contents ought to be made public in order to awaken, enlighten, and alarm our country. I rely upon your prudence, and am, dear sir, with my usual attachment to *you,* and to our beloved independence,

Yours, sincerely.

His excellency P. Henry.

———

Williamsburgh, March 5, 1778.

DEAR SIR,—By an express which Colonel Finnie sent to camp, I enclosed you an anonymous letter, which I hope got safe to hand. I am anxious to hear something that will serve to explain the strange affair, which I am now informed is taken up, respecting you. Mr. Custis has just paid us a visit, and by him I learn sundry particulars concerning General Mifflin, that much surprise me. It is very hard to trace the schemes and windings of the enemies to America. I really thought that man its friend: however, I am too far from him to judge of his present temper.

While you face the armed enemies of our liberty in the field, and, by the favour of God, have been kept unhurt, I trust your country will never harbour in her bosom the miscreant who would ruin her best supporter. I wish not to flatter; but when arts unworthy honest men are used to defame and traduce you, I think it not amiss, but a duty, to assure you of that estimation in which the public hold you. Not that I think any testimony I can bear, is necessary for your support, or private satisfaction, for a bare recollection of what is past must give you sufficient pleasure in every circumstance of life. But I can not help assuring you, on this occasion, of the high sense of gratitude which all ranks of men, in this your native country, bear to you. It will give me sincere pleasure to manifest my regards, and render my best services to you or yours. I do not like to make a parade of these things, and I know you are not fond of it; however, I hope the occasion will plead my excuse.

The assembly have at length empowered the executive here to provide the Virginia troops serving with you, with clothes, &c. I am making provision accordingly, and hope to do something towards it. Every possible assistance from government is afforded the commissary of provisions, whose department has not been attended to. It was taken up by me too late to do much. Indeed the load of business devolved on me is too great to be managed well. A French ship, mounting thirty guns, that has been long chased by the English cruisers, has got into Carolina, as I hear last night.

Wishing you all possible felicity, I am, my dear sir,
          Your ever affectionate friend,
                    and very humble servant,   P. HENRY.
His excellency General Washington.

———

                                        Valley Forge, March 27, 1778.

DEAR SIR,—About eight days past, I was honoured with
your favour of the 20th ultimo.

Your friendship, sir, in transmitting me the anonymous
letter you had received, lays me under the most grateful obligations; and, if any thing could give a still further claim
to my acknowledgments, it is the very polite and delicate
terms in which you have been pleased to make the communication.

I have ever been happy in supposing that I held a place
in your esteem, and the proof of it you have afforded on
this occasion makes me peculiarly so. The favourable light
in which you hold me is truly flattering, but I should feel
much regret if I thought the happiness of America so intimately connected with my personal welfare, as you so
obligingly seem to consider it. All I can say, is, that she
has ever had, and, I trust, she ever will have, my honest
exertions to promote her interest. I can not hope that my
services have been the best; but my heart tells me that they
have been the best that I could render.

That I may have erred in using the means in my power
for accomplishing the objects of the arduous, exalted station
with which I am honoured, I can not doubt; nor do I wish
my conduct to be exempted from the reprehension it may
deserve. Error is the portion of humanity, and to censure it,
whether committed by this or that public character, is the
prerogative of freemen.   *   *   *   *   *

*   *   *   *   *   *   *   *   *
*   *   *   *   *   *   *   *   *
*   *   *   *   *   *   *   *   *
*   *   *   *   *   *   *   *   *
*   *   *   *   *   *   *   *   *
*   *   *   *   *   *   *   *   *
*   *   *   *   *   *   *   *   *

This is not the only secret insidious attempt that has been
made to wound my reputation. There have been others
equally base, cruel, and ungenerous; because conducted with

as little frankness and proceeding from views perhaps as personally interested.

I am, dear sir, &c.

GEO: WASHINGTON.

To his excellency Patrick Henry, esquire, Governor of Virginia.

Camp, March 28, 1778.

DEAR SIR,—Just as I was about to close my letter of yesterday, your favour of the fifth instant came to hand.

I can only thank you again, in the language of the most undissembled gratitude, for your friendship: and assure you, the indulgent disposition which Virginia in particular, and the states in general entertain towards me, gives me the most sensible pleasure. The approbation of my country is what I wish; and, as far as my abilities and opportunity will permit, I hope I shall endeavour to deserve it. It is the highest reward to a feeling mind; and happy are they who so conduct themselves as to merit it.

The anonymous letter with which you were pleased to favour me, was written by **********, so far as I can judge from a similitude of hands.****   *   *   *   *
*   *   *   *   *   *   *   *   *

My caution to avoid any thing that could injure the service, prevented me from communicating, except to a very few of my friends, the intrigues of a faction which I know was formed against me, since it might serve to publish our internal dissensions; but their own restless zeal to advance their views has too clearly betrayed them, and made concealment on my part fruitless. I can not precisely mark the extent of their views, but it appeared in general, that General Gates was to be exalted on the ruin of my reputation and influence. This I am authorized to say from undeniable facts in my own possession, from publications the evident scope of which could not be mistaken, and from private detractions industriously circulated. *************, it is commonly supposed, bore the second part in the cabal; and General Conway, I know, was a very active and malignant partisan; but I have good reason to believe that their machinations have recoiled most sensibly upon themselves.

I am, dear sir, &c.

GEO: WASHINGTON.

His excellency Patrick Henry, esquire, Gov. of Virginia.

The following extract is taken from a letter written about the same time to a gentleman in New England, who had expressed some anxious apprehensions occasioned by a report that the commander-in-chief had determined to resign his station in the army:

"I can assure you that no person ever heard me drop an expression that had a tendency to resignation. The same principles that led me to embark in the opposition to the arbitrary claims of Great Britain, operate with additional force at this day; nor is it my desire to withdraw my services while they are considered of importance in the present contest; but to report a design of this kind, is among the arts, which those who are endeavouring to effect a change are practising to bring it to pass. I have said, and I still do say, that there is not an officer in the service of the United States, that would return to the sweets of domestic life with more heartfelt joy than I should. But I would have this declaration accompanied by these sentiments, that while the public are satisfied with my endeavours, I mean not to shrink from the cause: but the moment her voice, not that of faction, calls upon me to resign, I shall do it with as much pleasure as ever the wearied traveller retired to rest."

NOTE—No. XIII. *See Page* 456.

The following is an extract of a letter addressed on this occasion by General Washington to congress:

"Though I sincerely commiserate the misfortune of General Lee, and feel much for his present unhappy situation; yet, with all possible deference to the opinion of congress, I fear that their resolutions will not have the desired effect, are founded in impolicy, and will, if adhered to, produce consequences of an extensive and melancholy nature.

"Retaliation is certainly just, and sometimes necessary, even where attended with the severest penalties: but when the evils which may, and must result from it, exceed those intended to be redressed, prudence and policy require that it should be avoided.

"Having premised thus much, I beg leave to examine the justice and expediency of it in the instance before us. From the best information I have been able to obtain, General Lee's usage has not been so disgraceful and dishonourable, as to authorize the treatment decreed to these gentlemen, was it not prohibited by many other important considerations. His confinement, I believe, has been more rigorous than has been generally experienced by the rest of our officers, or those of the enemy who have been in our possession; but if the reports received on that head be true, he has been provided with a decent apartment, and with most things necessary to render him comfortable. This is not the case with one of the officers comprehended in the resolves, if his letter, of which a copy is transmitted, deserves your credit. Here retaliation seems to have been prematurely begun, or to speak with more propriety, severities have been, and are exercised towards Colonel Campbell, not justified by any that General Lee has yet received.

"In point of policy, and under the present situation of our affairs, most surely the doctrine can not be supported. The balance of prisoners is greatly against us, and a general regard to the happiness of the whole should mark our conduct. Can we imagine that our enemies will not mete the same punishments, the same indignities, the same cruelties, to those belonging to us in their possession, that we impose on theirs? why should we suppose them to have more humanity than we possess ourselves? or why should an ineffectual attempt to relieve the distresses of one brave man, involve many more in misery? At this time, however disagreeable the fact may be, the enemy have in their power, and subject to their call, near three hundred officers belonging to the army of the United States. In this number there are some of high rank, and the most of them are men of bravery and of merit. The quota of theirs in our hands bears no proportion, not being more than fifty. Under these circumstances, we certainly should do no act to draw upon the gentlemen belonging to us, and who have already suffered a long captivity, greater punishments than they now experience. If we should, what will be their feelings, and those of their numerous and extensive connexions? Suppose the treatment prescribed for the Hessian officers should be pursued, will it not establish what the enemy have been aiming to effect by every artifice, and the grossest misrepresentations? I mean, an opinion of our enmity towards them, and of the cruel conduct they experience when they fall into our hands; a prejudice which we, on our part, have heretofore thought it politic to suppress, and to root out by every act of kindness and of lenity. It certainly will. The Hessians will hear of the punishments with all the circumstances of heightened exaggeration, and would feel the injury without investigating the cause, or reasoning upon the justice of it. The mischiefs which may, and must inevitably flow from the execution of the resolves, appear to be endless and innumerable."

———

END OF VOLUME II.